Human Sexuality in Physical and Mental Illnesses and Disabilities

---

An Annotated Bibliography

Human Sexuality in Physical and Mental Illnesses and Disabilities

An Annotated Bibliography

by Ami Sha'ked

INDIANA UNIVERSITY PRESS

Bloomington & London

Manufactured in the United States of America

Library of Congress Cataloging in Publication Data

Sha'ked, Ami, 1945–
Human sexuality in physical and mental illnesses and disabilities.

"Media review, compiled and edited by Susanne M. Bruyer": p.

1. Handicapped—Sexual behavior—Bibliography.
2. Sex instruction for the handicapped—Bibliography.
I. Title. [DNLM: 1. Sex—Abstracts. 2. Handicapped —Abstracts. 3. Chronic disease—Abstracts. 4. Mental disorders—Abstracts. 5. Counseling—Abstracts. ZWM55 S527h]
Z7254.S43 [HQ30.5] 016.6139'5 78–17813
ISBN 0–253–10100–X 1 2 3 4 5 83 82 81 80 79

To D'rora

This book is dedicated with love

Contents

Preface

Contrary to common myths that portray the disabled person as sexless, there is accumulating clinical and research evidence suggesting that sexual interest and activity continue to be very important in the lives of many long-term patients and physically and mentally disabled persons. Furthermore, authorities assert that sexual adjustment is at the core of total medical and psychosocial rehabilitation of disabled patients. Consequently, health-care practitioners are confronted with increasing demands from disabled and chronically ill patients for counseling and advice in sexual matters. A comprehensive survey conducted in various Veterans' Administration spinal-cord-injury centers demonstrated an overwhelming interest on the part of veterans in receiving counseling and instruction in altered sexual function and activity. Those few spinal-cord-injury patients who have received sex counseling as part of their rehabilitation treatment reported that it was the most valuable of the human services they received. It seems that once past the acute phase of their illness or disability, most patients look forward to resuming sexual relations, and, if needed, actively search for professional help to enhance their sexual normalization. Recognizing the importance of sexual adjustment in total patient care, medical authorities throughout the world strongly suggest the restructuring of hospital and rehabilitation environments to allow and encourage greater intimacy for patients and their spouses. It has also been recommended that any medical work-up performed by a physician should include an evaluation of the patient's sexual functioning, and, if needed, individual or group sex counseling and sex education programs should be prescribed.

Despite the importance of sexuality and sexual adjustment for patients in medical and rehabilitation situations, sexual concerns and difficulties of disabled and chronically ill patients are not adequately attended to by health-care professionals. Sexual concerns and anxieties shared by these patients are compounded by the practitioner's reluctance, lack of training, and inexperience in dealing effectively with these issues. Contributing to this lack of quality sex counseling in medical and rehabilitation settings are the widespread myths and misconceptions surrounding sexuality and the disabled found among health-care workers. Above all, practitioners lack basic knowledge and information regarding the interrelationships between sexuality and various medical conditions and disabilities. It is primarily for the purpose of promoting knowledge in this field that this book was written.

The publication of this annotated bibliography was inspired and initiated in recognition of the increasing interest in sexuality and disabilities, and the urgent need for a comprehensive and extensive reference resource in the field of medical and rehabilitation sexology. This book is not intended to present in-depth discussions on the sexual aspects of various disabling conditions. However, most of the abstracts in this volume have been expanded to include important features and key information found in the original publications. This book, therefore, can meet an initial need for some basic information regarding sexual behavior, functioning, and difficulties associated with many physical and mental illnesses and handicapping conditions. This bibliography has been developed to serve the need for ready access to research and clinical work conducted in this field and to aid in locating precise sources of additional information. We hope that the reader will turn to these original sources when needed. The annotations will help the reader to decide on the nature and direction of further reading to expand his or her knowledge. We believe that this book is a must for all medical, rehabilitation, and other health-care practitioners, researchers, and educators who believe in total medical and rehabilitation care of patients and who recognize that sexual adjustment is an integral part of these processes.

A review of the literature published before 1940 revealed almost a complete lack of professionally meaningful discussion of sexuality in relation to any illness or disability. It was therefore decided to include in this volume material that was published from 1940 through 1977. In our search for relevant references, all possible sources of information and reference indices were thoroughly and carefully researched. These resources include: (1) Psychological Abstracts, (2) Index Medicus, (3) Excerpta Medica, (4) Social Science Citation Index, (5) Nursing Index, (6) International Nursing Index, (7) Current Index of Journals in Education, (8) Community Mental Health Review, (9) Child Development Abstracts and Bibliography, (10) Mental Retardation Abstracts, (11) Abstracts for Social Workers, (12) Social Science Index, (13) Exceptional Child Education Abstracts, (14) Cumulative Index of Nursing Literature, and others. When available, computerized search services were utilized in addition to man-search in libraries.

In the process of preparing this volume, similar previous bibliographic projects were studied. They were found either to be limited to a single disability—i.e., spinal-cord injury, mental retardation—or to include only a list of references without any description of their content. This book provides the reader with abstracts of journal articles, books, monographs, and other published material covering a wide range of physical and mental disabilities and medical conditions and illnesses. Materials reviewed and annotated have been grouped according to illness or disability type. In addition to abstracts, this book includes a chapter that provides important and practical information about various audio-visual materials on sexuality that are available and can be of help both to professionals and to patients. This chapter is of special value since current developments in sex education and counseling with physically and mentally disabled persons call for extensive use of audio-visual material for purposes of instruction and illustration. This media review is compiled and edited by Suzanne M. Bruyer, and is presented here by permission of the Human Sciences Press.

I would like to take this opportunity to extend my appreciation and gratitude to Rebecca J. Gosnell and Cathy Roundtree, reference librarians at Indiana University–Purdue University at Indianapolis, for their devoted and highly professional assistance in identifying and locating references reviewed in this book.

Ami Sha'ked
Institute for Sex Therapy, Education, and Research
Rehabilitation Center, Sheba Medical Center
Tel-Hashomer, Israel

Human Sexuality in Physical and Mental Illnesses and Disabilities

---

An Annotated Bibliography

Chapter One

General

Medical Sexology / Sex and the Disabled

Medical Sexology

Bailey, M. K. Organic causes of sexual impotence. *Digest of Neurology and Psychiatry*, 1950, *18*, 125–126.

Various medical conditions that can cause sexual dysfunctions in the male are discussed.

Belt, B. G. Some organic causes of impotence. *Medical Aspects of Human Sexuality*, 1973, *7*(1), 152–161.

Neurologic, chemical, endocrinologic, and surgical causes of sexual impotence are identified and discussed in view of research and clinical studies. The author asserts that while many causes of impotence can be diagnosed, only occasionally can a remedy be provided.

Burchell, R. C., Massie, E., Kurland, M. L., and Roen, P. R. Viewpoints: What conditions require a patient to abstain from sexual activity? *Medical Aspects of Human Sexuality*, 1976, *10*(9), 55–70.

Discussed in this paper are obstetric-gynecologic conditions, cardiac disorders, various infections, pregnancy, uterine cancer, and other medical conditions that may require a patient to abstain from sexual activity. Both myth and medical facts are presented.

Carey, P. Temporary sexual dysfunction in reversible health limitations. *Nursing Clinics of North America*, 1975, *10*(3), 575–586.

The main purpose of this article is to discuss male and female sexual dysfunctions associated with health problems, e.g., disease processes, surgical procedures, and drug treatment. The nursing management of temporary sexual dysfunctions resulting from these health problems is also discussed. The nurse's function includes identifying possible sexual dysfunctions in the patient and making an effort to open free communication with the patient. If necessary, the patient must be adequately referred to a professionally trained sex therapist.

Fine, H. L. Sexual problems of chronically ill patients. *Medical Aspects of Human Sexuality*, 1974, *8*(10), 137–138.

Studies dealing with sex and chronic illness show that sexuality continues to be an important part in the lives of many chronically ill patients. In this brief article, the author outlines and discusses some specific suggestions for sex counseling with the chronically ill patient and the disabled. The author concludes that "most sexual problems of chronically ill patients can be resolved through reassurance and encouragement as well as cooperation and patience from their spouse."

Ford, A. B., and Orfirer, A. P. Sexual behavior and the chronically ill patient. *Medical Aspects of Human Sexuality*, 1967, *1*(2), 51–61.

The authors discuss the relationship between sexual functioning and behavior and chronic illness. Specific illnesses and medical conditions presented include cerebrovascular disorders, endocrine diseases, spinal-cord injuries, and pelvic surgery. Also discussed are the role of the physician in facilitating sexual adjustment in patients, and patterns of adequate psychosexual adjustment.

Golden, J. S. How you can help patients with physical ailments to a better sex life. *Medical Times*, 1976, *104*(9), 83–91.

This article is addressed to health-care professionals in an attempt to increase their awareness of sexual difficulties in patients who suffer from physical ailments. The author stresses the importance of sex counseling with these patients, and indicates that the counselor has to be comfortable in discussing sexuality with patients.

Greene, F. T., Kirk, M., and Thompson, I. M. Retrograde ejaculation. *Medical Aspects of Human Sexuality*, 1970, *4*(12), 59–65.

The nature, incidence, and etiology of retrograde ejaculation are discussed. Various medical conditions and surgical procedures that may result in this ejaculatory disorder are identified and examined. Treatment suggestions are also made.

Griffith, E. R., and Trieschmann, R. B. Sexual function restoration in the physically disabled: Use of a private hospital room. *Archives of Physical Medicine and Rehabilitation*, 1977, *58*(8), 363–369.

The authors relate their experience in restoring sexual functioning in physically disabled patients through the use of a private room attached to the ward. The article describes the room and its purposes.

Hansen, D. D. Physical manifestations of sexual conflict. *Medical Aspects of Human Sexuality*, 1967, *1*(1), 31–34.

When direct sexual expression is unavailable or blocked, an alternative physical expression is needed to preserve psychological equilibrium. The association between various physical disturbances and sexual difficulties and conflicts is discussed in light of numerous case studies. Some specific suggestions for counseling are presented.

Hansen, D. D. Physical symptoms that may reveal sexual conflict. In C. W. Wahl (Ed.), *Sexual problems: Diagnosis and treatment in medical practice*. New York: Free Press, 1967.

The manifestation of sexual dysfunctions and conflicts in various physical symptoms is discussed and several case studies are presented for illustration.

Hirsch, E. W. Difficult ejaculation. *Sexology*, 1959, *26*, 303–307.

Organic, medical, and psychological factors in retarded ejaculation are identified and discussed along with some suggestions for treatment. Among the medical conditions associated with this sexual dysfunction are prolonged inflammation in seminal vesicles, intensive stricture formation within the posterior urethra, and Peyronie's disease.

Holsclaw, D. S., Perlmutter, A. D., Jockin, H., and Shwachman, H. Genital abnormalities in male patients with cystic fibrosis. *Journal of Urology*, 1971, *106*, 568–574.

This paper presents the authors' observation and examination of the clinical, chemical, surgical, and pathological aspects of the genital system of male patients with cystic fibrosis. Also described are findings relating to the reproductive capability of these patients. Abnormalities of the genital tracts were found to be an early constant feature of this disease. These changes are reported to be responsible for sterility and aspermia, and are reflected in the reduced volume and altered chemical composition of the ejaculate in these patients. The authors indicate, however, that testicular function and male sexual activity need not be affected by the disease. In female patients, cystic fibrosis does not cause comparable anatomic abnormalities. Most women with cystic fibrosis can bear children successfully.

Jacobson, L. Illness and human sexuality. *Nursing Outlook*, 1974, *22*(1), 50–53.

In the medical treatment offered the ill, the whole body is considered, but seldom is the sexual functioning of the individual integrated in the treatment. Among nurses there is little knowledge of sex counseling. In order for the health-care professional to fully "nurse" the ill person to health, the effects of illness on sexuality must be discussed and the patient must be counseled. The author discusses sexual aspects of various common health disorders, i.e., heart disease, pulmonary disease, obesity. She suggests that sex counseling needs to be an integral part of the health care of patients. The psychosexual aspects of the disfiguring and mutilating forms of cancer are also discussed. Specific suggestions for effective counseling by nurses are presented.

Jaffe, L. The terminally ill. In H. L. Gochros and J. S. Gochros (Eds.), *The sexually oppressed*. New York: Association Press, 1977.

Sexual problems and concerns of long-term hospitalized patients and their spouses are discussed. Medical and psychological aspects of the sexual dysfunctions experienced by these patients are presented.

Johnson, J. *Disorders of sexual potency in the male*. Oxford: Pergamon Press, 1968.

In general, this book discusses the symptoms, etiology, prognosis and treatment of sexual dysfunctions in the male, i.e., impotence, ejaculatory problems, and sexual deviations. Of special interest are chapters covering neurological, endocrinological, and other organic problems associated with sexual difficulties in the male. Also of interest is a chapter discussing disorders of potency related to and associated with psychiatric illness.

Kaufman, J. J. Organic and psychological factors in the genesis of impotence and premature ejaculation. In C. W. Wahl (Ed.), *Sexual problems: Diagnosis and treatment in medical practice*. New York: Free Press, 1967.

Psychological and organic factors causing impotence are discussed in this chapter. Of particular interest is the section identifying and discussing various physical illnesses and disabling conditions that may result in sexual dysfunction, e.g., vascular diseases, genitourinary failure, and others.

Kinch, R. A. H. Painful coitus. *Medical Aspects of Human Sexuality*, 1967, *1*(2), 6–12.

Organic and psychosomatic causes of dyspareunia are discussed along with various treatment modalities. The author concludes that "as soon as it is diagnosed, organic dyspareunia is easy to cure or refer, but the cure of psychosomatic dyspareunia requires a physician sensitive to the social environment of the marital unit."

Labby, D. H. Sexual concomitants of disease and illness. *Postgraduate Medicine*, 1975, *58*(1), 103–111.

The author asserts that "sexual functioning is responsive to stress and is thus influenced by emotional tensions and pressures, including those arising in the course of illness from any cause." The effects of various diseases and medical conditions on sexual functioning are identified and discussed along with the role and function of the physician in providing needed counseling and advice. Specific medical conditions discussed include cardiovascular diseases, hypertensive vascular disease, pulmonary diseases, renal disorders, diabetes mellitus, pelvic problems, and surgical intervention.

MacRae, I., and Henderson, G. Sexuality and irreversible health limitations. *Nursing Clinics of North America*, 1975, *10*(3), 587–597.

The main focus of this article concerns nursing assessment and intervention with patients who have irreversible health limitations. The article deals specifically with guidelines in approaching the patient regarding concerns about his or her sexuality. The second part of the article discusses specific activities in assessment of and intervention in the sexual aspects of a patient's care. The author suggests that before a nurse can effectively discuss a patient's sexuality, the nurse needs to be aware of and comfortable with her own sexuality. In addition to self-awareness, the nurse needs to have adequate knowledge of the anatomy and physiology of sexual functioning and of how irreversible health limitations affect this functioning.

Marbach, A. H., Mead, B. T., Rutherford, R. N., Wahl, C. W., Holmes, D. J., Fink, P. J., and Bernstein, W. C. Viewpoints: In what types of presenting complaints should physicians inquire about sexual practices or take a sexual history. *Medical Aspects of Human Sexuality*, 1973, 7(6), 34–44.

Various physical and mental symptoms that should alert the treating physician to possible sexual difficulties in the patient are discussed along with specific suggestions for effective sex-history interviews.

Money, J. Components of eroticism in man: II. The orgasm and genital somesthesia. *Journal of Nervous and Mental Disease*, 1961, *132*, 289–297.

The paper examines erotic arousal and orgasm in spinal-cord-injury patients, and other cases of unusual anomalies or impairments of the genital-reproductive system. Data were obtained from patients through extensive interviews conducted by the author. Based on his findings, the author concludes that sexual orgasm is coordinated by genitopelvic anatomy, hormones, and the brain, "any one of which may fail in its contribution without total destruction of orgastic function." Also, no one of these contributing components can be considered indispensable more than the others. Among the rare cases discussed are: extensive surgical resection of the genitals; prostatic resection; postpriapism impotence; eunuchism; and hypogonadism.

Money, J. Sexual problems of the chronically ill. In C. W. Wahl (Ed.), *Sexual problems: Diagnosis and treatment in medical practice*. New York: Free Press, 1967.

Problems of sexual functioning associated with various illness conditions, crippling and disfiguring injuries, specific sexual-system deformities, and other diseases are discussed in this chapter. Treatment and counseling possibilities are also presented.

Mozes, E. B. Treating organic impotence. *Sexology*, 1959, *25*, 568–573.

According to the author, about ten percent of all cases of sexual impotence are due to physical illness or organic faults. Some of these organic causes of impotence are discussed, along with some suggestions for treatment. Among the conditions discussed are paraplegia, diabetes, overweight, alcoholism, and drug abuse.

Naughton, J. Effect of chronic illness on sexual performance. *Medical Aspects of Human Sexuality*, 1975, *9*(10), 110–119.

Almost any form of chronic physical impairment or illness can adversely affect a patient's sexual functioning and behavior. The impact of spinal-cord injuries and coronary heart disease is the focus of discussion in this article. The author calls for more adequate sex counseling for the severely disabled person to assist him or her in obtaining some level of sexual adjustment.

Orfirer, A. P. Loss of sexual function in the male. In B. Schoenber, A. C. Carr, D. Peretz, and A. H. Kutscher (Eds.), *Loss and grief: Psychological management in medical practice*. New York: Columbia University Press, 1970.

In this chapter, the author discusses the traumatic psychological effects of the loss of sexual function in the male. Of particular interest is a section discussing the impact of feelings of loss on sexual functioning in illnesses which may physically involve the genital organs, e.g., genital surgery and spinal-cord injuries. The role of the physician in assisting patients in this area of concern is identified and described.

Paradowski, W. Socialization patterns and sexual problems of the institutionalized chronically ill and physically disabled. *Archives of Physical Medicine and Rehabilitation*, 1977, *58*(2), 53–59.

This article reports the results of a study aimed at examining sexual adjustment among institutionalized, long-term physically disabled patients (n=155). Results show that long institutionalization does not necessarily invalidate sexuality. Other results and conclusions are discussed.

Pearlman, C. K. Traumatic causes of impotence. *Medical Aspects of Human Sexuality*, 1975, *9*(6), 76–82.

Traumatic causes of impotence are discussed in light of clinical and research findings. Conditions presented include injuries to the penis, introduction of foreign bodies into the urethra, loss of the testicles, head injuries, spinal-cord injuries, and others.

Pinderhughes, C. A., Grace, E. B., Reyna, L. J., and Anderson, R. T. Interrelationships between sexual functioning and medical conditions. *Medical Aspects of Human Sexuality*, 1972, *6*(10), 52–76.

Both physicians and their patients hold various impressions regarding the relationships between medical conditions and sexual function and behavior. This article presents and discusses the results of a study aimed at the examination of these relationships. An attempt was made to study the degree to which patients and physicians think that there are relationships, the amount of communication that occurs between them regarding these relationships, the amount of information physicians believe is available on these matters, and the amount of information which is actually available. Data are summarized and conclusions are presented.

Rhodes, P. Psychosexual problems of chronic handicapped disease. *Medical Journal of Australia*, 1976, *2*(18), 688–692.

Psychological and sociosexual aspects of chronic illness and severe disabling conditions are discussed. The role of the health-care practitioner in alleviating sexual concerns of patients is identified and stressed.

Rubin, I. Climax without ejaculation. *Sexology*, 1964, *30*(1), 694–696.

In a number of cases, men may be rendered incapable of ejaculation as a result of physical diseases or surgery. The effects of various diseases (e.g., diabetes, urologic disorders) on the ejaculation mechanism are discussed. Aftereffects of prostate surgery, and the use of certain drugs, can result in retrograde ejaculation.

Rubin, I. Sexual adjustment in relation to pregnancy, illness, surgery, physical handicaps and other unusual circumstances. In C. E. Vincent (Ed.), *Human sexuality in medical education and practice*. Springfield, Ill.: Charles C. Thomas, 1975.

Physical aspects of sexual functioning are discussed with regard to various diseases, surgery, and physically handicapping conditions. Medical conditions included in this chapter are cardiac disorders, hypertension, pregnancy, and diabetes. Conditions relating to surgery that are discussed are prostatic surgery, hysterectomy, mastectomy, oophorectomy, colostomy and rectal surgery, and vaginal surgery. Alternatives for sexual expression for those with a physical handicap are discussed briefly. Other medical problems associated with sexuality which are presented include epilepsy, mental retardation, institutional isolation, and disfiguring injuries and diseases. The author emphasizes the physician's responsibility to determine the level of functioning of the patient and to freely discuss sexuality with the patient. The importance of sex counseling with patients is emphasized.

Spencer, R. F., and Raft, D. Somatic symptoms of sexual conflicts. *Medical Aspects of Human Sexuality*, 1967, *10*(6), 141–150.

The author presents case examples to illustrate direct somatic symptoms of sexual conflicts that result in shame, guilt, anxiety, and inhibition. The most common of these symptoms seems to be pelvic congestion, which is a result of chronic or repeated arousal without orgastic release, and which usually is perceived as discomfort in the pelvic area and back.

Taussig, L. M. Psychosexual and psychosocial aspects of cystic fibrosis. *Medical Aspects of Human Sexuality*, 1976, *10*(2), 101–102.

Sociomedical considerations and psychosocial and sexual aspects of cystic fibrosis are discussed and suggestions for counseling and therapy are presented.

Tyler, E. A. Sex and medical illness. In A. M. Freedman, H. I. Kaplan, and B. J. Sadock (Eds.), *Comprehensive textbook of psychiatry* (Vol. 2). Baltimore: Williams and Wilkins, 1975.

Medical illness and sexual behavior are commonly interrelated. The relationship between sexual function, dysfunction, and behavior and medical illness is discussed, along with some specific suggestions for counseling.

Tyler, E. A. Sex and medical illness. In B. J. Sadock, H. I. Kaplan, and A. M. Freedman (Eds.), *The sexual experience*. Baltimore: Williams and Wilkins, 1976.

The author asserts that "there is an increasingly widespread recognition that a reciprocal relationship probably exists between most medical illnesses and patients' sexual behaviors, attitudes, and expectations." He classifies sexual behavior problems associated with medical illness into four groups: disinterest, or lack of desire for sexual activity; physical incapacity or discomfort with sexual performance; fear of causing, precipitating, or aggravating a physical illness by sexual activities; and the use of physical illness as an excuse to avoid undesired sexual experiences. These four groups of possible sexual implications of physical illness are further discussed. In conclusion the author suggests that "when a latent sexual problem becomes manifest during medical illnesses, the physician managing the medical illness must recognize the relationship of the two problems and refer those he does not feel competent to treat."

Wilcox, R. Counseling patients about sex problems. *Nursing*, 1973, *3*(3), 44–46.

Sexual problems and concerns encountered by the practicing nurse in various medical fields, and the nurse's role in alleviating them, are discussed. Emphasis is placed on patients in intensive care units, where "sexual acting out is common," and on patients in trauma and neurosurgery wards, e.g., spinal-cord-injury patients. Also discussed is the role of the nurse in sex counseling with geriatric patients.

Wolfe, W. G., and Detmer, D. E. Disease, surgery, and family relationships. In D. W. Abse, E. M. Nash, and L. M. R. Louden (Eds.), *Marital and sexual counseling in medical practice* (2nd ed.). New York: Harper and Row, 1974.

Aimed at the practicing physician, this chapter identifies and discusses family, marriage, and sexual aspects associated with various chronic diseases. These include acquired and congenital heart disease, surgery of the head and neck, breast surgery, hysterectomy, colon surgery, renal transplantation, and other medical conditions. Possible sexual dysfunctions associated with some of these conditions are discussed and case reports of patients are presented to illustrate possible marital implications. The authors assert that the physician must be aware of and prepare the patient for the potential impact of a disease or its treatment on marriage and the family.

Woods, N. F. *Human sexuality in health and illness*. St. Louis: C. V. Mosby, 1975.

This book treats sexuality from biological, psychological, and social points of view. The book includes chapters on sexual adaptation to hospitalization and illness; sexuality and chronic illness, e.g., diabetes and heart diseases; sexual adjustment following enterostomy, mastectomy, and hysterectomy; sexuality and paraplegia; and the effects of drugs on sexual behavior and functioning. The role of the health-care professional in sex counseling and sex education is also discussed.

Zahn, M. Incapacity, impotence and invisible impairment: Their effects upon interpersonal relations. *Journal of Health and Social Behavior*, 1973, *14*, 115–123.

This study examines the impact of certain characteristics of physical impairments upon various interpersonal relations, i.e., relationships with spouse, general family relationships, relations with friends, and casual encounters. One of the functional limitations studied was sexual dysfunction. It was hypothesized that the loss of sexual function as a result of physical disability will be disruptive of interpersonal relations primarily within the family setting. Also, the younger the sexually dysfunctional person and the higher his social class status the greater will be the disruption in interpersonal relationships within the family structure. Results and conclusions are presented.

Zalar, M. Human sexuality: A total component of patient care. *NSHA* [*Imprint*], 1974, *21*, 22–23, 45, 47–48.

Sexual concerns of hospitalized patients, and the role of the nurse in dealing with sexual acting-out behavior of patients, are discussed. The importance of sex education within the context of nurses' training is emphasized.

Zalar, M. Human sexuality: A component of total patient care. *Nursing Digest*, 1975, *3*, 40–43.

Sexual concerns and difficulties of hospitalized patients are discussed along with some factors that facilitate better nurse-patient relationships and increase the nurse's ability to deal with the patient's sexuality.

Zinsser, H. H. Sex and surgical procedures in the male. In A. M. Freedman, H. I. Kaplan, and B. J. Sadock (Eds.), *Comprehensive textbook of psychiatry* (Vol. 2). Baltimore: Williams and Wilkins, 1975.

Sexual dysfunctions in the male secondary to various surgical procedures are discussed. Specific procedures described include colostomy, ileostomy, and renal transplant.

Zinsser, H. H. Sex and surgical procedures in the male. In B. J. Sadock, H. I. Kaplan, and A. M. Freedman (Eds.), *The sexual experience*. Baltimore: Williams and Wilkins, 1976.

The author asserts that many urological surgical procedures threaten sexual potency in the male. The sexual implications of various surgical treatments are identified and discussed. These procedures include sterilization and castration, vasectomy, colostomy, ileostomy, and renal transplant. Many operative procedures result in disorders of ejaculation, e.g., retrograde ejaculation, absent ejaculation. These sexual disorders and their association with various urological surgical procedures are also discussed. The author suggests that "the surgeon, as a key figure in bringing on the loss of function, has to weigh benefits and possible losses, but he usually accepts more readily than the patient the dysfunctions involved."

Sex and the Disabled

Anderson, T. P., and Cole, T. M. Sexual Counseling of the physically disabled. *Postgraduate Medicine*, 1975, *58*(1), 117–123.

Sexual satisfaction and adjustment play an important role in the individual's ability to adapt to an acquired physical disability. The authors present a framework that shows how sexual functioning is affected by various physically disabling conditions, such as brain injuries, spinal-cord injuries, muscular diseases, amputations, renal disease, diabetes, heart condition, multiple sclerosis, and enterostomy. The framework shows the areas of sexual function impaired by each disability for both males and females. According to the authors, sexuality has to be discussed with physically disabled patients within the context of other medical and rehabilitation problems and issues faced by them. A frank discussion of the sexual implication of a disability should take place when the patient is ready for such a discussion. The authors also stress the following points: (1) loss of sensation does not mean loss of feelings and emotions; (2) loss of potency does not mean loss of ability; (3) loss of urinary continence does not mean loss of penile competence, and (4) loss of genitalia does not mean loss of sexuality.

Attitudes on sexuality in rehabilitation. *Resource Guide*, 1976, *1*(1), 51–53.

Members of the Center for Independent Living discuss in this article their feelings and attitudes regarding their sexuality. The sexuality of the disabled person has been ignored far too long. Negative attitudes toward the disabled person as a sexual being have caused difficulties for the disabled in viewing themselves as sexual beings. The attitudes of health-care and rehabilitation personnel are a key factor in assisting the disabled person to achieve sexual adjustment and total rehabilitation and social integration.

The Center for Independent Living is "a support group owned and operated by persons with physical disabilities. . . . They work together on all aspects of creating an independent life style for the physically disabled." They use peer counseling programs to assist newly disabled persons with the mental preparation for independent living. CIL also works for political change, particularly within the medical profession and institutions which serve the disabled. The Center, located in Berkeley, California, offers consulting services to rehabilitation centers and hospital staff.

Ayrault, E. W. *Helping the handicapped teenager mature.* New York: Association Press, 1971.

According to the author, the main purpose of this book is to clarify the handicapped teenager's role in the home and society, and to assist him or her in dealing with daily problems imposed by the disabling condition. The book is also intended to assist parents and other family members in understanding the increased range of experience and maturity open to the teenager if he or she is properly directed and encouraged. Of particular interest is a chapter discussing sexuality and the handicapped teenager. Outlined in this chapter are common sexual problems faced by the handicapped and the importance of and the need for sex education for handicapped teenagers and their parents.

Barton, D. Sexually deprived individuals. *Medical Aspects of Human Sexuality*, 1972, *6*(2), 88–97.

Sexual deprivation as a result of physical illness or trauma, and its psychological impact on the patient and the patient's spouse, are among the topics discussed in this paper.

Bergström-Walan, M. B. Sex and handicap: Investigation of knowledge and attitudes toward sex among physically handicapped pupils at boarding school. Paper presented at the International Cerebral Palsy Society, April 1971.

Results of a study examining knowledge and attitudes toward sex and the handicapped person were discussed in this presentation.

Berkman, A. H. Sexuality: A human condition. *Journal of Rehabilitation*, 1975, *41*, 13–15, 37.

Sexuality is viewed as a dynamic, continuous process in human development, based on learning and developmental experiences. Disability in childhood usually affects the individual's sexual development and adult relationships. This paper describes the scope of the problem of sexuality in the disabled person and explores the role of the rehabilitationists in facilitating the client's sexual development. The author has developed a positive approach to sexuality and disability as a result of his experiences as a sex counselor with spinal-cord-injured veterans. He presents studies which indicate that sexual inadequacy can affect overall psychological adjustment because sexuality is an organizing factor forming the person's sense of identity. Sex education and sex counseling help the disabled to become more creative sexually, to communicate effectively with their sex partners, and to improve their sexual function.

Bidgood, F. E. Sexuality and the handicapped. *SIECUS Report*, 1974, *2*(3), 1–2.

The message of this article is that all human beings are sexual by nature, from the moment of their birth to the moment of death. This includes the handicapped person, who should enjoy equal rights for the expression of sexual feelings and needs. The article provides an analysis of the difference between the psychosexual and the social development of the disabled person and that of the able-bodied person. While the latter develops a more-or-less realistic sexual self-concept and is accepted as a sexual human being, the development of the former is one of frustration and denial, especially for those handicapped who are placed in an institution early in life. Those who become handicapped as teenagers or adults face greater problems because they have experienced the sexual attitudes of society, and "having internalized society's concept of the handicapped as asexual and something less than human, they apply it to themselves in their new state." As a result, their sexual self-concept is distorted. Professionals should accept the disabled person as a sexual human being and provide services that assist the individual in the expression of his or her sexuality.

Billington, R. Sexual self image and physical disability. *Midwife Health Visit Community Nurse*, 1977, *13*(2), 46–49.

Sexual adjustment is an important factor that promotes total rehabilitation of physically disabled persons. This article discusses psychosexual and social aspects of disability and identifies the role of the health-care practitioner in assisting patients toward improving their sexual self image.

Branson, H. K. When a mate is disabled, what sex solutions? *Sexology*, 1967, *34*, 98–100.

The author discusses problems of sexual and psychosocial adjustment faced by the physically disabled person and his or her spouse and suggests some readjustment possibilities. A case study is presented to illustrate both the difficulties and some possible solutions to the problems.

Branson, H. K., and Branson, R. Sex and the handicapped. *Sexology*, 1964, *30*, 561–564.

Sexual aspects in physical disabilities are discussed.

Carpenter, J. O. Changing roles and disagreement in families with disabled husbands. *Archives of Physical Medicine and Rehabilitation*, 1974, *55*, 272–274.

The purpose of this study was to identify some of the complex ways in which disabled husbands in families with employed wives and in families with nonemployed wives affect the family. Another goal of this study was to determine whether or not husbands of employed wives make fewer economic decisions than those with unemployed wives. Finally, an attempt was made to ascertain whether the severity of disability affects the performance of household roles by disabled husbands. Results of this study are analyzed and discussed.

Chigier, E. Sexual adjustment of the handicapped. Proceedings Preview: Twelfth World Congress of Rehabilitation International, Sydney, Australia, 1972, *1*, 224–227.

The author discusses the rights of the handicapped for culturally normative sexual expression, and the importance of sexual adjustment in the rehabilitation process of the disabled person.

Chigier, E. Sex counseling of the physically disabled. Paper read at the Thirteenth World Congress of Rehabilitation International, Tel Aviv, Israel, June 13–18, 1976.

The author describes the experiences gained in sex counseling of physically disabled patients at the Sex Adjustment Clinic for the Disabled at the Rehabilitation Center, Sheba Medical Center, Israel.

Cole, T. Reaction of the rehabilitation team to patients with sexual problems. Paper presented at the Thirty-Fifth Annual Assembly of the American Academy of Physical Medicine and Rehabilitation, Washington, D.C., October 24, 1973.

Various reactions of rehabilitation workers to the disabled person presenting sexual problems are discussed. The author asserts that, in contrast to ineffective reactions, the rehabilitation worker needs to consider sexuality a legitimate part of the rehabilitation process and facilitate sexual adjustment in the disabled person.

Cole, T. M. Sexuality and physical disabilities. *Archives of Sexual Behavior*, 1975, *4*(4), 389–403.

The author emphasizes the importance of sexual adjustment for total rehabilitation of physically disabled persons. Realistic acceptance of the disability is directly associated with realistic consideration of sexuality. Cole also presents physiological explanations of reflex erection and of the sexual response cycle in the spinal-cord-injured person as compared to able-bodied persons. A section on the spinal-cord-injured female is included. The author makes some suggestions for counseling the disabled person in the area of sexuality.

Cole, T. M., and Cole, S. S. The handicapped and sexual health. *SIECUS Report*, Special Issue on the Handicapped, 1976.

The authors discuss the importance of sexual expression and adjustment for the physically disabled person. The implications for rehabilitation and health-care professions are: (1) health-care practitioners must be comfortable with their own sexuality so that they can effectively assist the disabled person in the process of sexual adjustment; (2) practitioners should display a willingness to discuss sexuality with the disabled person; (3) mutual trust and open communication should be developed and maintained between the practitioner and the disabled client; (4) the health-care professional needs to accept the fact that sexuality is an important factor in the disabled person's rehabilitation process; and (5) professionals need to reexamine their sexual attitudes and gain understanding of their sexuality. The message to the handicapped person is that sexuality involves much more than the physical characteristics of sexual intercourse.

Cole, T. M., and Cole, S. S. Sexuality and physical disabilities: The physician's role. *Minnesota Medicine*, 1977, *60*(7), 525–529.

Although some disabilities directly affect sexual functioning, most do not. This article discusses sexuality in physical disabilities, identifies myths held by health-care practitioners, emphasizes the importance of sexual adjustment within the framework of total rehabilitation, and describes the physician's role in assisting the patient to reach sexual adjustment.

Coleman, N. J. Sexual information in the rehabilitation process. *Journal of Applied Rehabilitation Counseling*, 1974, *5*, 201–206.

Rehabilitation counselors are frequently confronted by clients who have problems of sexual nature. Counselors must be aware of the importance of sexual adjustment in the context of total rehabilitation of clients. The article reviews sex information and sources of such information that are of interest to rehabilitation counselors working with spinal-cord-injured clients, mentally retarded persons, or persons with other disabilities.

Diamond, M. Sexuality and the handicapped. *Rehabilitation Literature*, 1974, *35*, 34–40.

Various issues and problems related to the sexuality and sexual expression of the handicapped person are discussed, along with some recommendations for handling problems presented by the handicapped. The author also presents several general rules for improving sexual functioning that are pertinent for all, but especially so for the disabled person.

Egg, M. *The different child grows up*. New York: John Day Company, 1969.

This book discusses psychological, educational, and vocational aspects of mental retardation. Of special interest are two chapters discussing sexuality and the mentally retarded person. One of these chapters argues for the importance of sex education for mentally retarded persons and discusses an approach to take in teaching sex-related subjects to this population. The other chapter of interest discusses marriage for the retarded person.

Enby, G. *Let there be love: Sex and the handicapped*. New York: Taplinger, 1975.

This book, written by a young woman paralyzed and confined to a wheelchair, pinpoints the urgent need for a change in society's attitude toward the physically disabled person. The author asserts that the public as well as health-care professionals are far from aware that the handicapped are denied the most fundamental of human needs, the need to love and to express their sexuality. She gives an account of her experience of the repressive attitudes toward sex in rehabilitation and hospital settings and the isolation a disabled person has to cope with in a society largely ignorant of the disabled person's sexual needs and capabilities. Constructive proposals for alternatives are offered.

Ferro, J. M., and Allen, H. A. Sexuality: The effects of physical impairment. *Rehabilitation Counseling Bulletin*, 1976, *20*(2), 148–151.

Using a semantic differential scaling procedure, the authors compared the attitudes of physically disabled college students (n=23) with nondisabled students (n=47) on attitudes toward various sexual behaviors. Results show no significant differences between the two groups in this regard. However, the disabled group scored significantly lower in regard to feelings of their own sexuality.

Finch, E. Sexuality and the disabled. *Canadian Nurse*, 1977, *73*(1), 19–20.

The importance of sexual adjustment for the physically disabled person and chronically ill patient has been recognized by many. This article presents sexual problems and concerns experienced by patients and describes the role of the nurse in alleviating them.

Find, S. L., Skipper, J. K., and Hallenbeck, P. N. Physical disability and problems in marriage. *Journal of Marriage and the Family*, 1968, *30*, 64–73.

The major purpose of this study was to examine the effects of severe, long-term physically disabling conditions upon marital relationships in couples where the wife was the disabled individual (n=36). A Perception of Needs Scale and a Marital Satisfaction Scale were developed and used in this study. Results show that the physical condition of the disabled subjects cannot be used as a predictor of need or of marriage satisfaction in either member of the couple. Need satisfaction and marriage satisfaction were found to be highly correlated. The authors suggest areas for future research.

Frank, L. K. Social and emotional development in the adolescent crippled. *Crippled Children*, 1951, *29*(2), 4–5, 28.

The author is convinced that "much of the bitterness and life-long resentful hostility that handicapped adults often show could be avoided by more concern for the social, emotional, and sexual development of children." It seems that the handicapped adolescent is treated as a sexless person who lacks sexual needs and interests. Also, current rehabilitation practices give the disabled person little or no opportunity for social integration. Parents and professionals should recognize the need of adolescent disabled children to win attention and attract interest from the opposite sex. This is important in the developmental process of clarifying and establishing the masculine or feminine role.

Frankel, A. Sexual problems in rehabilitation. *Journal of Rehabilitation*, 1967, *33*, 19–20.

Anxiety after a devastating injury often brings to the surface hidden conflicts relating to the injured person's sex role. Often a patient displaces this sex-related anxiety to a concern about his physical status. This article discusses some of the sex-related problems that affect the rehabilitation process. It is important for the rehabilitation worker to be aware of the fact that a client's sexual behavior often reflects his characteristic style of participation in interpersonal relationships. In dealing with the patient's sexual rehabilitation, the health-care professional must also deal with the patient's family and must try to understand the problems and stresses that the patient might encounter while at home.

Gochros, H. L., and Gochros, J. S. (Eds.). *The sexually oppressed.* New York: Association Press, 1977.

This book discusses various groups that, according to the authors, are sexually oppressed. Of special interest are chapters presenting sexual concerns and problems of the physically disabled, the mentally retarded, the deaf, the aged, and the terminally ill patient.

Golub, S. When your patient's problem involves sex. *RN*, 1975, *38*(3), 27–31.

The author asserts that, "because of her own anxiety about sex, the nurse may avoid the patient's attempts to communicate his sexual concerns." Aimed at practicing nurses, this article discusses sexual difficulties and concerns associated with various medical conditions, such as hysterectomy, prostatectomy, and diabetes. The role of the nurse in assisting the patient in dealing with his or her sexual concerns and problems is also identified and discussed.

Gordon, S. Being attractive. *The Exceptional Parent*, 1975, *5*(5), 30–31.

This brief article stresses the importance for the disabled adolescent of self-acceptance as a core requirement to becoming well-accepted, socially and sexually, by others.

Gordon, S. On being the parent of a handicapped youth: A guide to enhance the self-image of physically and learning disabled adolescents and young adults. New York: Association for Brain Injured Children, 1973.

The author asserts that feelings of inferiority in handicapped youths can be reinforced by their parents' feelings of anxiety and guilt. The aim of this booklet is to discuss how handicapped persons feel about themselves and their relationships with other people. The message to parents is that "guilt, anxiety, self-pity, over-indulgence, ambivalence, or unrealistic demands help no one." To assist parents in their interaction with their disabled teenagers, the author presents a wide range of topics in question-and-answer format, including questions on sexuality, marriage, and children of handicapped persons.

Gordon, S. Sexual rights of people . . . who happen to be handicapped. Syracuse, New York: Center of Human Policy, 1974.

Professionals are gradually facing the realization that people with disabilities are not exceptional in their sexual impulses. This pamphlet proclaims that access to information about sex, sexual expression, and birth control services is a basic right of all handicapped persons. The author emphasizes: "The isolated among our handicapped cannot afford to be naive about sex. The retarded and their families must be prepared for making decisions about such matters as contraception and voluntary sterilization." The author discusses how parental attitudes, coupled with the general atmosphere of the family environment, affect the child's eventual sexual attitudes and behaviors in adulthood. Parents' reactions to the child's masturbation or his use of obscenity are discussed, and the problems of sexuality in an institutional setting are examined.

Greengross, W. *Entitled to love*. Horsham, Sussex, Great Britain: National Fund for Research into Crippling Disease, 1976.

The author stresses the importance of sexual expression and adjustment for the physically disabled person. This book discusses psychological, social, and sexual aspects of disability and the need for counseling and education for the improvement of sexual expression by the disabled.

Greengross, W. Sex problems of the disabled. *Rehabilitation*, 1975, *93*, 9–13.

In a paper presented at the Westminster International Seminar on "Rehabilitation—The New Era," Greengross strongly advocates the sexual rights of the disabled. She discusses the sexual problems of the disabled, "to give the subject the airing it so badly needs," and touches upon the topics of parental attitudes toward sex, sexual identity, masturbation, lack of privacy, lack of transportation, and inadequacy of sex counseling. She emphasizes that because the disabled are shut off from so many of the pleasures in life, they should be helped to develop all possible channels for pleasure, comfort, and personal exploration. These include all the joys of loving another human being and being loved in return.

Griffith, E. R., and Trieschmann, R. B. Treatment of sexual dysfunction in patients with physical disorders. In J. K. Meyer (Ed.), *Clinical management of sexual disorders.* Baltimore: Williams and Wilkins, 1976.

The authors assert that the "management of sexual problems in the physically disabled is a complex task because of the multiple etiological considerations and the varied treatment strategies with which the professional must be familiar." Therefore, they define the problems of sexual dysfunctions associated with physical disabilities by differentiating between the primary, organic dysfunctions and the secondary, behavioral ones. This chapter discusses the management and treatment procedures of both types of sexual dysfunctions. Aspects of treatment discussed are: when to initiate treatment; who is best qualified to treat; how to introduce the idea of treatment to the patient; and the need to recognize and accept the sexual value system of the treatment unit. Specific management procedures of primary and secondary sexual dysfunctions are identified and reviewed. The treatment modalities described included prostheses, drugs, exercises, surgery, behavior modification programs, training and practice of sexual activities, positions of sexual intercourse, alternate sexual behavior, group education and counseling, surrogate partner training, and sex education for disabled children.

Griffith, E. R., Trieschmann, R. B., Hohmann, G. W., Cole, T. M., Tobis, J. S., and Cummings, V. Sexual dysfunctions associated with physical disabilities. *Archives of Physical Medicine and Rehabilitation*, 1975, *56*, 8–13.

This paper is an abridgement of six addresses made at the 1973 joint annual meetings of the American Academy of Physical Medicine and Rehabilitation and the American Congress of Rehabilitation Medicine. In general, the papers emphasize the psychosocial aspects of sexuality which the rehabilitation team should consider in dealing with disabled persons. The role of learning, the importance of communication between partners, and the necessity of integrating sex drives, sex acts, and sexuality are discussed, along with principles of management of sexual dysfunctions in three disabilities, i.e., cardiovascular disorders, spinal-cord injuries, and amputations.

Guthrie, D. Sexual problems of disabled people: The work of SPOD. Paper presented at the Thirteenth World Congress of Rehabilitation International, Tel Aviv, Israel, June 13–18, 1976.

In 1973 a Committee on Sexual Problems of the Disabled (SPOD) was set up in England. The committee was initiated by the National Fund for Research into Crippling Diseases to study and advise on sexual problems as these might occur among disabled persons. A study of the sexual problems of physically disabled people, carried out on behalf of the Committee in 1974/75 by the Research Institute of Consumer Affairs, demonstrates clearly that: (a) the majority of disabled people encounter sexual problems associated with their disability. (b) Generally speaking, the more severe the overall handicap, the more probable is associated sexual difficulty. (c) Sexual problems arise in relation to all major groups of disability and are not linked only with disorders of the sexual system itself or with psychogenic elements of sexuality. (d) Until recently, little attention has been paid to such problems by the public or by professional workers in the field of disability. Indeed, the sexuality of the disabled man or woman has been ignored or tacitly denied by society in general. (e) Any thorough knowledge of the problems and of solutions to them is rare in the helping professions. Most training courses for medical, paramedical, and social workers take little account of them. (f) Most disabled people who encounter sexual difficulties receive little or no advice or counsel directed at solving or ameliorating their problems. These findings have been amply borne out by the Committee's experience, and SPOD has adopted an ongoing function aimed at public and professional education in these matters, accumulation and dissemination of information concerning them, and setting up a service for advice or referral for ongoing counsel where these are required by disabled clients or those concerned with them.

Heslinga, K., Scheller, A. M., and Berkuyl, A. *Not made of stone: The sexual problems of handicapped people.* Springfield, Ill.: Charles C. Thomas, 1974.

The idea that handicapped persons also have sexual needs is being realized more and more. This book discusses various motor disabilities and their impact on the sexual functioning of the handicapped person.

Also presented are the sexual implications of respiratory disorders and skin diseases. For the reader's clearer understanding of the physical and sociological aspects of sex, chapters on the reproductive system, its disorders and treatment, and adult sexuality are included.

Hoch, Z. Sex therapy and marital counseling for the disabled within the framework of a sex therapy center. Paper read at the Thirteenth World Congress of Rehabilitation International, Tel Aviv, Israel, June 13–18, 1976.

The author describes a sexual and marital counseling program conducted at Rambam Hospital in Haifa, Israel.

Hohmann, G. W. Reactions of the individual with a disability complicated by a sexual problem. Paper read at the Thirty-fifth Annual Assembly of the American Academy of Physical Medicine and Rehabilitation, Washington, D.C., October 24, 1973.

Sexual problems associated with a physical disability and the role of the rehabilitation staff in dealing with the sexuality of the disabled person are the two main topics discussed in this presentation. Also presented are a few precautions that should be considered when counseling the disabled person regarding his or her sexuality.

Lancaster-Gaye, D. (Ed.). *Personal relationships, the handicapped and the community: Some European thoughts and solutions.* London: Routledge and Kegan Paul, 1972.

Part two of this book discusses sexuality and marriage in physically disabled persons. Sex education and counseling programs in Holland, England, Sweden, and Denmark are presented.

Lindner, H. Perceptual sensitization to sexual phenomena in the chronic physically handicapped. *Journal of Clinical Psychology*, 1953, *9*, 67–68.

This study examined the hypothesis that sexual functioning is a crucial aspect in the development of psychological adjustment in paraplegics. Based on other research, it was felt that the chronically physically handicapped who retain their sexual potency after their injury differ significantly from those who are impotent. Twenty paraplegics who had retained some measure of sexual functioning were matched to twenty who had no sexual functioning. All were randomly selected. Each person was given two tests of perceptual function devised by the author. Results indicated that sexually potent patients have more ability to perceive and form concepts involving sexual identification. This study also helped to confirm that impotent paraplegic patients reject the notion of the loss of sexuality and express their sex function disability symbolically through feelings of insecurity and helplessness; they are preoccupied with their own bodies and physical complaints and find it difficult to socialize or to engage in vocational training. Sexual functioning seems to be a central factor in the readjustment process of paraplegics.

Ludwig, E. G., and Collett, J. Disability, dependency, and conjugal roles. *Journal of Marriage and the Family*, 1969, *31*, 736–739.

This study examined the effects of disability on conjugal behavior and role definition in marriage. It was found that disabled persons who were dependent on their spouses spent more time with their spouses and less time with friends and relatives. They were also less likely to be involved in decision making and were more likely to reflect conjugal role flexibility than disabled persons who were not dependent on their spouses.

Mowatt, M. H. Emotional conflicts of handicapped young adults and their mothers. *Cerebral Palsy Journal*, 1965, *26*, 6–8.

The need for opportunities for sexual expression and social integration is raised by a group of young persons with cerebral palsy. Other psychosocial aspects of this condition are presented.

Nagi, S. Z., and Clark, D. L. Factors in marital adjustment after disability. *Journal of Marriage and the Family*, 1964, *26*, 215–216.

Various demographic variables related to the impact of physical disability on the maintenance of intact marriages were examined by comparing a group of disabled persons who remained married with a group who were separated or divorced. Variables studied include sex, race, age, religious affiliation, occupation, level of education, level of earnings, number of children, and place of residence.

Nigro, G. Sexuality in the handicapped: Some observations on human needs and attitudes. *Rehabilitation Literature*, 1975, *36*(7), 202–205.

The author offers some personal observations on sexuality in physically and mentally disabled persons based on her extensive experience in working with this population. She asserts that health-care professionals, educators, and the general public should accept the fact that the disabled are sexual persons who should enjoy equal opportunities for sexual development and expression. Professionals need to assist the disabled person in developing sexual identity and to promote social and sexual opportunities and integration. Sex education programs are needed to help disabled persons to understand their sexuality and to express it meaningfully.

Nigro, G. Some observations on personal relationships and sexual relationships among lifelong disabled Americans. *Rehabilitation Literature*, 1976, *37*(11–12), 328–330.

In this article, the author, a recreation specialist, presents her observations and concepts regarding social relationships, interpersonal interaction, and sexuality in severely disabled adults participating in a United Cerebral Palsy Association recreational program. An attempt is made to explain these concepts from a developmental point of view which shows that handicapped children "become further handicapped because they don't have the same opportunity for self-assertion and self-determination and the opportunity to gradually grow away from their families." This may limit their ability for satisfying interpersonal and sexual relationships in their adult life. Given the fact that the disabled person still has sexual and interpersonal interaction needs, there are four areas where assistance is needed: (1) improving the attitude of the public and encouraging the public to accept the fact that the disabled person is also a sexual human being; (2) providing knowledge and information about sex to the disabled person to replace ignorance and misconceptions about this subject; (3) promoting opportunities for increased social interaction and sexual experiences for the disabled; and (4) improving the disabled person's ability to establish meaningful personal relationships.

Nordqvist, I. *Life together: The situation of the handicapped.* Stockholm: The Swedish Central Committee for Rehabilitation, 1975 (English translation).

This book is an account of the Nordic Symposium on Sexual and Allied Problems Among the Orthopedically Handicapped, held in Stockholm, Sweden, in 1969. Among the topics discussed in this book are sex education for handicapped pupils, sexual needs of the handicapped, sexual functioning and fertility in orthopedically disabled males, sexual functioning and pregnancy in orthopedically disabled females, and contraceptive methods.

Nordqvist, I. The home and institutional environments in relation to the sexual development of orthopedically handicapped children and young people. In I. Nordqvist, *Life together: The situation of the handicapped.* Stockholm: The Swedish Central Committee for Rehabilitation, 1975 (English translation).

The orthopedically handicapped person has special needs for sex education both at home and in institutional environments. This chapter discusses these special needs in light of the person's psychosocial and sexual development. The parents' role in the sex education and development of their handicapped child is also identified and discussed. The author concludes that there is a need to promote understanding on the part of parents and health-care staff for sexual behavior and special needs of the handicapped child, and to enhance acceptance of the handicapped child as a sexual human being. Also needed are increased opportunities for better social interaction and integration for the handicapped.

Nordqvist, I. Sexual education for orthopedically handicapped pupils. In I. Nordqvist, *Life together: The situation of the handicapped.* Stockholm: The Swedish Central Committee for Rehabilitation, 1975 (English translation).

Results of a study conducted in Swedish schools showed that, compared to the nonhandicapped, orthopedically disabled pupils had a lower level of sexual knowledge. The author makes various suggestions to improve this situation. There is a need to facilitate a positive attitude toward sexuality among teaching and nursing staff and to increase their knowledge concerning sex and sexuality. The need for sensitivity training and sex counseling for handicapped students is identified, and some steps in promoting sexual knowledge are outlined and discussed.

Nordqvist, I. The sexual life of the orthopedically handicapped: Needs and opportunities. In I. Nordqvist, *Life together: The situation of the handicapped.* Stockholm: The Swedish Central Committee for Rehabilitation, 1975 (English translation).

The author stresses that "ignorance among many categories of staff as to the needs of the orthopedically handicapped and their ability to function sexually has unnecessarily restricted the chances of achieving a harmonic sexual life." The handicapped person's sexual needs are not different from those of the able-bodied. The handicapped person needs an equal opportunity to express his or her sexuality. The author discusses ways to promote the recognition of the sexual needs of the handicapped person. Factual information should be provided so that the individual can assume responsibility for his or her sexual life, obtain knowledge about how to function sexually despite the disability, and acquire greater opportunities for social contacts and integration.

Nordqvist, I. The sexual life of the orthopedically handicapped male. In I. Nordqvist, *Life together: The situation of the handicapped.* Stockholm: The Swedish Central Committee for Rehabilitation, 1975 (English translation).

Sexual functioning and fertility in male paraplegic patients are discussed in light of research and clinical findings. The need for sexual adjustment, its importance, and measures to promote its achievement by the handicapped are identified and discussed.

Nordqvist, I. The sexual life of orthopedically handicapped women. In I. Nordqvist, *Life together: The situation of the handicapped.* Stockholm: The Swedish Central Committee for Rehabilitation, 1975 (English translation).

Sexual functioning and pregnancy in orthopedically handicapped women are discussed in this chapter. Some suggestions for increasing sexual satisfaction are also presented. The author notes that the disabled woman has fewer sexual difficulties than does the disabled man. According to the author, this is due primarily to the more passive role that women usually assume in sexual intercourse, compared to the more active and physically involving role of men.

Partridge, J. C. A right to love? *Lancet*, 1972, *1*, 1057–1058.

This is an editorial review of a report that was written by Ann Shearer for England's National Association for Mental Health. The report presents the findings of a study examining attitudes, both in institutions and in the general public, toward the handicapped person's sexual needs and emotions. Myths and misconceptions were found in both samples. This article reviews and comments on the results of this study in light of current needs for improvement of society's attitudes toward the disabled person and for the promotion of normative sexual life and social integration for the disabled person.

Romano, M. D. The physically handicapped. In H. L. Gochros and J. S. Gochros (Eds.), *The sexually oppressed.* New York: Association Press, 1977.

Sexuality as it relates to physical disability in both male and female patients is discussed in light of numerous case studies.

Romano, M. D. Sexuality and the disabled female. *Accent on Living*, Summer 1973, 7–13.

Sexual function of the physically disabled woman is discussed in light of old and new perceptions and attitudes relating to feminine sexuality. Specific considerations affecting the sexual expression and function of the disabled woman are presented. These are: (1) "logistical" problems, such as sensory and motor changes, pain, spasticity, and urinary and bowel problems; (2) the need for greater verbal communication in order that the disabled woman may express her sexual desires and communicate to her partner the activities and positions she finds most pleasurable; (3) the need for the disabled woman to plan and prepare for sexual activity more than does the able-bodied woman; and (4) the creation of appropriate social encounters and opportunities that may lead to sexual expression.

Sadoughi, W., Leshner, M., and Fine, H. L. Sexual adjustment in a chronically ill and physically disabled population: A pilot study. *Archives of Physical Medicine and Rehabilitation*, 1971, *52*, 311–317.

This was a questionnaire study of patients discharged from a physical medicine and rehabilitation service regarding their sexual adjustment (n=55). Disabling conditions and illnesses included were emphysema, arthritis, stroke, and amputation. Seventy-eight percent of the subjects reported a decline in the frequency of sexual intercourse following disability. Many subjects indicated they would like to have sex counseling and advice. Other results are discussed and conclusions are presented. The authors point to the need for further investigation of specific disabilities and their psychosexual aspects.

Schlesinger, B. Sexuality and the physically handicapped. *Canadian Medical Association Journal*, 1976, *114*(9), 772–773, 809.

The impact of physical disability on sexuality is discussed in light of the importance of sex education for handicapped persons. Sex education can alleviate concerns and teach needed social skills.

Sex and the handicapped: A selected bibliography (1927–1975). Cleveland, Ohio: Veterans' Administration Hospital, 1975.

Five hundred and twenty-five references dealing with psychosocial and sexual aspects of various disabling conditions are listed in this booklet. Subject headings include: sex education, drug addiction, amputation, burns, spinal-cord injury, urogenital disorders, neoplasia, the aged, endocrine disorders, ostomy patients, cystic fibrosis, the mentally retarded, and other disabling conditions.

Sex Information and Education Council of the U.S. special issue on the handicapped. *SIECUS Report*, 1976.

This special issue of *SIECUS* includes the following articles: (1) the handicapped and sexual health; (2) sexuality and the handicapped; (3) a sex education program for the visually impaired in a residential school; and (4) sex education for the deaf adolescent. Also presented in this publication is a thorough review of audio-visual and written materials on sexuality, sex education with special groups, sex counseling, and sex and the disabled. Finally, a selective annotated bibliography on sex and the handicapped is included.

Sha'ked, A. Psychosexual aspects in the readjustment process of the disabled person: Counseling and curricular applications. Paper read at the International Conference on Psychology and Human Development, Jerusalem, December 30, 1976.

Contrary to common myth, the physically disabled individual, like the able-bodied person, is a sexual being. Studies show that sexual adjustment is indeed at the core of the disabled person's total psychosocial adjustment and rehabilitation processes. However, despite the importance of sexuality, the disabled person is not receiving adequate sex counseling and advice from the health-care professional. The disabled person's anxieties and concerns about sexuality are compounded by the rehabilitation worker's reluctance and lack of training and expertise in dealing effectively with this issue. The main objective of this project was to fill the gap in needed training in rehabilitation by developing a curriculum in human sexuality within the context of concepts of normalization and social integration. This is a timely and important project since current trends and emphases in rehabilitation are toward the normalization of the disabled person. Currently there is a surprising lack of such a curriculum in rehabilitation psychology training.

Shearer, A. *A right to love?* London: The Spastics Society and the National Association for Mental Health, May 1972.

This report is based on a study conducted in England to examine attitudes toward the sexual and emotional needs of handicapped persons. The results of this study reflect not only the frustrations and difficulties of the handicapped, but also the shortcomings, ambivalence, and misconceptions of the professional staff of institutions regarding normative sexual needs of the handicapped. It was found that professional staff have reinforced the stereotyped reaction to disabled persons by denying them knowledge about their sexuality and by denying them the means of expressing their needs. The public in general is disturbed at the idea that the disabled person has the same sexual feelings, desires, and needs as does the rest of the population. The impact of these negative attitudes on the development of the disabled person is further discussed.

Sidman, J. M. Sexual functioning and the physically disabled adult. *American Journal of Occupational Therapy*, 1977, *31*(2), 81–85.

The impact of various disabling conditions on sexuality is discussed. Disabilities presented include stroke, cardiac disease, spinal-cord injury, pulmonary disease, arthritis, and alcoholism.

Skipper, J. K., Fink, S. L., and Hallenbeck, P. N. Physical disability among married women: Problems in the husband-wife relationship. *Journal of Rehabilitation*, 1968, *34*, 16–19.

Interviews with 36 disabled women and their husbands were conducted to examine the effects of a wife's long-term disability on the marital relationship. The focus was on the disabled woman's needs and their satisfaction and her satisfaction with marriage. A high correlation was found between the husband's need satisfaction and his satisfaction with marriage. A high correlation was also found between satisfaction with sex and general marriage satisfaction, suggesting that the greater the disabled woman's sexual satisfaction the greater will be her marriage satisfaction in general. Only one woman in the study sample was not participating in sexual activities because of her disabling condition.

Slootwig, H. Sexual help for the disabled in Holland. Paper read at the Thirteenth World Congress of Rehabilitation International, Tel Aviv, Israel, June 13–18, 1976.

Functions and activities of the Dutch Society for Sexual Reform as they relate to assisting the disabled person to attain sexual adjustment were discussed in this presentation.

Smith, G. K. Sex and the young sheltered workshop employee. *Rehabilitation in Australia*, 1970, 7(4), 11–14.

Physical problems, the prospects, difficulties, and possibilities of marriage, and some of the behavior problems relating to sex life for the handicapped are the topics discussed in this article. Erection through local stimulation only is reported to be possible for 46 percent of male paraplegics, and through psychic and local stimulation for an additional 20 percent. Diseases of the hips and pelvis, while rarely interfering with sexual activity in males, may cause practical difficulties with females, particularly in that the course of pregnancy and labor becomes complicated. The author feels that the most important ingredient for successful sexual experiences is a spouse who is mature enough to be as helpful as necessary, and reassuring and encouraging as well.

Smith, J., and Bullough, B. Sexuality and the severely disabled person. *American Journal of Nursing*, 1975, *75*, 2194–2197.

Based on personal experience and on interviews and observations made with persons with various severe disabling conditions, the authors present the psychosocial and sexual implications of these disabilities. The role of the practicing nurse in providing primary and secondary sex counseling for disabled persons is discussed and practical suggestions for effective approaches to counseling patients regarding sexuality are presented.

Spock, B., and Lerrigo, M. O. *Caring for your disabled child.* New York: Macmillan, 1965.

Of special interest in this book is a chapter discussing sexual and social developments and difficulties in disabled children and adults. Topics covered include childhood sex-play, body changes, marriage and sexuality in the spinal-cord-injured person, and other related issues.

Stewart, W. F. R. Sexual rehabilitation: A gap in provision for the disabled. *Nursing Mirror and Midwives Journal*, 1976, *142*, 47–49.

This article presents the results of a study examining sexual problems encountered by physically disabled persons and some implications for sexual counseling and advice. It was found that sexual problems could be broken down into the following broad categories: those of sexual potency and capacity; those of physical comfort; those of physical safety; problems of paralysis; psychoemotional difficulties affecting sexuality; and problems in establishing social and sexual relationships.

Thompson, B., and Clifford, K. The disabled person and family dynamics. *Accent on Living*, Summer 1972, 1–6.

The interrelationships between problems of physical disability and marital difficulties are discussed within the framework of marriage dynamics and family interaction. Sexuality is one area of possible conflict and difficulty for the disabled person and his spouse. Rehabilitation counselors need to allow the disabled person to talk freely and openly about sexual and marital problems, and assist him in achieving sexual adjustment. Results of a study on sexuality following spinal-cord injury are presented, indicating that 56 percent of the subjects had experienced complete sexual intercourse since their injury. All subjects had engaged in some petting and lovemaking since their injury. The authors indicate that, based on other studies they examined, somewhere between 52 percent and 75 percent of spinal-cord-injured persons can achieve a satisfactory sexual adjustment.

Tobias, A. Marriage and handicapped people. *Case Conference*, 1968, *6*, 218–223.

Problems relating to marriage and sexual relations in handicapped people and to adequate preparation of the handicapped for marriage are discussed in this article.

Toward intimacy: Family planning and sexual concerns of physically disabled women. Task Force on Concerns of Physically Disabled Women. Everett, Washington: Planned Parenthood of Snohomish County, 1977.

This book is aimed at the physically disabled woman, and attempts to foster her sexual adjustment. Sections on body image, relationships with sex partners, and relationships with parents and self are presented. Also included is a discussion on contraceptive methods.

Trieschmann, R. B. Sex, sex acts and sexuality. Paper read at the Thirty-fifth Annual Assembly of the American Academy of Physical Medicine and Rehabilitation, Washington, D.C., October 24, 1973.

The author discusses and makes a distinction between sex, sex acts, and sexuality in light of the sexual needs and function of the physically disabled person. She concludes that a disability does not eliminate sexual feelings and needs.

Trippe, M. J., and Mathey, J. P. Helping special people be sexual people: First us, then them. Paper read at the Thirteenth World Congress of Rehabilitation International, Tel Aviv, Israel, June 13–18, 1976.

The authors describe a program aimed at facilitating sexual adjustment in physically disabled persons.

Withersty, D. J. Sexual attitudes of hospital personnel: A model for continuing education. *American Journal of Psychiatry*, 1976, *133*(5), 573–575.

The author presents a continuing education program aimed at improving the effectiveness of health-care practitioners in dealing with the sexual concerns and difficulties of physically disabled persons and chronically ill patients. The program involves group activities and role-playing techniques.

Young, B. M. Sex and the handicapped adolescent. *Rehabilitation Digest*, 1972, *4*, 12–13.

Concerns of physically disabled adolescents about sexual functioning and fertility are discussed, and some suggestions for better treatment of these subjects by health-care practitioners are made.

Chapter Two

Internal Medical Conditions

Cardiovascular Diseases / Diabetes and Other Endocrine Disorders / Renal Failure / Cancer / Obesity

Cardiovascular Diseases

Abramov, L. A. Sexual life and sexual frigidity among women developing acute myocardiac infarction. *Psychosomatic Medicine*, 1976, *38*(6), 418–425.

The purpose of this study was to examine various aspects in the sexuality of 100 women with acute myocardial infarction. A control group consisted of 100 patients hospitalized for other reasons. Results and conclusions are presented and discussed.

Bakker, C. Heart disease and sex: Response to questions. *Medical Aspects of Human Sexuality*, 1971, *5*, 24–35.

A panel of authorities participating in a seminar on Counseling the Cardiac Patient on Work and Sex answers various questions relating to sexuality in heart disease. Questions answered include: (1) How does the physiological cost of sexual activity compare with other daily work activities? (2) How long is it necessary to forbid sexual activity following onset of cardiac illness? (3) What factors determine success in returning to sexual activity following a heart attack? (4) Is sudden death during sexual intercourse a realistic danger? (5) Can graded sexual activity be utilized for the purpose of increasing colateral circulation in patients? Also discussed are some guidelines for the counseling of cardiac patients in sexual matters.

Block, A., Maeder, J. P., and Haissly, J. C. Sexual problems after myocardial infarction. *American Heart Journal*, 1975, *90*(4), 536–537.

The authors present the results of a follow-up study examining adjustment of former myocardial infarction patients. Results show that although most of the patients resumed a normal life, there was a sharp decrease in the frequency of their sexual intercourse. Reasons for this change were: decrease in sexual libido and desire, depression, anxiety, wife's fears, patient's fear of sudden death during intercourse, fatigue, angina, and impotence.

Brenton, M. *Sex and your heart.* New York: Coward-McCann, 1968.

The main purpose of this book is to offer information about sexual and emotional aspects of heart disease. Topics discussed include the sexuality of the middle-aged man, sexual problems and heart disease, pregnancy and heart disease, and others.

Canning, J. R., Bowers, L. M., Lloyd, F. A., and Cottrell, T. L. C. Genital vascular insufficiency and impotence. *Surgical Forum*, 1963, *14*, 298–299.

This is a report of a study aimed at the examination of the association between sexual impotence and vascular insufficiency. Some of the patients examined were suffering from pelvic vascular insufficiency resulting from vascular disease. Results and conclusions are presented and discussed.

Cohen, B. D., Wallston, B. S., and Wallston, K. A. Sex counseling in cardiac rehabilitation. *Archives of Physical Medicine and Rehabilitation*, 1976, *57*(10), 473–474.

To fill the gap in needed services, a sex counseling program in cardiac rehabilitation was developed. Aspects of this program and reactions of patients and their spouses are discussed along with recommendations for further investigation of this process.

Eliot, R. S., and Miles, R. R. Advising the cardiac patient about sexual intercourse. *Medical Aspects of Human Sexuality*, 1975, *9*(6), 49–50.

Sexual difficulties, fears, and anxieties associated with cardiac disorders are discussed in light of the physiology of the sexual response cycle. Also presented are specific suggestions for office counseling and advice by a physician.

Green, A. W. Sexual activity and the post-myocardial infarction. *American Heart Journal*, 1975, *89*(2), 246–252.

This article discusses various myths and misconceptions held by both cardiac patients and health-care practitioners regarding sexual activity. Information is presented in regard to heart rate during the sexual response cycle, and to training the heart to tolerate a higher level of work load. It is recommended that the topic of sex should be discussed with the patient as soon as his condition stabilizes.

Griffith, G. C. Sexuality and the cardiac patient. *Heart and Lung*, 1973, *2*, 70–73.

In this article the author discusses concerns facing the cardiac patient. Cardiac illness brings many questions and fears to the patient regarding sexual functioning. Many patients fear the possibility of dying during intercourse. The author feels that through open discussion with the nurse or physician, the patient can become more knowledgeable about his personal condition and alter his activity to agree with his heart problems and thus alleviate the fears and anxiety associated with sexual intercourse. The author also discusses various aspects of sex counseling with cardiac patients, outlining specific precautions for the patient before or during sexual intercourse. He concludes that as soon as the cardiac patient can resume his former life patterns, sexual relations can also be resumed.

Hellerstein, H. K., and Friedman, E. H. Sexual activity and the postcoronary patient. *Medical Aspects of Human Sexuality*, 1969, *3*(3), 70–96.

The purpose of this study was to obtain data to provide a base for counseling postcoronary patients regarding sexuality. The study compared the sexual activity of postcoronary and highly coronary-prone subjects, identified modifying factors compromising optimal sexual activity, and compared physiologic changes during sexual coitus to changes occurring during other activities. Various means of data collection were used to obtain a full psychophysiologic and sexual profile of each patient (n=91), and EKG tracings which compared heart rates and changes during sexual activity and other activities were obtained. Many factors which could modify sexual activity were explored. The results indicate that sexual activity in the postcoronary patient is based on an interaction of pre-illness status and the direct and indirect effects of heart disease. It was found that sexual activity decreased markedly in subjects with higher blood pressure, more passive dependency, and lower incomes. There was an increase in sexual activity with decrease in cholesterol. The physiologic stress of coitus was found to be minimal. The authors concluded that sexual activity depends on: (1) sexual drive and performance in earlier life; (2) the effects of aging; (3) the spouse's health, attitudes, and decisions; (4) physiologic factors after myocardial infarction; (5) cardiovascular function prior to myocardial infarction; and (6) response to medical intervention to enhance heart function.

Hellerstein, H. K., and Friedman, E. H. Sexual activity and the postcoronary patient. *Archives of Internal Medicine*, 1970, *125*, 987.

This paper presents the results of a study which examined sexual functioning and activity in postcoronary patients (n=91). A subsample of 14 patients was monitored by EKGs during work and sexual activity. Results of the study show a decrease in sexual activity in these patients after myocardial infarct. Other results are discussed and conclusions and specific recommendations are presented.

Howard, E. J. Sexual expenditure in patients with hypertensive disease. *Medical Aspects of Human Sexuality*, 1973, *7*(10), 82–92.

The author describes and discusses cardiac response and expenditure during sexual activity in patients with hypertensive disease. Also presented are the effects of antihypertensive drugs on sexual behavior. Finally, specific measures to give protection from hypertensive complications are outlined.

Knoller, R., Kennedy, J. W., Butler, J. C., and Wagner, N. N. Counseling the coronary patient on sexual activity. *Postgraduate Medicine*, 1972, *51*, 133–136.

The need for the physician to counsel the coronary patient on sexual activity is the major theme of this article. The authors assert that in determining when sexual activity can resume after the coronary episode the minimum considerations should be the extent of recovery, the physiologic costs of sexual activity, and the level of precoronary sexual activity. If the patient can climb two flights of stairs without difficulty, he is usually considered to be able to engage in sexual activity. Both the patient and his spouse should be counseled on when sexual activity can be resumed and on alternate positions for sexual intercourse in order to keep stress factors at a minimum.

Laver, M. Sexual behavior patterns in male hypertensives. *Australian and New Zealand Journal of Medicine*, 1974, *4*, 29–31.

The results of a study aimed at the examination of sexual behavior patterns in male hypertensive patients (n=88) are presented and discussed. It was found that 50 percent of the patients had decreased sexual potency. The patients attributed this to their drug therapy. While no one specific drug was blamed, the incidence was higher in patients who were severely hypertensive and on larger doses of all drugs. The author suggests that questions related to sexual activity in males should be included in all questionnaires about hypotensive drugs.

Lawson, B. Easing the sexual fears of the cardiac patient. *RN*, 1974, *37*, 1–5.

After the immediate life-threatening crisis of cardiac illness has subsided, the patient shifts his energies to other concerns. Two of these concerns are returning to work and resuming sexual activities. The latter seems to be the most difficult for the patient and the health professionals to handle. The author discusses ways of facilitating communication between nurse and patient in dealing with the patient's sexual concerns. The nurse or physician should include the patient's spouse or usual sex partner whenever plans for discharge are made. The patient's sex partner usually has fears and concerns of his or her own that need to be discussed. Fears or concerns of either the patient or the patient's sex partner that are not openly discussed may hamper optimal recovery of the patient.

Levenson, R. M., Rosenman, R. H., and Schwab, J. J. A summary of a symposium on counseling the cardiac on work and sex. *Ohio State Medical Journal*, 1970, *66*, 1003–1007.

This article summarizes a seminar discussion dealing with counseling the cardiac patient regarding work and sexuality. The actual physiologic cost of sexual intercourse is reported to be equivalent to that of climbing one flight of stairs at a medium pace. At orgasm the heart rate usually averages between 120 and 140 beats per minute in most of the postinfarction patients studied. A physical conditioning program usually improves sexual activity in both quantity and quality. The physician must evaluate the physiological as well as the psychosocial aspects of the patient before making a rehabilitation program recommendation.

Lord, J. W. Peripheral vascular disorders and sexual function. *Medical Aspects of Human Sexuality*, 1973, *7*(9), 34–43.

The relationship between peripheral vascular disorders and sexual functioning is discussed in this article. The effects of therapy on sexuality are also discussed.

Massie, E., Rose, E. F., and Cupp, J. C. Sudden death during coitus—fact or fiction? *Medical Aspects of Human Sexuality*, 1969, *3*(6), 22–26.

The occurrence of sudden death during sexual intercourse as a result of a coronary occlusion is discussed. The viewpoints of four authorities are presented.

Moor, K., Folk-Light, M., and Nolen, M. J. The joy of sex after a heart attack: Counseling the cardiac patient. *Nursing*, 1977, *7*(6), 53–55.

Essential questions asked by cardiac patients regarding their sexuality are discussed in this article. Also presented are numerous guidelines for sexual intercourse which could help patients minimize the work load on the heart.

Muckleroy, R. N. Sex counseling after stroke. *Medical Aspects of Human Sexuality*, 1977, *11*(12), 115–116.

This article discusses the effects of stroke on sexual libido and functioning. The average age at stroke is approximately 70 years, and the patient is likely to have preexistent health problems such as diabetes, hypertension, or coronary artery disease. Also, the patient may have taken either pre- or post-stroke medication which tends to decrease libido and limit sexual functioning. Other causes of sexual dysfunctioning associated with stroke and some suggestions for counseling are presented.

Oaks, W. W., and Moyer, J. H. Sex and hypertension. *Medical Aspects of Human Sexuality*, 1972, *6*(11), 128–137.

To elicit information relating to preexisting sexual practices as well as to the dysfunctions superimposed by hypertension and its therapy, the authors examined 50 hypertensive patients. Results of this study and conclusions are presented and discussed.

Page, L. B. Advising hypertensive patients about sex. *Medical Aspects of Human Sexuality*, 1975, *9*(1), 103–104.

Anxieties about the association between hypertension and cardiovascular disease result in many cases of sexual dysfunctions and difficulties. The author discusses these problems and presents some specific suggestions for office counseling by a physician. Specific topics discussed include blood pressure and sexual coitus, effects of antihypertensive medications on sexual functioning, and counseling the patient.

Proger, S., Scherf, D., and Massie, E. What do you tell post-coronary patients regarding sex activity? *Medical Aspects of Human Sexuality*, 1968, *2*(11), 22–23.

Sexual activity should be frankly discussed with every patient suffering from coronary disease. These authors present their opinions regarding the sex counseling and advice a coronary patient should receive from his physician. In general, there is agreement among the authors that when a patient is fully recovered from a heart attack he "may lead a reasonably normal life" which includes sexual activity.

Reichert, P. Does heart disease end sex activity? *Sexology*, 1962, *29*, 76–81.

The effect of heart disease on the patient's sexual functioning and behavior is discussed. Physiological changes during sexual intercourse are also considered.

Renshaw, D. C. Emotional links to coronary disease: Impact on sexual activity. *Practical Psychology for Physicians*, March 1976, 30–35.

Careful and thoughtful psychosexual counseling and advice should be an integral part of the physician's work with cardiac patients. In most cases, sexual dysfunctions in patients are a result of psychosocial factors caused by the illness and not the result of the illness per se. The author discusses the impact of these factors, which she calls the "As and Ds of sexual dysfunction in heart disease." These are: anxiety, anger, aging, depression, dissociation, deliberate sexual control, and drugs. It is important to attempt to prevent sexual dysfunction as a result of these factors by providing the cardiac patient with adequate counseling before he or she leaves the hospital.

Renshaw, D. C. Emotional reactions to cardiac disease. *Chicago Medicine*, 1976, *79*(2), 53–55.

Concerns and anxieties about sexual activity and the possibility of heart attack during sexual intercourse is one of the areas of emotional reactions to cardiac diseases discussed in this paper. These fears may be shared by the patient's spouse, and if not openly discussed may result in complete avoidance of physical contact between the anxious couple. Sexual dysfunction, usually secondary impotence, may occur as a consequence of the patient's anxiety over his sexual performance or his cardiac situation and life. The author concludes that "it is wise to suggest some relaxed sexplay for the couple as an alternate to coitus until he is reassured about the quality and duration of his erections." Also effective is an open and frank discussion with the couple which allows them to raise questions and voice concerns and anxieties.

Renshaw, D. C. Sexual problems in stroke patients. *Medical Aspects of Human Sexuality*, 1975, *9*(12), 68–74.

Autonomical, emotional, and chemical factors associated with possible sexual dysfunctions in stroke patients are discussed in light of existing research and clinical knowledge. Some of the sexual dysfunctions are psychogenic in origin. Overwhelming fear and ongoing anxiety about recurrent stroke, anxiety over sexual performance, unresolved guilt feelings associated with the stroke, and depression are some psychological causes of dysfunctional sex. The author suggests that an explicit and frank discussion of sexuality with both the stroke patient and his or her partner "can make the most profound change in the way the couple either endures their separate loneliness or live out their remaining years in optimum closeness."

Rogers, S. Viewpoints: What do you tell post-coronary patients regarding sex activity? *Medical Aspects of Human Sexuality*, 1968, *2*, 22–28.

A panel of five physicians discuss their clinical opinions in regard to counseling the postcoronary patient about future sexual activity. A general consensus is that sexuality needs to be discussed openly with every patient suffering from coronary disease. One opinion presented is that sexual intercourse may be resumed in six to eight weeks after the attack if no subsequent significant anginal pains have occurred. The preferable time for intercourse is in the morning when the patient is rested.

Scheingold, L. D., and Wagner, N. N. *Sound sex and the aging heart*. New York: Human Science Press, 1974.

Reflecting upon their clinical experience and a review of the literature, the authors discuss the sexual aspects of aging with special emphasis on cardiac problems. Expanding upon results of research on sexual response in older people, the authors abolish common myths and misconceptions by proving that older persons have sexual interests and ability. Indicating that sex does not put an excessive strain on the heart, they present concrete sexual stimulation exercises for the cardiac patient and his or her spouse. They devote a chapter to a discussion of the resumption of sexual activity following a heart attack and other heart diseases. This is followed by a discussion of the role of the spouse of the cardiac patient in the sexual adjustment of the couple. Finally, the authors address themselves to the sexual problems of older single, widowed, or divorced individuals and assert that "the game-playing nature of traditional courtship could be abandoned in the later years in favor of more honest communication."

Schirger, A., and Gifford, R. W., Jr. Guanethidine, a new antihypertensive agent: Experience in the treatment of 36 patients with severe hypertension. *Mayo Clinic Proceedings*, 1962, *37*, 100.

The authors report that of 22 men treated for hypertension with guanethidine, 5 experienced retrograde ejaculation and 4 others became sexually impotent. In the case of retrograde ejaculation, an orgasm occurs and the semen reaches the prostatic urethra, but it then passes into the bladder rather than to the outside. This condition results from failure of the vesical neck to close during orgasm. Inasmuch as closure of the vesical neck is under control of the sympathetic nervous system, the development of retrograde ejaculation following a chemical sympathectomy produced by guanethidine is understandable.

Skelton, M., and Dominian, J. Psychological stress in wives of patients with myocardial infarction. In D. W. Abse, E. M. Nash, and L. M. R. Louden (Eds.), *Marital and sexual counseling in medical practice* (2nd ed.). New York: Harper and Row, 1974.

The authors report the results of a study they conducted with 65 wives of patients with myocardial infarction. The initial impact, the reaction after hospital discharge, and the adjustment one year after the onset of illness are discussed. Data showing the frequency of sexual intercourse before and after the illness are also presented. Many wives reported that the frequency of sexual coitus had been decreasing as they became older and that the illness only accelerated this trend. Nine wives expressed concern and anxiety about the effect of sexual activity on their husbands. By six months after the onset of the illness all but one of these nine couples had resumed sexual activity. The authors conclude that their findings confirmed the psychological difficulties experienced by wives of myocardial infarction patients reported by previous studies.

Stein, R. A. Resuming sexual relations after myocardial infarction. *Medical Aspects of Human Sexuality*, 1976, *10*(6), 159–160.

This is a guide to office counseling related to the resumption of sexual activity after myocardial infarction. The author identifies and discusses the factors causing alteration in sexual functioning and activity following a myocardial infarction. These factors include previous sexual pattern, physiological aspects, self-image, and fear of precipitating another heart attack.

Tobis, J. S. Cardiovascular patients and sexual dysfunction. Paper read at the Thirty-fifth Annual Assembly of the American Academy of Physical Medicine and Rehabilitation, Washington, D.C., October 24, 1973.

Sexual aspects and concerns associated with cardiovascular diseases, and the spouse's role in the sexual adjustment of the patient, are discussed in light of clinical and research findings.

Trimble, G. X. The coital coronary. *Medical Aspects of Human Sexuality*, 1970, *4*(5), 64–72.

The incidence and nature of death during coitus due to cardiac disorder is discussed in light of the findings of clinical studies and observations.

Tuttle, W. B., Cook, W. L., and Fitch, E. Sexual behavior in postmyocardial infarction patients. *American Journal of Cardiology*, 1964, *13*, 140.

The aim of this study was to examine sexual functioning and activity in patients who had had myocardial infarction one to nine years prior to the study. The interval from myocardial infarction to first sexual intercourse averaged three months. Results of the study showed that a third of the patients resumed their normal pattern of sexual activity. Two-thirds had a marked and lasting reduction in the frequency of sexual intercourse. Impotence was reported in 10 percent of the study sample. These patterns bore no relation to the age of the patient, or to the severity of the heart disease. It was suggested that changes in sexual activity and pattern resulted from fear and lack of adequate advice and counseling. The authors urge physicians to be more specific in their recommendations for postmyocardial infarction patients.

Van Bree, N. S. Sexuality, nursing practice, and the person with cardiac disease. *Nursing Forum*, 1975, *14*(4), 397–411.

The impact of cardiac disease on sexual function and behavior of patients and the role of the practicing nurse in alleviating sexual problems and concerns are the topics discussed in this paper. Attention is given to the physiological effects of sexual intercourse on the cardiovascular system, the psychosocial aspects of cardiac disease, and to the implications for sex counseling. If the nurse is to be effective in this role, she has to assess her own attitudes toward sexuality, develop interpersonal skills necessary to discuss sexuality freely, assess and increase her sexual knowledge, be able to assess the patient's sexual concerns, and explore the role of the nurse in the intervention of sexual concerns of patients.

Wagner, N. N. Sexual activity and the cardiac patient. In R. Green (Ed.), *Human sexuality: A health practitioner's text.* Baltimore: Williams and Wilkins, 1975.

Due to limited sex counseling and advice provided by physicians, cardiac patients usually act according to their limited knowledge, fears, myths, and misconceptions. This may lead to unwarranted decrease in sexual activities, even to the point of complete abstinence. The author discusses sexuality in cardiac patients in light of research and clinical data accumulated in this area. The physiology of the sex act is described with special attention given to changes that occur in the heart function during the sexual response cycle in coitus and masturbation. Finally, some specific implications for counseling are identified and discussed. The author concludes that when the cardiac "patient has returned to mild to moderate physical activity, he can also return to the level of sexual activity he was experiencing prior to the onset of cardiac difficulties. Patients should not be deprived of assistance in this area of their rehabilitation."

Watts, R. J. Sexuality and the middle-aged cardiac patient. *Nursing Clinics of North America*, 1976, *11*(2), 349–359.

Sexual implications of cardiac disease in middle-aged patients are discussed. Specific topics presented include the male sexual response cycle, depression in patients and its effect on sexuality, spouse's role, and the role of the nurse in alleviating the patient's concerns.

Diabetes and Other Endocrine Disorders

Abelson, D. Diagnostic value of the penile pulse and blood pressure: A Doppler study of impotence in diabetics. *Journal of Urology*, 1975, *113*, 636–639.

Doppler measurements of penile blood pressure and penile pulse measurements were taken from 15 impotent diabetics and 29 controls. The pulses were palpable in all subjects in the control group but not in 6 diabetic patients. While the penile blood pressure was obtainable in all control subjects it was not obtained in 2 diabetics. The author concludes that "using the penile pulse data and a comparison of the penile with the brachial systolic pressures, 2 or possibly 3 grades of penile ischemia are definable, providing a measure of pelvic vascular insufficiency."

Allen, C., and Carlyle-Gail, C. A depression hyposexual-alopecia syndrome. *British Medical Journal*, 1942, *2*, 67–68.

This is a detailed clinical case report of a 33-year-old male patient who had a combined syndrome of depression-hyposexuality and alopecia (excessive loss of hair). The authors point out the similarity of this syndrome to some other characteristics of endocrine diseases. Although they refrained from indicating the causation of the syndrome described in their paper, the authors do suggest that it might have an endocrine origin.

Anhalt, M. A., and Carlton, C. E. Hypospadias and epispadias. *Medical Aspects of Human Sexuality*, 1973, 7(9), 218–226.

The symptoms, etiology, and sexual aspects of hypospadias and epispadias are discussed in this article.

Antonini, F. M., and Petruzzi, E. Sexual disturbances in male diabetics. Paper read at the Seventh Congress of the International Diabetes Federation. Buenos Aires, August 23–28, 1970.

There is a high incidence of impaired sexual function among male diabetic patients. This study examined plasma testosterone in 10 diabetic patients. Results indicate that in patients affected by sexual dysfunction, plasma testosterone levels are maintained, at least until the eighth decade of life.

Berggvist, N. The gonadal function in male diabetics. *Acta Endocrinologica*, Suppl., 1954, *18*, 1–29.

The author studied 63 diabetic patients, 8 of whom complained of sexual dysfunction. Results show a decrease of 17-ketosteroids in the younger group.

Birnbaum, M. D., and Eskin, B. A. Psychosexual aspects of endocrine disorders. *Medical Aspects of Human Sexuality*, 1973, *7*(1), 134–150.

This paper discusses the interplay between endocrinopathies and psychosexual disturbances. The authors suggest that "many endocrinopathies produce serious psychological disturbances, either directly or via their secondary effects." The authors discuss various endocrine disorders associated with childhood, adolescence, and adulthood, e.g., precocious puberty, acne, polycystic ovarian disease, menstrual irregularity, adrenal hyperactivity syndrome, Klinefelter's syndrome, infertility, menstrual dysfunction, menopause, and other abnormalities. The psychological and sexual implications of each disorder are identified and discussed. Commentaries by two authorities follow this presentation.

Bobrow, N. A., Money, J., and Lewis, V. G. Delayed puberty, eroticism, and sense of smell: A psychological study of hypogonadotropinism, osmatic and anosmatic (Kallmann's syndrome). *Archives of Sexual Behavior*, 1971, *1*(4), 329–343.

The main purpose of this study was to examine the social and psychosexual development and personality function in a group of male patients (n=13) with chronically delayed spontaneous puberty attributed to hypogonadotropinism. In five cases this condition was associated with verified hyposmia (Kallmann's syndrome). Patients revealed an inhibition or lack of sexual interest and arousability alone or with a sexual partner. This absence of sexual interest and activity remained following initiation of sex hormone treatment. This led the authors to conclude that "one may speculate that it is a matter of generalized inhibition secondary to histories of prolonged infantilism and apprehension about nondevelopment rather than the simple absence of hormonal puberty."

Brooks, M. H. Effects of diabetes on female sexual response. *Medical Aspects of Human Sexuality*, 1977, *11*(2), 63–64.

According to the author, sexual dysfunction occurs with similar frequency in diabetic males and females. A careful evaluation of sexual functioning in the patient should be conducted. The author suggests the following steps in evaluation: obtain a complete sex history and physical examination in an attempt to distinguish psychological from physiological dysfunctions; inquire about intermittent sexual dysfunction; look for signs of depression, anger, fear, and anxiety—all can cause sexual dysfunction; inquire about medication and alcohol use; determine if the patient's diabetes is under control; look for endocrine abnormalities or organic diseases. After eliminating all these possibilities, the physician should consider "diabetic sexual dysfunction."

Campbell, I. W., and Clarke, B. F. Sexual dysfunction in diabetic men. *Medical Aspects of Human Sexuality*, 1975, *9*(3), 157–158.

This brief guide to office counseling concentrates on a discussion of the sexual dysfunctions associated with diabetes in male patients. Types of diabetic impotence and other dysfunctions are described along with their causes, and specific guidelines for counseling by a physician are presented.

Campbell, I. W., Ewing, D. J., Clarke, B. F., and Duncan, L. J. P. Testicular pain sensation in diabetic autonomic neuropathy. *British Medical Journal*, 1974, *2*, 638–639.

The purpose of this study was to examine a group of male diabetics with autonomic neuropathy to determine the possible usefulness of testicular pain sensation. The subjects were 32 male diabetics with autonomic neuropathy. The most common symptom of autonomic neuropathy was impotence. In 14 of the subjects it was the only symptom. In 17 patients impotence was accompanied by other signs of autonomic neuropathy, such as postural hypotension, intermittent nocturnal diarrhea, and gastric fullness or delay in emptying. Only 1 subject denied impotence. The mean age of the subjects was 48 years and the average duration of diabetes was 17 years (range 2–33 years). All but 4 of the subjects were using insulin. The results showed that 14 subjects had normal responses to testicular pain. Of the rest, 2 subjects had no response and 6 subjects had diminished response to testicular pain. Of the 14 subjects with impotence alone, only 2 had diminished testicular sensation, whereas of the 18 subjects with other features of autonomic neuropathy, 11 had absent and 5 had diminished testicular sensation. The subject who reported no impotence had normal testicular pain sensation. The authors concluded that absent or diminished testicular sensation correlated well with objective evidence of autonomic neuropathy. Those subjects with impotence alone usually had a normal testicular pain response. Subjects with other signs of autonomic neuropathy tended to have abnormal pain response.

Cherlin, R. S., and Appel, G. B. Sexual function in Addison's disease. *Medical Aspects of Human Sexuality*, 1977, *11*(3), 129–130.

Addison's disease refers to primary adrenal insufficiency. This brief article presents the symptoms, diagnostic tests, and treatment of this disease. Sexual problems, including impotence and decreased sexual libido, are not infrequent in patients with Addison's disease. The author discusses various therapy modalities in the treatment of sexual dysfunctions associated with this disease.

Clopper, R. R., Jr., Adelson, J. M., and Money, J. Postpubertal psychosexual function in male hypopituitarism without hypogonadotropinism after growth hormone therapy. *Journal of Sex Research*, 1976, *12*(1), 14–32.

This article presents various aspects of sex, eroticism, and social behavior found in nine postpubertal male hypopituitary patients without hypogonadotropinism. Results show that in the patients studied, sexual inertia was expressed as a relatively low frequency of erection, ejaculation, masturbation and fantasy, as well as decreased incidence of dating and erotic behavior. A tendency toward social isolation was also observed.

Cooper, A. J. Diagnosis and management of endocrine impotence. *British Medical Journal*, 1972, *2*, 34–36.

A long list of causes for endocrine impotence is presented, with diabetes mellitus given the strongest emphasis. The relationship of testosterone to potency and impotency is also discussed, with supportive data. A sex history taken from both partners and a thorough physical examination are important before treatment can begin. The steps for treatment where an endocrine disorder is present include replacement measures to restore physical health, and psychophysiological therapy aimed at the impotence. There is better success if both types of treatment are done by the same person. In the absence of an endocrine disorder, psychophysiological treatment should be initiated.

Dingman, J. R. Endocrine aspects of impotence. *Medical Aspects of Human Sexuality*, 1969, *3*(4), 57–66.

Endocrine disturbances associated with sexual impotence are discussed and suggestions for treatment are presented.

Ehrhart, A. A., and McCauley, E. Sexually precocious girls. *Medical Aspects of Human Sexuality*, 1975, *9*(11), 63–64.

Psychological, social, and sexual aspects of idiopathic sexual precocity are discussed and specific suggestions for treatment, counseling, and sex education are presented.

Eliasson, R., Wide, L., Wiklund, B., and Ostman, J. Sexual function in male diabetic patients. Paper read at the Seventh Congress of the International Diabetes Federation, Buenos Aires, August 23–28, 1970.

Sexual dysfunctions in diabetic patients were examined. The authors conclude that the occurrence of impotence could not be related to either pituitary or testicular dysfunction.

Ellenberg, M. Impotence in diabetes: The neurologic factor. *Annals of Internal Medicine*, 1971, *75*, 213–219.

An underlying neurologic factor associated with impotence in diabetes was suggested by the fact that penile erection depends on the autonomic nervous system, which is frequently involved in diabetic neuropathy. This study examined this neurogenic basis of impotency in 45 impotent diabetic patients whose average age was 43.2 years. Seventy-five percent of the patients had had diabetes for less than 10 years. The control group consisted of 30 male diabetic patients who were sexually potent. Results of an extensive examination revealed that of the 45 impotent patients studied, 37 showed neurogenic vesical abnormalities and 38 had neuropathy. In the control group, 3 of 30 patients had bladder involvement, and neuropathy was detected in 6 patients. Results of a random survey of 200 diabetic male patients indicate that 59 percent were sexually impotent, and 82 percent of these impotent patients had neuropathy. Only 12 percent of the potent patients showed neuropathy. Plasma testosterone levels were also examined to discover any possible endocrine cause for the diabetic impotence. Results showed normal testosterone levels. Testosterone therapy produced no successful results in patients. The author concludes that the results of his study "imply a significant neuropathic factor in diabetic impotence and minimize an endocrine basis."

Ellenberg, M. Impotence in diabetics: A neurologic rather than an endocrinologic problem. *Medical Aspects of Human Sexuality*, 1973, 7(4), 12–28.

Impotence in male diabetic patients is far more frequent than in nondiabetic persons. In this article, the author discusses the effect of diabetes on male potency. The emphasis in discussion is on the endocrine and neurologic factors underlying impotence. The author concludes that "the findings of normal plasma testosterone values and the completely negative response to the use of testosterone in full measure are strong arguments against the significance of endocrine factors in the pathogenesis of diabetic impotence." He adds that his studies imply that impotence in the diabetic male is based on neurologic factors, and is usually associated with neurogenic bladder involvement.

Ellenberg, M. Sex and the female diabetic. *Medical Aspects of Human Sexuality*, 1977, *11*(12), 30–38.

The effect of diabetes on female sexuality was studied in 100 patients. This group included relatively equal numbers of women with and women without neuropathy. Results show that 44 of the 54 patients with neuropathy had normal libido and orgasmic reaction. Only 7 women in this group indicated diminished libido and orgasmic responsivity. Of the 46 patients without neuropathy, 38 reported normal libido and orgasmic reaction, 6 showed diminished responses, and 2 reported absent libido and orgasmic responsivity.

Ellenberg, M., and Weber, H. Retrograde ejaculation in diabetic neuropathy. *Annals of Internal Medicine*, 1966, *65*, 1237–1246.

This paper presents five case reports of retrograde ejaculation associated with diabetes. The reports document this syndrome as a diabetic autonomic neuropathic manifestation, and indicate the sequential developments in relation to its pathogenesis.

Escamilla, R. F. Physical diseases which cause disturbance of sexual development and function. *Medical Aspects of Human Sexuality*, 1975, *9*(11), 47–48.

Physical diseases, particularly of an endocrinologic nature, may affect sexual functioning and development. This brief guide to office counseling identifies some of these diseases and discusses sexual problems associated with each of them. The medical conditions discussed include acromegaly, pituitary dwarfism, pituitary tumors, extreme obesity, hyperthyroidism, parathyroids, and others.

Faerman, I., Glocer, L., Fox, D., Jadzinsky, M. N., and Rapaport, M. Impotence and diabetes: Histological studies of the autonomic nervous fibers of the corpora cavernosa in impotent diabetic males. *Diabetes*, 1974, *23*, 971–976.

In searching for a neurological lesion of the nerves that control erection, the authors conducted this histologic study to examine the nerve fibers of the corpora cavernosa of the penis in a group of impotent diabetic males. Autopsies were performed on five impotent diabetics, mean age 51, with an average duration of diabetes of 9.6 years. Results of this study and some conclusions are presented and discussed in this article. The authors conclude that their study lends strong support to the opinion that sexual impotence in diabetics is due to neurological lesion of the nerve fibers that control erection.

Faerman, I., Vilar, O., Rivarola, M. A., Rosner, J. M., Jadzinsky, M. N., Fox, D., Lloret, A. P., Berstein-Hahn, L., and Saraceni, D. Impotence and diabetes: Studies of androgenic function in diabetic impotent males. *Diabetes*, 1972, *21*, 23–30.

In order to study sexual functioning in male diabetics, the authors examined the plasma concentration of testosterone, the biosynthesis of androgens, and testicular morphology in seven male diabetic patients who were sexually impotent. For comparative purpose these examinations were performed also in a group of five paraplegic patients. Results of this study and some specific conclusions are presented and discussed. The authors conclude that "the present study suggests that the impotence and the testicular abnormalities found in diabetics may be secondary to a lesion of the autonomic nerves."

Ford, C. V. Hypoglycemia, hysteria, and sexual function. *Medical Aspects of Human Sexuality*, 1977, *11*(7), 63–72.

To investigate possible sexual dysfunctions in patients with hypoglycemia, the author reviewed 25 case histories of patients referred to him. This article presents and discusses the results of this review. The author suggests that the patient's evaluation should include a comprehensive sex history, as sexual conflicts and difficulties may be an important source of the patient's discomfort.

Frawley, T. F. Physical and psychological sexual effects of hyperadrenocorticalism. *Medical Aspects of Human Sexuality*, 1973, *7*(5), 39–57.

The physical, psychosocial, and sexual aspects of hyper-adrenocorticalism are identified and discussed. This condition is due to an excess of adrenocortical hormones, which occurs more frequently in the female than in the male. In the female, this condition leads to defeminization, i.e., amenorrhea, breast atrophy, decreased pelvic adiposity, acne, and hirsutism. In the adult male, acne and increased muscle strength and sex drive occur initially, followed by weakness and impotence.

Gaskell, P. The importance of penile blood pressure in cases of impotence. *Canadian Medical Association Journal*, 1971, *105*, 1047–1051.

The author was confronted with the problem of deciding "whether, in the presence of clinical evidence of obliterative vascular disease in the lower limbs, impotence could be ascribed to obstruction to blood flow in vessels supplying the penis." To examine this problem, penile blood pressure of impotent subjects was compared to that of potent healthy male subjects. Some of the impotent subjects were diabetic patients. The author concludes that the results of the study indicate that "obstruction to blood flow was identified as a cause of impotence in patients with little other evidence of peripheral vascular disease."

Greene, L. F., Kelalis, P. P., and Weeks, R. E. Retrograde ejaculation of semen due to diabetic neuropathy. *Fertility and Sterility*, 1963, *14*(6), 617–625.

In retrograde ejaculation, an orgasm occurs and the semen reaches the prostatic urethra, but it then passes into the bladder rather than to the outside. The authors have extensively studied four patients who were experiencing retrograde ejaculation. Clinical studies indicated that each patient had experienced a functional sympathectomy secondary to diabetic neuropathy, and it is the authors' opinion that this complication of diabetes was the etiologic basis for the retrograde ejaculation. These four case studies are presented and discussed. In all cases, diabetic visceral neuropathy appeared to result in a disturbance of the sympathetic nerves supplying the bladder. This in turn prevented closure of the vesical neck and allowed retrograde ejaculation of semen.

Hemphill, R. E. Return of virility after prefrontal leucotomy. *Lancet*, September 1944, 345–346.

The author presents a case history of a 33-year-old patient with a long-standing case of obsessional neurosis with emaciation, sexual impotence, and hypogonadism. Four months after he underwent prefrontal leucotomy he was obese, with gonads of normal size, and experienced adequate sexual functioning and activity.

Klebanov, D., and MacLeod, J. Semen quality and certain disturbances of reproduction in diabetic men. *Fertility and Sterility*, 1960, *11*, 255–261.

The authors examined 28 diabetics, 18 of whom complained of diminished sexual potency. In 9 of these patients there was no ejaculate, and in 4 patients the ejaculate volume was less than normal. The sperm count was diminished in 5 patients, and in 14 patients there was abnormal motility.

Kolodny, R. C. Sexual dysfunction in diabetic females. *Medical Aspects of Human Sexuality*, 1972, *6*(4), 98–106.

This article presents the results of a study aimed at the examination of sexual function in diabetic women (n=125). Results show that 35 percent of the patients had complete absence of orgasmic response during the year preceding this study, whereas only 6 percent of nondiabetic controls reported nonorgasmic response during the same period. The author urges further research in this area.

Kolodny, R. C., Kahn, C. B., Goldstein, H. H., and Barnett, D. M. Sexual dysfunction in diabetic men. *Diabetes*, 1974, *23*, 306–309.

The purpose of this study was to obtain further data on sexual dysfunction in male diabetics. Subjects were 175 men, 18 to 83 years of age, with diabetes mellitus. These men were interviewed during outpatient visits. The study involved obtaining a sex history and a medical history, performing a physical examination, and obtaining lab studies. The sex history included questions covering sexual distress, the mode of impotency, the onset, duration, frequency, and degree of impotence, and the current existence of intact neurovascular function. Results show that of the 175 men, 85 (48.6 percent) were impotent. No relation was found between duration of diabetes and impotence, which was usually gradual in onset. Incidence of neuropathy was found to be significantly higher in impotent males. The authors assert that the pathophysiologic mechanism of impotence in diabetic men is unclear. Since there is no known therapy for these men, the physician must first rule out curable impotence. The authors suggest that counseling of both husband and wife is vital, especially in relieving tension and anxiety for the incurably impotent diabetic male.

Koncz, L., Balodimos, M. C. Impotence in diabetes mellitus. *Medical Times*, 1970, *98*(8), 159–170.

This is an extensive discussion of the effects of diabetes on sexual potency and functioning of male patients. A comprehensive review of relevant literature is presented and conclusions are drawn. Tables showing the percentage of impotent diabetic patients in different studies and the prevalence of impotence in different age groups of diabetic and nondiabetic subjects are presented and discussed. Other topics covered are the pathogenesis of impotence, failure of ejaculation, endocrine factors in diabetic impotence, hystological and seminal fluid examination in diabetics, vascular aspects of impotence, and impotence on a psychogenic basis. The authors conclude that "although impaired sexual function in diabetics is a frequent and serious complication, the pathogenesis is poorly understood and the therapy of this condition leaves much to be desired."

Kupperman, H. S., and Vaughan, C. Impotence in nondiabetic endocrine disease. *Medical Aspects of Human Sexuality*, 1974, *8*(11), 112–123.

According to the authors, the endocrine basis in organic impotence is by far the most significant factor. This article examines the sexual implications of nondiabetic endocrinopathies that can result in impotence. The authors suggest that impotence in patients with endocrinopathies may be reversible by correct diagnosis and early therapy. A wide variety of endocrinopathies associated with sexual dysfunctions is presented and discussed.

Miller, S., and Mason, H. L. The excretion of 17-ketosteroids by diabetics. *Journal of Clinical Endocrinology*, 1945, *5*, 220.

The authors found that in five of seven diabetics with diminished sexual libido and potency there was a significant decrease in the level of 17-ketosteroids.

Money, J., and Alexander, D. Eroticism and sexual function in developmental anorchia and hyporchia with pubertal failure. *Journal of Sex Research*, 1967, *3*(1), 31–47.

This article presents and discusses the results of a study aimed at the examination of the psychosexual function of four patients with anorchia and four patients with nonfunctional testes. A case study of a patient with bilateral anorchia, who was functioning satisfactorily in sexual coitus for over two years before treatment, is presented in detail. Analysis of the data obtained shows a wide range of erotic imagery and sexual behavior in the subjects. Testosterone treatment caused an increase in the level of sexual activity in all subjects, though to different degrees.

Money, J., and Alexander, D. Psychosexual development and absence of homosexuality in males with precocious puberty. *Journal of Nervous and Mental Disease*, 1969, *148*(2), 111–123.

The purpose of this report was to present the findings of an investigation of psychosexual development and sexual behavior of 18 precocious boys. Results show that, generally, "psychosexual development, in the precocious boys under study, clearly was not an automatic by-product of the precocious pubertal appearance of sex hormone." Distinguishing psychological characteristics of the study subjects were a tendency to high IQ, increased energy expenditure, early occurrence of the capacity for frankly sexual imagery in dreams, and early establishment of the capacity for sexual excitation by visual imagery and perception as well as by tactile sensation.

Money, J., and Clopper, R. R., Jr. Postpubertal psychosexual function in post-surgical male hypopituitarism. *Journal of Sex Research*, 1975, *11*(1), 25–38.

The authors discuss various aspects of psychosexual development, sexual behavior, eroticism, and social development in postpubertal male patients diagnosed as having hypopituitarism secondary to the surgical removal of a pituitary tumor. Data collected and analyzed include information on erection, ejaculation, masturbatory behavior, erotic imagery, sexual intercourse, dating, socialization, and love. Problems of case management are discussed and suggestions for counseling are presented.

Money, J., and Walker, P. A. Psychosexual development, maternalism, nonpromiscuity, and body image in 15 females with precocious puberty. *Archives of Sexual Behavior*, 1971, *1*(1), 45–59.

Fifteen females with precocious puberty were followed and examined. Results reported in this paper relate to the subjects' intellectual levels, school achievements, friendship choices, play interests, moods, maternalism, masturbation and sex play in childhood, romantic and erotic imagery and dreams, sexual intercourse, marriage, and pregnancy. Also reported are findings describing body image of the patients. Suggestions for counseling are presented.

Morris, H. J., and Yunis, E. Age changes of seminal vesicles and vasa deferentia in diabetics. *Archives of Pathology*, 1964, 77, 126–131.

Morphological changes with age in the seminal vesicles and vasa deferentia of diabetic and nondiabetic patients were examined and compared in the study presented in this article. Results and conclusions are discussed.

Pollitt, E., Hirch, S., and Money, J. Priapism, impotency and human figure drawings. *Journal of Nervous and Mental Disease*, 1964, *139*(2), 161–168.

The purpose of this study was to examine human figure drawings of six postpriapism sexually impotent patients and one postpriapism sexually potent patient. Subjects were also interviewed for a psychosexual assessment of genitopelvic eroticism. Results show that "all the impotent patients indicated their sexual inadequacy and incompetence to satisfy their partners in sexual intercourse." The human figure drawings did not present any sign that could reveal that impotence was the patients' specific disability.

Pool, T. L., Cook, E. N., and Kepler, E. J. Endocrine therapy of cryptorchidism, impotence and prostatic obstruction. *Medical Clinics of North America*, 1940, *24*, 1057–1067.

Of special interest is a section in this article discussing various medical conditions and diseases associated with organic impotence, e.g., diabetes mellitus, multiple sclerosis, pernicious anemia, and others. The authors also discuss the etiology, diagnosis, and endocrine therapy of impotence resulting from these conditions.

Rausch-Stroomann, J. G., Petry, R., Mauss, J., Hienz, H. A., Jakubowski, H. D., Senge, T., Muller, K. M., Eckardt, B., Berthold, K., and Sauer, H. Studies of sexual function in diabetes. Paper read at the Seventh Congress of the International Diabetes Federation, Buenos Aires, August 23–28, 1970.

Sexual functioning in 175 male diabetic patients was studied. Of these patients, 40 percent had lost sexual potency. Other results are discussed.

Renshaw, D. C. Impotence in diabetics. *Diseases of the Nervous System*, 1975, *36*, 369–371.

The author indicates that this brief presentation "overviews what little has been done in the specific study of diabetic impotence, [and] reveals many uncertainties regarding the actual mechanisms responsible for the symptom." Three clinical case studies are presented to illustrate the role of various psychogenic factors in the development of a sexual dysfunction in the diabetic male. The author suggests that it is very difficult to make a diagnosis for organic impotence in a diabetic.

Rubin, A. Studies in human reproduction, IV. Diabetes mellitus and seminal deficiency. *American Journal of Obstetrics and Gynecology*, 1962, *83*, 200–202.

The author describes disorders of production of spermatozoa and of seminal fluid in ten of eleven diabetic patients he examined.

Rubin, A. Studies in human reproduction: The influence of diabetes mellitus in men upon reproduction. *American Journal of Obstetrics and Gynecology*, 1958, *76*, 25–29.

This study examined reproductive histories of 198 diabetic men attending diabetes clinics. Twenty-five percent of the sample 30 to 34 years of age were sexually impotent. The incidence gradually increased with age so that by 50 to 54 years 53.6 percent were impotent. The incidence of impotence was not related to the age of onset of the illness, its duration, its severity, or the presence of vascular or neurological complications associated with the diabetes. There were no significant differences between the study and control groups in regard to incidence of conceptions, premature births, stillbirths, malformations, sex ratio of the offspring, and birth weights of offspring.

Rubin, A. Sexual behavior in diabetes mellitus. *Medical Aspects of Human Sexuality*, 1967, *1*(4), 23–25.

Impotence occasionally seems to be the first symptom presented by a diabetic patient when he first seeks medical aid. The relationship between diabetes and sexual functioning and behavior is discussed in light of the findings obtained by examining 198 diabetic patients.

Rubin, A., and Babbott, D. Impotence and diabetes mellitus. *Journal of the American Medical Association*, 1958, *168*(5), 498–500.

A sample of 198 diabetic males was studied regarding the frequency of difficulties they experienced in obtaining and maintaining erections. Impotence was found to occur at an earlier age and more frequently among the patients than in the general population. The incidence of impotence in diabetics in the age group 30 to 34 was two to five times higher than in the population studied by Kinsey and his associates. The incidence gradually increased with age, to 53.6 percent for diabetic men 50 to 54 years of age. Thirty percent of those who became impotent did so within one year after the clinical recognition of their illness. Sixty percent became impotent within five years of the onset of their diabetes. There was no apparent association between the age of the patient at onset of the illness, its duration, its severity, or the presence of vascular or neurological complications and the presence of impotence. Libido persisted for some time after the onset of impotence in most of the cases studied. The authors suggest that men complaining of premature impotence should be examined for possible diabetes mellitus.

Rubin, I. Diabetes and impotence. *Sexology*, 1963, *30*, 83–85.

A definite connection between diabetes and problems with penile erection exists. This paper discusses impotence in diabetic patients in light of the clinical experience gathered in two diabetes treatment clinics. An unusually high incidence of impotence was found among 198 men attending these clinics. The author asserts that for many of the patients who become impotent, potency returns when the diabetes is controlled.

Schoffling, K. Hypogonadism in male diabetic subjects. In B. S. Leibel and G. A. Wrenshall (Eds.), *On the nature and treatment of diabetes*. Amsterdam: Excerpta Medica Foundation, 1965.

This chapter reports and discusses the results of histological examinations of testicular biopsies in diabetic patients with sexual dysfunctions. Results revealed hypospermatogenesis with partial arrest in the maturation of the germinal epithelium. Case histories and clinical findings in 160 sexually impotent diabetic patients are summarized and compared to those in 154 diabetics without sexual dysfunctions. The author asserts that research results "suggest that impotence and infertility in male diabetics are due to secondary hypogonadotropic hypogonadism."

Schoffling, K., Federlin, K., Ditschuneit, H., and Pfeiffer, E. F. Disorders of sexual function in male diabetics. *Diabetes*, 1963, *12*, 519–527.

This paper presents data on sexual development, libido, potency, and fertility in a selected group of male diabetic outpatients (n=314). The authors also conducted extensive laboratory investigation of endocrine and testicular function in patients with clinical evidence of sexual disorder. Results of this investigation are presented and discussed.

Schon, M., and Sutherland, A. M. The role of hormones in human behavior, III. Changes in female sexuality after hypophysectomy. *Journal of Clinical Endocrinology and Metabolism*, 1960, *20*, 833–841.

This study examined the sexual functioning of 50 women with metastatic breast cancer who had undergone hypophysectomy as a therapeutic measure to check the progress of the disease. In the first stage of the study, 20 women were interviewed before and after hypophysectomy with regard to their sexual functioning and activity. In the second phase of the study, 30 women were studied after hypophysectomy. Of these women, 23 had previously undergone mastectomy. Results showed that mastectomy did not have a significant influence on the patients' sexual functioning, whereas hypophysectomy resulted in a sharp decrease of sexual desire, activity, and gratification. The decline in sexual functioning was attributed to the absence of the tropic pituitary hormone which activates the adrenal androgens. Other results are discussed and conclusions are presented.

Singhal, K. C. Impotence in male diabetics. Unpublished thesis for M.D. degree. Punjab University, Chandigarh, 1967.

This thesis presents the results of a detailed clinical investigation of the sexual functioning of 216 male diabetics and 1,010 age-matched healthy controls. Subjects ranged from 20 to 55 years of age. Impotence was found to be 15 to 30 times more prevalent in diabetics than in the healthy controls. In the diabetic patients 20 to 35 years of age, 53.6 percent admitted to being impotent, and in the patients between 36 and 55 years of age, the incidence of impotence was 79 percent. Psychiatric histories and examinations taken from patients, and the fact that 60 percent of the impotent diabetics were experiencing morning erections, led the author to suggest that impotence in the majority of cases was psychologic and not organic in nature.

Singhal, K. C., Rastogi, G. K., Aikat, B. K., and Chhuttani, P. N. Testicular histology in diabetics with impotence. *Indian Journal of Pathology and Bacteriology*, 1969, *12*, 145–148.

This study examined testicular histology in diabetic patients who were sexually impotent. Testicular biopsy was performed in 11 diabetic patients with normal sexual function, 25 diabetics who were sexually impotent, and 20 nondiabetic, healthy persons. Of 11 sexually functioning diabetics, 5 showed changes in testicular histology. Of the 25 impotent patients, 4 had no pathological changes and 7 showed complete atrophy. The remaining cases had variable degrees of basement membrane thickening, maturation arrest, atrophy of germinal epithelium, and relative preponderance of Sertoli cells. These changes were found more frequently in the diabetic patients than in controls. There was no significant correlation between impotence and histological findings.

Sprague, R. G. Impotence in male diabetics: Editorial. *Diabetes*, 1963, *12*(6), 559–560.

In this editorial, Sprague presents his commentary on the findings of a study conducted by Schoffling and his associates regarding impotence in diabetic patients. The unusual extent of this study and the fact that some of its findings appear to be at variance with the observations of many physicians are discussed. Schoffling's study is described as "a provocative report of an extensive, ambitious study of the endocrinology of sexual disorders in male diabetics, involving complex technics of endocrine investigation." One of this study's striking findings was the successful therapeutic results obtained by testosterone therapy alone. This was contrary to the observation of many clinicians that testosterone has little therapeutic value in the treatment of impotence associated with diabetes. Schoffling's study is presented in this issue of *Diabetes*.

Waxenberg, S. E., Drellich, M. G., and Sutherland, A. M. The role of hormones in human behavior, I. Changes in female sexuality after adrenalectomy. *Journal of Clinical Endocrinology and Metabolism*, 1959, *19*, 193–202.

The purpose of this study was to examine sexual functioning and activity in 29 women, mean age 51 years, following oophorectomy and adrenalectomy for metastatic breast cancer. Of the 17 patients reporting some sexual desire before operation, 16 experienced a decrease in sexual desire after surgery. Of the 17 patients sexually active preoperatively, all reduced their frequency of sexual activity postoperatively, almost half stopping entirely. The authors conclude that the adrenal glands and, more specifically, the androgens of adrenal origin play a critical part in maintaining the patterns of sexual behavior in women.

Whitehouse, F. W. Two minutes with diabetics. *Medical Times*, 1977, *105*(11), 61–63.

Physiological and medical aspects of retrograde ejaculation associated with diabetes are briefly discussed in this article.

Renal Failure

Abram, H. S., Hester, L. R., Epstein, G. M., and Sheridan, W. F. Sexual activity and renal failure. Proceedings of the Fifth International Congress of Nephrology, Mexico, 1972, *3*, 207–210.

The main purpose of this study was to examine the sexual histories of male patients with chronic renal failure and the effect of intermittent dialysis and renal transplantation on their sexual functioning (n=32). Results are presented and discussed.

Abram, H. S., Hester, L. R., Sheridan, W. F., and Epstein, G. M. Sexual functioning in patients with chronic renal failure. *Journal of Nervous and Mental Disease*, 1975, *160*(3), 220–226.

This article discusses psychological and sexual function implications involved in chronic renal failure and its treatment. The researchers studied sexual functioning in 32 dialysis and transplant patients. For some subjects it was possible to obtain a profile of sexual activity prior to the onset of the disease, while on dialysis treatment, and after transplantation. The major indicator of sexual activity was the frequency of sexual intercourse. Results showed that approximately 20 percent of the patients reported no decreased sexual functioning at any point during the course of their illness and treatment; 45 percent showed decrease in sexual activity after the onset of chronic renal disease, and 35 percent had reduced potency after the beginning of dialysis treatment. Therefore, the institution of dialysis cannot be considered the main etiological factor in all patients with reduced sexual potency. In the group of patients with functioning homografts, 20 percent maintained their sexual functioning as before the onset of illness or while on dialysis, and 40 percent reported that they regained their sexual potency after experiencing reduced sexual activity after onset of the disease or while on dialysis. Another 40 percent did not regain potency. The authors encourage more in-depth and longitudinal studies in this area.

Bommer, J., Tschope, W., Ritz, E., and Andrassy, K. Sexual behavior of hemodialyzed patients. *Clinical Nephrology*, 1976, *6*(1), 315–317.

In this study, 18 married men on home dialysis and 10 of their wives were interviewed to evaluate sexual adjustment. Results regarding frequency of intercourse, libido, and other variables are presented.

Cohen, A. D., Gower, P. E., Rogers, K. L., Pegrum, G. D., and Wardener, H. E. Reproductive potential in males treated by chronic haemodialysis. Proceedings of the European Dialysis and Transplant Association Annual Conference, 1970, *10*, 282–288.

An investigation of 35 patients on maintenance hemodialysis suggested that most of them enjoyed an active sex life.

Hickman, B. W. All about sex . . . despite dialysis. *American Journal of Nursing*, April 1977, 606–607.

Psychosexual aspects in hemodialysis patients are discussed in light of the nurse's role in providing needed counseling.

Kretser, D., Atkins, R., Hudson, B., and Scott, D. Disordered spermatogenesis in patients with chronic renal failure undergoing maintenance hemodialysis. *Australian and New Zealand Journal of Medicine*, 1974, *4*, 178–181.

Male patients with chronic renal failure undergoing maintenance hemodialysis were evaluated with regard to testicular function. The patients included two unmarried men, ages 19 and 23, and four married men, ages 30 to 54. The length of renal failure was six months to five years. Significant abnormalities in spermatogenesis were found in all patients. However, one patient had exhibited potency only nine months before the onset of renal failure. It was tentatively concluded by the authors that the renal disease contributed to the spermatogenic disorder.

Levy, N. B. The psychology and care of the maintenance hemodialysis patient. *Heart and Lung*, 1973, *2*(3), 400–405.

Psychosocial aspects in hemodialysis patients are identified and discussed in light of recent literature and clinical observation. Topics covered are the stages of adaptation to hemodialysis, psychological defense mechanisms employed by patients, personality structures and special psychological problems of patients, depression, suicidal behavior, and marital and sexual problems. The author reviews findings of previous studies examining sexual functioning in hemodialysis patients. He suggests that problems of potency may be related to the "impact of the reversal of family role upon the tenuous masculine identity of these patients." It was noted that seven of eleven male patients studied were masturbating openly during the process of hemodialysis. The author attributed this primarily to a manifestation of anxiety from the stress of hemodialysis. It is the author's general impression that female patients as a group manifest fewer difficulties in sexual functioning.

Levy, N. B. Sexual adjustment to maintenance hemodialysis and renal transplantation: National survey by questionnaire: Preliminary report. *American Society for Artificial Internal Organs*, 1973, *19*, 138–143.

This paper evaluates sexual functioning of 56 male kidney transplant recipients and 287 males who were on hemodialysis without transplantation. These subjects responded to a questionnaire mailed to transplant and dialysis patients in a nationwide survey. In the transplant patients, sexual functioning prior to uremia was compared with that after transplantation only, without a comparison to sexual activity in the same group while on dialysis. It was concluded that sexual functioning was markedly reduced following transplantation. However, 72 percent of those who replied to the questionnaire did report having intercourse after transplantation, while 26 percent reported a minimum frequency of two times per week. Of the hemodialysis patients, 10 percent reported absence of sexual intercourse prior to illness, compared with 50 percent while on dialysis. The author concludes that emotional factors play a role in the cause of sexual dysfunction among hemodialysis patients. Sexual problems which did not diminish with the improvement of physical conditions seemed to support this hypothesis.

Levy, N. B., and Wynbrandt, G. D. The quality of life on maintenance haemodialysis. *Lancet*, June 1975, 1328–1330.

Eighteen hemodialysis patients were interviewed in an attempt to rate their quality of life. Sexual functioning was one of the variables studied.

McKevitt, P. M. Treating sexual dysfunction in dialysis and transplant patients. *Health and Social Work*, 1976, *1*(3), 133–155.

The special needs of dialysis and transplant patients for sexual counseling, and the role of health-care professionals in meeting these needs, are discussed.

Renshaw, D. C. Sexual function and renal dialysis. *Journal of Sex Education and Therapy*, Spring-Summer, 1976, 47–50.

The author discusses psychosocial and sexual aspects of dialysis patients. Recent advances in the treatment of severe renal disease have greatly improved the patient's chances for survival. However, despite these advances, the renal patient undergoing dialysis is subject to physical, psychological, social, and sexual stresses. Psychophysical stresses include fear of disability, fear of death, depression, and loss of self-esteem. Social stresses include job loss and financial difficulties. Very few studies have been done regarding the sexual stresses of the renal patient. Generally the studies of males have found a decrease in frequency of intercourse from pre-uremia to the uremic phase, and a further decrease from the uremic phase to the dialysis phase. Health-care workers must deal with the psychosexual difficulties of the patient in an attempt to alleviate these problems.

Salvatierra, O., Fortmann, J. L., and Belzer, F. O. Sexual function in males before and after renal transplantation. *Urology*, 1975, *5*, 64–66.

The purpose of this study was to examine changes in sexual function after renal transplantation. Subjects were 130 male patients between the ages of 20 and 60 who have received kidney transplants. The average follow-up period on subjects after transplantation was 36 months. Subjects were given a questionnaire specifically developed for this study to assess changes in level of libido and sexual potency. Results show a marked decrease in frequency of successful sexual coitus in patients with end-stage renal failure. After a kidney transplant, most patients reported a return to a pre-illness level of sexual functioning. Fourteen percent of the subjects reported that they had no sexual intercourse prior to illness, compared with 47 percent during end-stage renal failure and 22 percent after kidney transplantation. The authors concluded that "this study indicates that the majority of men with functioning kidneys can look forward to a return of sexual activity comparable to the pre-illness state."

Sherman, F. P. Impotence in patients with chronic renal failure on dialysis: Its frequency and etiology. *Fertility and Sterility*, 1975, *26*(3), 221–223.

Fourteen patients with chronic renal failure and on a hemodialysis program underwent neurologic, psychiatric, and endocrine studies to determine the frequency and etiology of impotence among them. Results are presented and discussed.

Thurm, J. A. Effect of chronic renal disease on sexual functioning. *Medical Aspects of Human Sexuality*, 1976, *10*(8), 81–82.

The ability to maintain sexual adequacy is one concern of patients with renal disease. In this brief guide to office counseling, the author outlines and discusses the effects of renal disease on sexual functioning in both hemodialysis and renal transplantation patients. Specific suggestions for counseling are also presented.

Thurm, J. Sexual potency of patients on chronic hemodialysis. *Urology*, 1975, *5*(1), 60–62.

This study evaluated the sexual functioning of 22 male patients undergoing chronic hemodialysis for longer than six months. Of these patients, 46 percent maintained some sexual function. Sexual activity was more apparent among the home dialysis patients. Generally, loss of desire for sexual activity appeared to be more prevalent than loss of potency. The author concludes that "patients on chronic hemodialysis may produce a model for the etiology and treatment of organic impotence."

Cancer

Abitbol, M. M., and Davenport, J. H. The irradiated vagina. *Obstetrics and Gynecology*, 1974, *44*, 249–256.

The purpose of this study was to investigate the anatomic and histologic alterations in the vagina and its surrounding structures following irradiation. The report presented in this article is based on a study of 97 cases of invasive carcinoma of the uterine cervix. Features frequently present in radiotherapy patients were narrowing or obliteration of the vagina, pelvic fibrosis, and pain or discomfort on pelvic examination. No specific sexual dysfunctions are described.

Abitbol, M., and Davenport, J. H. Sexual dysfunction after therapy for cervical carcinoma. *American Journal of Obstetrics and Gynecology*, 1974, *119*, 181–189.

The authors, motivated by the lack of research on the sexual function of women following therapy for cervical carcinoma, conducted this major study. The main purpose of the study was to examine the effect of different therapeutic approaches for invasive carcinoma of the cervix on the sexual function of patients (n=97). Three modes of therapy were used: radiotherapy alone, surgery alone, and a combination of both. Frequency of sexual intercourse was the major criterion for assessing sexual function or dysfunction in the subjects. That is, only when there was a decrease in the frequency of sexual intercourse were there also other sexual dysfunctions in patients, such as painful intercourse, lack of libido, etc. Results showed that shortening of the vagina interfered markedly with the sexual function of most of the women treated with radiotherapy, while only 2 of 32 surgically treated patients reported sexual dysfunction. The authors therefore give preference to radical surgery in the management of early carcinoma of the cervix. It was also found that the percentage of patients having anatomical distortions and sexual dysfunctions was similar in the three groups regardless of treatment mode.

Aso, R., and Yasutomi, M. Urinary and sexual disturbances following rectal cancer, and pudential nerve block as a countermeasure for urinary disturbance. *American Journal of Proctology*, 1974, *25*, 60–69.

This paper presents the results of a study examining urinary disturbance and sexual difficulties in patients following rectal cancer. An evaluation of a new method of pudential nerve block as a countermeasure for vesical disturbance is also given. Subjects were 296 patients who had radical surgery for cancer. Results show that 96 percent of 101 patients less than 60 years of age reported being sexually active before surgery. Postoperatively, however, 4.2 percent reported accelerated sexual functioning, 15.2 percent maintained usual functioning, 43.1 percent reported reduced sexual activity, and 37.5 percent abstained completely. Of the patients over 60 years of age, 41.4 percent reported reduced sexual function following surgery, and 51.7 percent abstained. Other results are discussed.

Bernstein, W. C. Sexual dysfunction following radical surgery for cancer of rectum and sigmoid colon. *Medical Aspects of Human Sexuality*, 1972, *6*, 156–163.

The author discusses the effects of surgical operations for cancer of the sigmoid colon and rectum on sexual functioning of male patients. Detailed descriptions of the anatomy and physiology of both erection and ejaculation are presented, with specific implications of possible dysfunctions in the patient following radical surgery for cancer of the rectum and colon. Possibilities for preserving sexual functioning in such patients are also discussed. Reports of the incidence of sexual impotence in these patients vary from 53 to 100 percent, with an average reported incidence of 76 percent. When surgery carries with it possible sexual complications, "the surgeon should be prepared to intelligently and tactfully discuss the subject with the patient and to counsel him in the event that dysfunction or impotence does occur." Several forms of noncoital sexual techniques are still available for the patient who loses sexual potency.

Binder, D. P. Sex, courtship and the single ostomate. Los Angeles: United Ostomy Association, 1973.

Many questions and concerns enter the mind of the new ostomate regarding social interaction, sexual functioning, and marriage prospects. This booklet discusses these and other areas of interest such as sexual incapabilities, sexual techniques, birth control, and homosexuality.

Brown, R. S. Sexual life of women following pelvic exenteration. In D. W. Abse, E. M. Nash, and L. M. R. Louden (Eds.),

Marital and sexual counseling in medical practice (2nd ed.). New York: Harper and Row, 1974.

The author presents the results of a study he conducted with 15 female patients following pelvic exenteration. The purpose of the study was to assess in these patients (1) social adjustment following the operation; (2) psychological adjustment to mutilation, especially the desexualization and the loss of bowel control following colostomy; (3) correlation of personality factors and the course of malignancy; and (4) the role of psychiatric support in treating the responses of these patients. The author, from his data, concluded that "despite the stresses to which these patients were subjected, overall social and psychological adjustment was favorable." Autoerotic practice and sexual dreams were reported by some women after the operation took place.

Burnham, W. R., Lennard-Jones, J. E., and Brooke, B. N. The incidence and nature of sexual problems among married ileostomists. *Gut*, 1976, *17*, 391–392.

This is an abstract of a paper presented by the authors at the British Society of Gastroenterology. The purpose of the study presented was to examine sexual functioning and the nature of sexual problems experienced by ileostomy patients. Results and conclusions were reported.

Byrd, B. F. Sex after mastectomy. *Medical Aspects of Human Sexuality*, 1975, *9*(4), 53–54.

The author asserts that following mastectomy the patient needs counseling in three major areas regarding her sexuality: (1) her image to the world; (2) her image to her mate; and (3) her sexual self-image. These three areas are discussed in relation to sexual adjustment, and specific guidelines for office counseling by a physician are presented.

Daly, M. J. Psychological impact of surgical procedures on women. In A. M. Freedman, H. I. Kaplan, B. J. Sadock (Eds.), *Comprehensive textbook of psychiatry* (Vol. 2). Baltimore: Williams and Wilkins, 1975.

The psychosexual impact of various surgical procedures in women is discussed. Specific procedures described include bilateral oophorectomy, hysterectomy, colpocleisis, radical pelvic operations, and other forms of surgery.

Daly, M. J. Psychological impact of surgical procedures on women. In B. J. Sadock, H. I. Kaplan, and A. M. Freedman (Eds.), *The sexual experience*. Baltimore: Williams and Wilkins, 1976.

The emotional, sexual, and conception implications of various operative procedures performed on the pelvic and reproductive organs of women are identified and discussed. These include the psychological and sexual impact of castrating and sterilizing procedures, bilateral oophorectomy, hysterectomy, vaginal procedures, obstetrical operations, and radical pelvic operative procedures. The author concludes by suggesting that "proper preoperative evaluation for any pelvic surgery should be comprehensive, dealing with fantasies and expectations, so that the resulting emotional response will be positive. In this way the postoperative recovery of women will be enhanced."

Dlin, B. M., and Perlman, A. Sex after ileostomy or colostomy. *Medical Aspects of Human Sexuality*, 1972, *6*(7), 32–43.

Psychosexual problems associated with ileostomy or colostomy are discussed in light of research and clinical findings. Also presented are data obtained by the authors from 500 questionnaires and personal interviews with patients in psychotherapy. Questions were patterned on those of Kinsey, covering various aspects of the patients' sexual activities, attitudes, and adjustments.

Dlin, B. M., Perlman, A., and Ringold, E. Psychosexual responses to ileostomy and colostomy. *American Journal of Psychiatry*, 1969, *126*, 374–384.

In an attempt to dispel myths and taboos surrounding colostomy and ileostomy, the authors conducted this study to examine the psychosexual implications and adjustment following these operations. A questionnaire survey was conducted among 500 members of various ostomy associations. Results show that potency and fertility do suffer somewhat, but not to the extent and degree previous estimates would indicate. The importance of counseling and the role of the physician in facilitating the patients' psychosexual adjustment are stressed and discussed.

Drellich, M. G. Sex after hysterectomy. *Medical Aspects of Human Sexuality*, 1967, *1*(11), 62–64.

The underlying message of this report is that when sexual dysfunctions occur in postoperative hysterectomy patients it is mostly a result of psychosocial factors and not of the physical condition per se. The major factor is related to irrational fears and the psychological effects of surgery in the female genital area. Other intervening aspects may include preoperative regret for the loss of childbearing ability; ambivalence about loss of menstruation; fear of the effects of surgery on everyday feminine activities and roles; fear of sexual unacceptability to spouse or partner; actual postoperative side-effects of hysterectomy that indirectly affect sexuality, e.g., bowel irregularities, loss of appetite, weight gain, feelings of weakness, fragility, and vulnerability; and the belief that hysterectomy was a punishment for sexual sins. The author concludes that "the physician is best equipped to handle these sexual problems when he clearly recognizes that hysterectomy and the surgical menopause in mature females need not, in themselves, cause a decrease in sexual desire, sexual pleasure, or ability to participate in sex."

Drellich, M. G., and Bieber, I. The psychologic importance of the uterus and its functions: Some psychoanalytic implications of hysterectomy. *Journal of Nervous and Mental Disease*, 1958, *126*, 322–336.

This paper presents the findings of a series of psychological observations made on randomly selected premenopausal women who had undergone hysterectomies (n=23). The purpose of the study was to determine the importance of the possession of the uterus in female adaptation. Most subjects viewed the uterus as a sexual organ, childbearing organ, reservoir of strength, and maintainer of youth and attractiveness. Surgery was sometimes viewed as punishment for guilt-laden attitudes involving sexual activities. The authors suggest that "the uterus is regarded by many women as an important symbol of femininity, onto which is projected attitudes towards sexual and nonsexual female functions." Most of the subjects expressed some anxiety concerning their ability to participate in sexual relations, the possibility of sexual rejection by husbands, the loss of sexual attractiveness, and their ability to satisfy their husbands sexually.

Druss, R., O'Connor, J., and Stern, W. Changes in body image following ileostomy. *Psychoanalytic Quarterly*, 1972, *41*, 195–207.

The case histories of four women who had permanent ileostomy after total colectomy for ulcerative colitis are studied and discussed. Five phenomena were observed in these four women: (1) Phantom rectum: For a couple of weeks after the surgery they had a sense of fullness and an urge toward bowel movement. The rectum, of course, did not exist, so this was perhaps the patient's denial of the loss of a body part through surgery. (2) The stoma as phallus: While many patients felt a loss of a major organ, the bowel, these four women reacted as if they had a gain. To them the stoma looked like a penis. (3) Exhibitionism: All four women were happy to disrobe for medical personnel in mixed audiences. (4) Erotic feelings toward the surgeon: These women felt conscious excitement sexually for their surgeons. (5) Changes in personality and life style: Denial and hypomania were used as defense mechanisms against depression and anxiety about bodily mutilation. Also noticed was an actively directed aggressive behavior.

Dyk, R. B., and Sutherland, A. M. Adaptation of the spouse and other family members to the colostomy patient. *Cancer*, 1956, *9*, 123–138.

Intensive interviews were conducted with 29 men and 28 women to determine the psychosocial impact of abdominoperineal resection with establishment of a dry colostomy. The focus of these interviews was on the adaptation of the spouse and other family members to the colostomy patient. Adaptation was examined in the areas of work, sexual functioning and activity, and social life. Results and conclusions of this extensive study are presented.

Ervin, C. V., Jr. Psychologic adjustment to mastectomy. *Medical Aspects of Human Sexuality*, 1973, *7*(2), 42–65.

Emotional reactions to and psychosocial and sexual problems associated with mastectomy are discussed in this article.

Finkle, A. L. Sex after prostatectomy. *Medical Aspects of Human Sexuality*, 1962, *2*(3), 40–41.

The effect of prostatectomy on the patient's sexual function, and suggestions for treatment and sexual counseling are discussed. The majority of more than 200 aging men examined, who were sexually active prior to operation, retained their sexual function postoperatively.

Finkle, A. L. Sexual potency after perineal prostatectomy. *Western Journal of Surgery, Obstetrics and Gynecology*, 1962, *70*(2), 55–57.

This article presents and discusses the results of a study aimed at examining sexual functioning in patients following perineal prostatectomy (n=26). Results revealed that there was preservation of sexual potency in about 70 percent of the patients. Age, per se, was not found to be a limiting factor in maintaining sexual potency. The author concludes that "sexual impotency is no more common following perineal prostatectomy than other surgical approaches to the gland."

Gambrell, E. Sex and the male ostomate. Los Angeles, California: United Ostomy Association, 1973.

This booklet was written for both the male ostomate and his sexual partner in order to assist them in achieving a psychological adjustment to sex with an ostomy and to provide advice for the management of the ostomy for a satisfying sex life. Information was gathered from various sources, including a survey of 95 male ostomates who answered a lengthy questionnaire which covered a wide range of aspects of their sexual functioning. There are four major sections in this publication: (1) the anatomy of ostomy, i.e., ileostomy, urostomy, and colostomy; (2) psychological problems following surgery, i.e., fear of failure in sexual functioning; (3) making love, including ostomy management, sexual positions, overcoming sexual difficulties; and (4) organic problems following surgery, including impotence, orgasmic dysfunctions, ejaculatory incompetence, and sterility.

Gold, F. M., and Hotchkiss, R. S. Sexual potency following simple prostatectomy. *New York State Journal of Medicine*, 1969, *69*, 2987–2989.

The purpose of this study was to examine the status of sexual potency in men one year following prostate surgery. Ninety-four individuals, from 41 to 82 years of age, were studied. A control group of 34 aging men who had undergone inguinal herniorrhaphy one year before the study was also included. The results show that 80 percent of the patients in the youngest age group (50 to 60 years) reported no change in sexual potency following prostatectomy, compared to only 32 to 34 percent of the patients in the two older groups (61 to 80 years). No significant relation was found between the type of prostatectomy undergone and resulting impotency. Of the entire group, 81 percent reported the presence of retrograde ejaculation. In the control group it was found that 97 percent of the men reported no change in sexual potency, which excludes lower abdominal surgery per se as a contributing factor to prostatectomy impotency. In conclusion, it appears that the age of an individual undergoing a prostatectomy is a very significant factor in determining how his sexual potency will be affected. In addition, it appears that a great proportion of the men who have undergone a prostatectomy experience a sizable reduction in sexual performance.

Goligher, J. C. Sexual function after excision of the rectum. *Proceedings of the Royal Society of Medicine*, 1951, *44*, 824.

This article presents and discusses the results of a study aimed at the examination of sexual functioning in male patients following excision of the rectum (n=95). The author reports that penile erections occurred in 72 percent of the patients, and that sexual intercourse was successful in 64 percent of those. All patients who had intercourse experienced orgasm, but 39 percent had retrograde ejaculation. This condition results from failure of the vesical neck to close during orgasm.

Grabstald, H. Postradical cystectomy impotence treated by penile silicone implant. *New York State Journal of Medicine*, 1970, *15*, 2344–2345.

The author notes that "organic sexual impotence in the male patient is virtually an inevitable consequence of radical cystectomy or radical prostatectomy." This article presents case reports of two patients who underwent radical cystectomy and whose resulting impotence was successfully managed by the insertion of a silicone plastic prosthesis. Based on these experiences the author concludes that impotence resulting from radical cystectomy can be successfully managed by this surgical procedure in carefully selected patients who are mentally stable, relatively young, and free of diseases two or more years after surgery.

Greenberg, E. Effects of testosterone in women with breast cancer. *Medical Aspects of Human Sexuality*, 1975, *9*(9), 135–143.

The treatment of metastatic breast cancer, with an emphasis on testosterone treatment, and its effect on sexual functioning and behavior is the main subject discussed in this article.

Grinker, R. R. Sex and cancer. *Medical Aspects of Human Sexuality*, 1976, *10*(2), 85–89.

The paper examines the impact of cancer on marital, sexual, and family relationships, and its similarities to other traumatic events, such as loss of a loved one, divorce, or loss of a job. Case histories of six patients are presented to illustrate the psychosocial and sexual aspects of cancer.

Hollender, M. H. Hysterectomy and feelings of femininity. *Medical Aspects of Human Sexuality*, 1969, *3*(7), 6–15.

Following a review of relevant literature, the author concludes that the evidence suggests that hysterectomy often sets off profound psychological problems in postoperative patients. He adds: "it is my contention that the operation is perceived as a blow to femininity by almost all women." The author presents four detailed case studies of hysterectomy patients and discusses the psychosocial and sexual difficulties and problems faced by these women. Reassuring the patient about her femininity can be supportive and helpful. The gynecologist needs to provide accurate information and encouragement by informing the patient that the removal of the uterus does not mean the end of her sexual life or feminine attractiveness.

Huffman, J. W. Hysterectomy: Procedure and aftermath. *Medical Aspects of Human Sexuality*, 1975, *9*(11), 123–124.

Psychosexual difficulties and specific steps in counseling the patient who is to undergo a hysterectomy are discussed in this brief guide to office counseling.

Lyons, A. S. Sex after ileostomy and colostomy. *Medical Aspects of Human Sexuality*, 1975, *9*(1), 107–108.

Ileostomy or colostomy can result in some sexual difficulties for the patient. This brief paper discusses these difficulties and presents suggestions for counseling to be provided by the physician. A thorough sex history and physical examination, coupled with indicated laboratory procedures, are essential to counseling the patient regarding sexuality. The psychological impact of the stoma, interpersonal relationship problems faced by the patient, and the mechanics of sexual activities following ileostomy or colostomy are also discussed. The physician is encouraged to make referrals to a sex therapist when needed.

Montague, D. K. Sex after cystectomy. *Medical Aspects of Human Sexuality*, 1977, *11*(12), 91–92.

According to the author, cystectomy always results in significant sexual dysfunction in the male patient and frequently in the female patient. After cystectomy, a man is unable to obtain an erection, and seminal emission and ejaculation are absent. Sex counseling and penile prostheses for these patients are two additional topics discussed.

Norris, C., and Gambrell, E. Guess who's pregnant? A discussion on sex and pregnancy for the female ostomate. *Ostomy Quarterly*, 1972, *9*(2), 4, 42–56.

Written to answer some of the questions and alleviate apprehensions that the female ostomate might have concerning her sexual attractiveness or her ability to handle the problems of pregnancy and birth, this article was compiled from responses made by ostomate mothers to a questionnaire survey carried out by the United Ostomy Association. These responses indicated that ostomies present no untoward problems in themselves and that courting, romance, sex, and pregnancy can and do proceed normally for most ostomates. Practical suggestions are made for adjustments to the stoma or the appliance that might be necessary during sexual activity and during pregnancy, with explanatory quotations from doctors and ostomates.

Norris, C., and Gambrell, E. Sex, pregnancy and the female ostomate. Los Angeles: United Ostomy Association, Inc., 1972.

Aimed primarily at the female ostomate, this booklet discusses various physical, psychological, social, and sexual implications of ostomy for both the patient and her spouse. Sexual functioning, pregnancy, diet, and delivery in these patients are also covered.

Rent, C. S., Rent, G. S., and Northcutt, T. J. Behavioral factors related to the onset of cervical cancer. *Journal of Health and Social Behavior*, 1972, *13*, 437–445.

The purpose of this study was to identify behavioral characteristics associated with contracting cervical cancer. A group of fifty women with the malignancy and an equal number of controls were compared in terms of past and present sexual behavior and hygiene practice. The study group was found to display higher rates of venereal diseases, less douching after intercourse, less use of contraceptives such as jellies and foams, greater use of Lysol solution as a first douche, and more births outside a medical setting than in the control group. This finding suggests that cervical cancer could be related to some unknown agent which might be transmitted through sexual activities.

Rotkin, I. D., Quenk, N. L., and Couchman, M. Psychosexual factors and cervical cancer. *Archives of General Psychiatry*, 1965, *13*, 532–536.

The authors report selected early data from a large multivariate study they conducted in an attempt to investigate components possibly associated with the onset and incidence of cervical cancer. The selected psychological and sexual variables in this article were studied for interrelationships and for differences between patients and controls. It was found that there was no clearly significant difference between patients and controls in general affect toward sexual intercourse as determined from responses to the question "what do you think about during the act of sexual intercourse?" Sexual affect scores were found to be related positively to presence or absence of orgasm, frequency of orgasm, and presence or absence of masturbation.

Sopchak, A. L., and Sutherland, A. M. Psychological impact of cancer and its treatment: Exogenous sex hormones and their relation to lifelong adaptations in women with metastatic cancer of the breast. *Cancer*, 1960, *13*, 528–531.

Thirty-two female patients with carcinoma of the breast who had had radical mastectomies were studied in order to examine the effects of sex hormone therapy on sexual behavior and functioning. Results led the authors to conclude that 1) androgens heighten sexual desire in breast cancer patients, whereas estrogens do not; 2) the types of changes brought about by sex hormone treatment can sometimes be traceable to earlier patterns of the person's sexual adjustment; and 3) the less sexually inhibited patients were more strongly affected by the androgens, the more sexually inhibited women were either less affected or not affected at all by this treatment.

Steele, R. Sexual factors in prostatic cancer. *Medical Aspects of Human Sexuality*, 1972, *6*(8), 70–81.

Unusually great sexual drive, multiple partners, and history of venereal disease appear to be related to prostatic cancer. These and other sexual aspects of this disease are discussed. Also presented are the results of a study conducted by the author to examine patterns of sexual behavior exhibited by prostatic cancer patients.

Vasicka, A., Popovich, N. R., and Brausch, C. C. Postradiation course of patients with cervical carcinoma: A clinical study of psychic, sexual, and physical well-being of sixteen patients. *Obstetrics and Gynecology*, 1958, *11*(4), 403–414.

The purpose of this study was to evaluate the psychologic, sexual, and physical well-being of a group of postradiation patients treated for cervical carcinoma (n=16). The patients' case histories, results, and recommendations for evaluation and treatment of this disease are presented.

Waxenberg, S. E., Finkbeiner, J. A., Drellich, M. G., and Sutherland, A. M. The role of hormones in human behavior: Changes in sexual behavior in relation to vaginal smears of breast-cancer patients after oophorectomy and adrenalectomy. *Psychosomatic Medicine*, 1960, *22*(6), 435–442.

Data concerning sexual behavior were obtained from a group of women following oophorectomy and adrenalectomy for metastatic cancer of the breast. Vaginal smears from most of the patients were also available. Decreased cytological activity in the vaginal mucosa and decreased sexual desire, activity, and responsiveness were found in these patients. Other findings are analyzed and discussed.

Weinberg, P. C. Psychosexual impact of treatment in female genital cancer. *Journal of Sex & Marital Therapy*, 1974, *1*(2), 155–157.

The purpose of this article was to examine the psychosexual impact of various modes of therapy utilized in the treatment of gynecic malignancy. It emphasizes the necessity for sensitivity on the part of physicians so as to avoid postoperative sexual dysfunction in patients. The methods of treatment and therapy differ with the various types of lesions and the extent of the disease at the time of surgery. In general, early lesions are treated surgically with less posttherapy dysfunction. This reduces the chances of vaginal stenosis and atrophy. The earlier the surgery, the better the prognosis for continued normal coital function. In cases of more radical surgery, radiotherapy is often necessary. These treatments can often be severely destructive to coital function. There is a possibility that this can be avoided with intensive posttherapy care and counseling. The physician must be aware of the fears and anxieties suffered by patients with a malignant disease. With proper care, education, and counseling, almost all sexual dysfunctions can be avoided.

Witkin, M. H. Sex therapy and mastectomy. *Journal of Sex & Marital Therapy*, 1975, *1*(4), 290–304.

According to the author, the emotional trauma of mastectomy is greater than the physical trauma. More should be done to prepare the patient and her spouse to work together toward a resolution of the crisis. This article is an effort in that direction, aimed primarily at sex therapists. The therapist is encouraged to help both the patient and her partner to confront the mastectomy experience. Intercourse should occur as soon as possible following surgery. The husband should be as compassionate, supportive, and expressive of his love and concern for his wife and her feelings as possible. All efforts should be directed at prevention of loss of self-esteem on the part of the patient. Certain sex therapy exercises (body imagery and sensory focus) are described. Their aim is to promote acceptance of the loss and the sharing of the emotional experience between the sexual partners.

Woods, N. F. Facts and opinion: Influence on sexual adaptation to mastectomy. *JOGN Nursing*, 1975, *4*, 33–37.

Mastectomy may have a negative effect on the woman's sex life if she believes the disfiguring surgery has left her sexually unacceptable or inadequate. The biologic, psychologic, and sociocultural factors affecting the postoperative sexual adjustment of the patient are outlined and discussed. Pain in the operation area, the patient's perception of her sex partner's reaction, and societal standards of sexual desirability are a few of the factors affecting the sexual adjustment of mastectomy patients. Also discussed is the practicing nurse's role and function in the sexual adjustment process of these patients. The nurse has to evaluate the patient's ability for adjustment and her need for counseling and advice in this area.

Obesity

Allon, N. The relationship between overweight and sexual orientation. Paper presented at the Seventieth Annual Meeting of the American Sociological Association, August 25–29, 1977.

Allon conducted 200 open-ended interviews with female participants in group dieting meetings. The interviews focused on the relationships between overweight and sexual orientation. Four major themes about the relationship between overweight and sexuality were found: (1) 75 percent of the subjects made reference to sexual promiscuity in regard to their losing or not losing weight; (2) the next most common theme cited by subjects was labeled by the author as "feelings of sexiness." Some 55 percent of the sample made reference to their gaining or losing sexiness as a result of losing weight; (3) about 40 percent of the subjects reported a relationship between eating or food and sexuality. Most of these women stressed the idea of food as a substitute for sexual activity; (4) 35 percent of the participating women showed signs of poor body image and its relationship to overweight and sexuality. Many women labeled themselves "ugly" and sexually "unattractive" because of their overweight.

Beigle, H. G. Sex and overweight. *Sexology*, 1964, *30*, 664–666.

Sexual conflicts and difficulties resulting from and associated with overweight and obesity are discussed.

Bruch, H. Obesity and sex. *Medical Aspects of Human Sexuality*, 1969, *3*(2), 42–52.

Weight increase may be a response to sexual frustration or may be a defense against sexuality. This and other relationships between obesity and emotional and psychosexual problems are discussed in this article. Therapeutic management of those obese persons with difficulties demands evaluation of the individual circumstances.

Buchanan, J. R. Sexual problems of obese women. *Medical Aspects of Human Sexuality*, 1976, *10*(1), 49–50.

The author identifies and discusses the psychosexual implications of obesity in women. Negative self-image, fear of competition with other, more attractive women, and the adjustment to changed body image are some of the problem areas covered. Some specific suggestions for counseling are also presented.

Dwyer, J. T. Psychosexual aspects of weight control and dieting behavior in adolescents. *Medical Aspects of Human Sexuality*, 1973, *7*(3), 82–114.

Psychological, social, and sexual difficulties and problems associated with obesity and weight control are discussed in light of a comprehensive review of the literature.

Friedman, A. I. *Fat can be beautiful*. New York: Berkley Publishing Corporation, 1974.

Of particular interest in this book is a chapter discussing the association between obesity and sexuality, and various techniques of sexual coitus for obese couples.

Friedman, A. I. *How sex can keep you slim*. Englewood Cliffs, N.J.: Prentice-Hall, 1972.

The association between obesity and sexuality, the impact of obesity on sexual functioning, and sexual stimulation techniques for obese couples are some of the topics discussed in this book. Numerous case histories from the author's clinical practice are presented for illustration.

Ishida, Y. Sexuality after small bowel bypass. *Current Medical Dialog*, 1974, *41*(12), 659–662.

Long-standing obesity was treated in a 34-year-old woman by means of surgical bypass of the small bowel. This paper presents and discusses this woman's case report, emphasizing her sexuality after undergoing such a procedure.

Volkan, V. D. Food, body shape and sexuality. In D. W. Abse, E. M. Nash, and L. M. R. Louden (Eds.), *Marital and sexual counseling in medical practice* (2nd ed.). New York: Harper and Row, 1974.

The author asserts that "a patient preoccupation with eating, dieting and weight control may be symptomatic of psychopathologic condition, the appreciation of which aids the family physician in his diagnosis and management and alerts him to those situations in which a psychiatric consultation may be indicated." Reflecting upon his clinical experience and a thorough review of relevant literature, the author outlines and discusses the psychological and sexual aspects of eating and weight problems and the specific medical disorders that may accompany them. Several case reports are presented and analyzed to illustrate these relationships. One of the cases involved a depressed 23-year-old woman whose conflicts were related to orality, sexuality, and dependence-independence. The patient was denying her husband sex, and finding "self-gratification in the bizarre ritual of eating and vomiting."

Chapter Three

Genitourinary Conditions

Urologic Illness / Gynecologic Diseases

Urologic Illness

Culp, O. S. Anomalies of male genitalia. *Medical Aspects of Human Sexuality*, 1974, *8*(9), 126–147.

Various genital anomalies in the male and their effect on sexual functioning are discussed in this article, with some suggestions for corrective surgery and treatment. The author suggests that "many hypospadias, epispadias, and associated anomalies can be corrected if well established surgical techniques are employed at the most opportune time." He adds that congenital urethral defects will not impair sexual functioning if an adequate reconstruction surgery is conducted.

Dahlen, C. P., and Goodwin, W. E. Sexual potency after perineal biopsy. *Journal of Urology*, 1957, *77*(4), 660–669.

The purpose of this study was to assess the effect of open perineal prostatic biopsy on sexual potency of patients (n=24). Results show that there were no changes in potency in one-third of the patients, while 37 percent reported diminution of potency after perineal biopsy, and 29 percent had complete loss of potency. The average age of those who suffered complete loss was 64.4 years, whereas the average age of those whose potency was unchanged was 53.7 years. Other results and conclusions are presented.

Davis, J. E., and Mininberg, D. T. Prostatitis and sexual function. *Medical Aspects of Human Sexuality*, 1976, *10*(8), 32–40.

The relationship between prostatitis and sexual function is the main topic discussed in this article. Also presented are some ideas for accurate diagnosis and treatment of the condition.

Dubin, L., and Amelar, R. D. Urologic disease and sexual function. *Medical Aspects of Human Sexuality*, 1971, *5*(10), 108–117.

According to the authors, the belief that urologic disease implies termination of sexual activity is in most cases unfounded. This paper discusses the psychosexual implications of urologic disease and the effects of urologic surgery on sexual functioning. It is concluded that most urologic conditions, whether medical or surgical in nature, usually do not result in permanent sexual dysfunction.

Finkle, A. L. The relationship of sexual habits to benign prostatic hypertrophy. *Medical Aspects of Human Sexuality*, 1967, *1*(2), 24–25.

The relationship between infrequent sexual activity or inadequate sexual gratification and benign prostatic hyperplasia is examined and discussed. The author could not find a one-to-one correlation between benign prostatic hyperplasia and sexual functioning in aging men.

Gibson, G. R. Impotence following fractured pelvis and ruptured urethra. *British Journal of Urology*, 1970, *42*, 86–88.

Sexual dysfunction is one of the long-term hazards of fractured pelvis and ruptured urethra. Subjects in this study were 35 male patients who were admitted to Sydney Hospital with fractured pelvis and ruptured urethra and who were available for follow-up examination over a period of three years or longer. Impotence was found in 13 patients (37 percent). Of the 26 patients who sustained a complete rupture of the membranous urethra, 11 were impotent (42 percent). Only 5 of the 35 patients fathered children after injury. The author indicates that the cause of impotence in these patients seems to be an interference with neural control. Damage with thrombosis of the dorsal and deep arteries of the penis in the region of the perineal membrane may also be responsible for impotence in some patients who had experienced ejaculation without erection.

Hyzer, W. J. Elephantiasis of male genitalia: Surgical treatment. *Medical Aspects of Human Sexuality*, 1973, *7*(5), 218–224.

Elephantiasis of the male genitalia is a physically, psychosocially, and sexually debilitating disease. These aspects of the disease are discussed, as are its etiology and treatment. Sexual rehabilitation usually follows treatment in otherwise well-motivated and adjusted patients.

Kaufman, J. J. Urologic factors in impotence and premature ejaculation. *Medical Aspects of Human Sexuality*, 1967, *1*(1), 43–48.

Various urologic factors and diseases affecting sexual potency are presented. The medical conditions that may cause impotency and difficulties in ejaculation include diseases of the nerve or blood supply, prostatic and urethral disease, and diabetes. Also discussed are the effects of surgery and of drug treatment on sexual functioning in male patients.

Kobshi, L. I. Sex after urologic surgery. *Medical Aspects of Human Sexuality*, 1974, *8*(12), 63–64.

Physiologic and psychogenic considerations associated with sexual difficulties following urologic surgery are discussed, and specific suggestions for treatment and counseling are presented.

McDonald, D. F. Peyronie's disease. *Medical Aspects of Human Sexuality*, 1972, *6*(5), 65–67.

The clinical presentation of Peyronie's disease includes tumors in the corpora cavernosa, associated with curved and painful penile erections. The physical, sexual, and treatment aspects of this disease are discussed. It was found that painful erections are present in 56 percent to 64 percent of patients. This complaint is more prevalent in younger patients.

Madorsky, M., Drylie, D. M., and Finlayson, B. Effect of benign prostatic hypertrophy on sexual behavior. *Medical Aspects of Human Sexuality*, 1976, *10*(2), 8–22.

The authors discuss the relationship between benign prostatic hyperplasia and associated alteration in sexual functioning and activity. Reduced sexual libido in older patients seems to complicate the evaluation of sexual potency following surgery. However, there is evidence that prostatectomy is associated with a decrease or loss of sexual potency. The authors state that "the consensus of opinion is that perineal prostatectomy will cause impotence in 30–40 per cent of patients, suprapubic and retropubic prostatectomy in 15–20 per cent of patients, and transurethral prostatectomy in 5–40 per cent of patients." Also discussed are the physiology of erection and the treatment of impotence.

Malin, J. Sex after urologic surgery. *Medical Aspects of Human Sexuality*, 1973, *7*(10), 245–264.

In this article the author discusses several types of urologic surgery and their effects on sexual functioning in the male. While some surgical procedures result in impotence and/or sterility in the male, psychogenic causes account for a significant amount of postoperative impotence. The urologic procedures discussed are total and partial penectomy, prostatectomy for malignant and benign tumors, and vasectomy. Regardless of the urologic surgery it is vital for the physician to explain the procedure adequately to the patient and his wife. Since many urologic surgeries threaten the male's body image and sexuality, adequate psychological preparation for the patient and his wife is also necessary. The attitude of the physician toward the patient and his surgery can influence the outcome of the surgery. If the physician takes the time to explain thoroughly the possible and/or inevitable effects of the surgery to the patient and his wife, much can be done to prevent psychogenic impotence.

Marshall, S. Painful urogenital conditions which impede coitus. *Medical Aspects of Human Sexuality*, 1976, *10*(12), 111–112.

Urogenital conditions affecting male and female patients and their impact on sexual intercourse are discussed in this brief communication. Also presented are suggestions for therapy and office counseling by a physician. Specific urogenital problems presented include infectious urethritis, herpes, traumatic urethritis, prostatitis, anatomical deformities, and vaginitis.

Poutasse, E. F. Peyronie's disease. *Medical Aspects of Human Sexuality*, 1976, *10*(1), 92.

The author defines Peyronie's disease as "a plaque-like fibrous induration of the penis accompanied by a painful erection and eventual chordee." The pathology, symptoms, clinical course, and medical and surgical treatment of the condition are discussed in this paper.

Roen, P. R. Urologic causes of frigidity. *Medical Aspects of Human Sexuality*, 1968, *2*(8), 20–21.

Urologic conditions affecting sexual responsivity and enjoyment are discussed in light of a case report that illustrates the difficulties involved.

Rowan, R. L. The problems of urine stoppage. *Sexology*, January 1970, 59–61.

The author discusses sexual difficulties and dysfunctions associated with urethral stricture, a narrowing and hardening of a portion of the urinary canal. This condition occurs mostly in men. Also presented is a case study to illustrate the sexual complications of this condition. Suggestions for treatment are given.

Sadoughi, W., and Bush, I. M. Urologic symptoms as a psychological crutch for underlying sex problems. *Medical Aspects of Human Sexuality*, 1974, *8*(7), 130–143.

Based on their clinical observations and experience, the authors stress that "many patients experience sexual difficulties as a result of genitourinary problems. In others, the inadequacy of their sexual experience may be one of the underlying causes of their urologic complaints." In this paper, the authors discuss the relationships between urological symptoms and sexual dysfunctions in light of several case studies from their clinical practice.

Smith, A. M., and Lattimer, J. K. Psychosexual impact of undescended testes and implantation of prostheses. *Medical Aspects of Human Sexuality*, 1975, *9*(5), 62–70.

The psychosocial and sexual development aspects of undescended testes are discussed in this paper, followed by a commentary by another authority. Based on their clinical experience and other findings, the authors conclude that the psychological factor is very important in the timing of therapy, and they advise that both testes be in the scrotum by the fifth birthday.

Walker, K. Urinary complaints. *Sexology*, 1961, *27*, 620–624.

Because of their close relationship, any disturbance in the urinary system may affect sexual functioning. The impact of various urinary disorders on sexual function and behavior is examined in this paper.

Wershub, L. P. Male genital abnormalities which interfere with intercourse. *Medical Aspects of Human Sexuality*, 1968, *2*(9), 53–58.

Various organic disorders and diseases of the male's genital organs and their effect on sexual function and behavior are presented and discussed. Specific abnormalities discussed include hypoplasia of the penis, hypospadias, epispadias, Peyronie's disease, monorchism, anorchism, and other conditions.

Gynecologic Diseases

Easley, E. B. Atrophic vaginitis and sexual relations. *Medical Aspects of Human Sexuality*, 1974, *8*(11), 32–58.

Dyspareunia resulting from atrophic vaginitis often interferes with satisfactory sexual intercourse in menopausal women. This and other sexual dysfunctions and behavior associated with atrophic vaginitis are discussed in this paper in light of the author's clinical experience. The prevention and treatment of this condition becomes clinically important after the menopause and after childbirth, especially with lactation. Low estrogen levels and thin vaginal epithelium are biologically normal in these two periods. The author stresses that "it is not unusual for a tiny dose of exogenous estrogen to help appreciably" in cases of dyspareunia associated with atrophic vaginitis. A commentary by two medical authorities follows this article.

Easley, E. B. Marital and sexual problems in gynecological practice. In D. W. Abse, E. M. Nash, and L. M. R. Louden (Eds.), *Marital and sexual counseling in medical practice* (2nd ed.). New York: Harper and Row, 1974.

Reflecting upon her extensive clinical experience, the author identifies and discusses the relationships between various gynecological problems and marital and sexual dysfunctions. She presents several clinical case reports to illustrate these relationships. Also outlined are the gynecologist's responsibilities in alleviating marital and sexual problems associated with gynecological conditions.

Fitzpatrick, G. Gynecologic surgery and its sexual impact. *Nursing Care*, 1977, *10*(7), 16–17.

The effects of gynecologic surgery on the patient's sexual behavior and functioning is discussed in light of the nurse's role and responsibility in alleviating the patient's concerns and difficulties. The importance of preoperational counseling is stressed.

Francis, W. J. A., and Jeffcoate, T. N. A. Dyspareunia following vaginal operations. *Journal of Obstetrics and Gynecology of the British Commonwealth*, 1961, *68*(1), 1–10.

Follow-up study was conducted with 243 women who underwent various types of vaginal operations. Coital function before and after operation was studied and compared. Apareunia and dyspareunia were commonly found in postoperative patients. Conclusions are presented in light of detailed results of this study.

Greer, B. E. Painful coitus due to hymenal problems. *Medical Aspects of Human Sexuality*, 1975, *9*(2), 160–169.

Various coital problems and difficulties related primarily to abnormalities of the hymen are discussed in this paper. One of the main problems identified is hymenal dyspareunia, which can be relieved by appropriate medications, psychotherapy, or surgery.

Huffman, J. W. Sexual relations after gynecologic surgery. *Medical Aspects of Human Sexuality*, 1969, *3*(11), 48–57.

The purpose of this study was to further examine the effects of gynecologic surgery on sexual function. The report was prepared after reviewing the records of 317 private patients who were seen over a period of one year. The study excluded women less than 16 years of age, single, widowed, or divorced women, those whose husbands were impotent, those in whom vaginal obliteration was necessary, and those in whom reconstructive surgery had been performed without genital excision. Results show that of the 317 women, 10 reported a decrease in their sexual reactions, 40 stated their sex life was better, and 267 found no change. Of the 10 who reported a decrease in sexual activity, 9 were found to have extraneous factors diminishing sexual capacity. The report hypothesized on the emotional stress of surgery and discussed the importance of preoperation screening and patient education. The author concludes that following gynecologic surgery alterations in sexual reactions are infrequent if the patient is stable and has been adequately prepared preoperatively as to what to expect. If physicians fail to instruct, the author predicts, a great many women will have emotional and sexual problems.

Huffman, J. W. Uterine displacement as a cause of dyspareunia. *Medical Aspects of Human Sexuality*, 1976, *10*(12), 62–71.

The author asserts that when dyspareunia is present and there is a retrodisplacement of the uterus the pain is, "in the majority of cases, due to other pelvic disorders rather than the retrodisplacement itself." This article discusses various pelvic disorders associated with coital pain and presents some therapeutic modalities.

Jacobs, T. J. Secondary amenorrhea and sexual conflicts. *Medical Aspects of Human Sexuality*, 1972, *6*(5), 87–97, 102.

Amenorrhea is the pathological absence of menstruation in a woman who has previously experienced normal menstrual cycles. The psychological and sexual aspects of this condition are discussed.

Jacobs, T. J. Sexual aspects of dysmenorrhea. *Medical Aspects of Human Sexuality*, 1976, *10*(5), 58–70.

Painful menstruation may reflect or contribute to sexual conflicts and difficulties. In this article, the author discusses the psychosexual aspects of dysmenorrhea, outlining the sexual problems, the effect of the condition on feminine self-image, and therapy.

Kerr, C. H. Obstetric trauma and subsequent sex relations. *Medical Aspects of Human Sexuality*, 1971, *5*(11), 28–41.

The effect of obstetric trauma on sexual function and activity of women is examined and discussed. Some preventative measures are presented. The author concludes that "proper emotional preparation of the patient for labor during her prenatal course, along with prevention of obstetric trauma, is the best means of assuring satisfactory sex relations after the puerperium."

Marbach, A. H. Sexual problems and gynecologic illness. *Medical Aspects of Human Sexuality*, 1970, *40*(12), 48–57.

The effect of gynecologic illness and surgery on sexual function and activity is discussed. The author asserts that "sexual problems can be intertwined with gynecologic illness, can be influenced, can be ameliorated, can be exacerbated, and can be eradicated by such illness, but rarely does gynecologic illness of itself create a severe and lasting sexual problem." Several case histories are presented for illustration, and suggestions for management are made.

Melody, G. F. Gynecologic illness and sexual behavior. *Medical Aspects of Human Sexuality*, 1968, *2*(11), 6–11.

The complaint of change in a woman's sexual behavior pattern may be an indication of an underlying gynecologic illness. The relationship between gynecological disorders and sexual function and interest is discussed, and treatment and counseling modalities are presented.

Mueller-Heubach, E. Prolapse of the uterus: Its effects on sexual behavior. *Medical Aspects of Human Sexuality*, 1972, *6*(11), 114–121.

Some women with uterine prolapse experience painful intercourse which may lead to alterations in sexual behavior. This and other sexual aspects of this medical condition are discussed. The importance of preoperative counseling is stressed.

Park, I. J. Vaginal anomalies. *Medical Aspects of Human Sexuality*, 1973, 7(12), 89–99.

The psychosocial, developmental, and sexual aspects of various vaginal anomalies are discussed, along with suggestions for treatment and counseling.

Trelford, J. D., Hanson, F. W., and Anderson, D. G. The feasibility of making an artificial vagina at the time of anterior exenteration: Case report. *Oncology*, 1973, *28*, 398–401.

The authors complain that "when a patient requires an exenterative procedure for carcinoma of the cervix, the surgeon seldom gives any thought to sexual activity of the patient." They present a case report of a patient whose postoperative sexual activity was considered. The paper reports on the use of amniotic membrane to maintain a vaginal opening in a 54-year-old patient. The authors conclude that "it is possible that in the future more consideration to the production of an artificial vagina at the time of exenterative procedures may be undertaken."

Chapter Four

Disorders of the Nervous System

Neurologic Disorders / Spinal-Cord Injury / Brain Injury / Epilepsy / Parkinson's Disease / Cerebral Palsy / Multiple Sclerosis

Neurologic Disorders

Horenstein, S. Sexual dysfunction in neurological disease. *Medical Aspects of Human Sexuality*, 1976, *10*(4), 7–31.

Neurological disease may adversely affect sexual functioning and behavior directly by altering physiology, or indirectly by creating psychological side-effects. The effect of neurological disease on sexual activity is discussed in this article. Specific conditions covered include cerebral disease, spinal-cord injury, and peripheral nerve lesions such as those associated with diabetes, uremia, or malnutrition. Some aspects of treatment, sex education, and rehabilitation are also presented.

Kott, J. A., and Kline, D. G. Neurologic diseases causing hypersexuality. *Medical Aspects of Human Sexuality*, 1977, *11*(11), 71–72.

This discussion of neurologic diseases causing hypersexuality includes the following disorders: temporal lobe epilepsy, encephalitis, and head injury. Also discussed is the impact of cerebral arteriosclerosis on sexual behavior of elderly men.

Levens, A. J. Impotence as a manifestation of neurologic disease. *Medical Annals of the District of Columbia*, 1964, *33*, 209–213.

Three detailed clinical case reports of intrinsic neurologic diseases are discussed to demonstrate that impotence may be a prominent symptom in neurologic conditions, as well as one of the early or presenting complaints of patients. One of the cases reported reveals that the medical treatment of the underlying neurologic condition, pernicious anemia, resulted in a recovery of potency in the patient. A variable impotence is reported in association with multiple sclerosis discussed in another clinical case report.

Poeck, K., and Pilleri, G. Release of hypersexual behavior due to lesion in the limbic system. *Acta Neurologica Scandinavica*, 1965, *41*, 233–244.

This is a report of a case history of a patient who had periodic release of aggressive and hypersexual behavior that seemed to be attributed to lesions in the patient's limbic system. The results of various clinical observations with postmortem examination of the lesions are discussed in light of earlier clinical research findings.

Rosenblum, J. A. Human sexuality and the cerebral cortex. *Diseases of the Nervous System*, 1974, *35*, 268–271.

The physiological relationships between the cerebral cortex and various aspects of sexual behavior and functioning are discussed. Also presented are sexual disorders associated with temporal lobe dysfunction.

Shapiro, A. K., and Shapiro, E. Sexuality and Gilles de la Tourette's syndrome. *Medical Aspects of Human Sexuality*, 1975, *9*(2), 100–109.

The authors suggest, based on clinical evidence, that the sexual and aggressive components of the Gilles de la Tourette's syndrome may result from neurophysiological, not psychological, causes. This syndrome is characterized by involuntary movement and utterances and the use of foul language. This article discusses the psychosexual aspects of this syndrome.

Silver, J. R. Sexual problems in disorders of the nervous system. I. Anatomical and physiological aspects. *British Medical Journal*, 1975, *59*, 480–482.

Silver discusses patients who are likely to be affected by sexual problems, the anatomy and physiology of intercourse and its impairment in men and women with chronic diseases of the nervous system, and the practical aspects of intercourse, marriage, pregnancy, and labor.

Silver, J. R., and Owens, E. Sexual problems in disorders of the nervous system. II. Psychological reactions. *British Medical Journal*, 1975, *59*, 532–533.

In counseling spinal-cord-injured patients with impaired sexual function, the doctor must not only be aware of the sexual problems in disorders of the nervous system, but must also know how to advise the patient. The authors discuss how to approach the subject, and consider role expectations and other psychological reactions that should be explored. Kinds of questions that may be investigated in interviews are listed and various therapeutic procedures are presented.

Walinder, J. Transvestism: Definition and evidence in favor of occasional derivation from cerebral dysfunction. *International Journal of Neuropsychiatry*, 1965, *1*, 567–573.

Some association between transvestism and cerebral disorder is suggested in this report. The author reviews pertinent literature and reports on twenty-six cases of transvestism who were examined electroencephalographically. Twelve patients showed abnormal records, and six patients had "probably normal" readings. In eight of the eighteen records which were not completely normal, the abnormality was present in one or both temporal lobes.

Weig, E. H. Counseling the adult aphasic for sexual readjustment. *Rehabilitation Counseling Bulletin*, 1973, *17*(11), 110–119.

The aphasic person is subjected to complex and conflicting experiences, including those connected with sexuality and sexual identity. The intimate relationship between sexual and social readjustment may prevent total rehabilitation, if proper attention is not directed at sexual problems. The author presents observations and problems encountered in counseling 100 ambulatory adults with various degrees of chronic aphasia, 85 of whom exhibited nonfluent aphasia, while 15 were fluent aphasics. Results show that sexual identity and role changes which occurred varied in severity depending on age, marital status, degree of motor impairment, and type of aphasia. Sexual inadequacy, loss of masculinity or femininity, impotency, and frigidity were frequent. Feelings of rejection were often at the basis of these feelings. The author asserts that the attitude of the unimpaired spouse is very important to the total rehabilitation of the patient.

Spinal-Cord Injury

Andres, P. Sexual and genital prognosis in adult paraplegics. *Paraplegia*, 1972, *10*, 218.

This is a summary of a paper presenting the author's findings relating to the sexual functioning of one hundred paraplegic patients examined by him. He indicates that, in general, erections are more frequent than ejaculations in this population. While in complete spastic lesions the reflex erections are common, ejaculations are more rare, occurring in approximately one-third of the cases. Sexual intercourse is difficult because of motor difficulties; however, if they can be solved, successful intercourse can be enjoyed. Results of an examination of twenty patients showed that if the spasticity is above level T10, ejaculation is possible. In cases where spasticity was below T10, five succeeded with good sperm and seven trials showed success with average sperm quality. As a rule, the value of the obtained ejaculations in these cases is average or mediocre as far as the number of sperm and their motility are concerned. In patients with incomplete spastic lesions the erections achieved were more reflexogenic than psychogenic, and they were very often accompanied by ejaculation. In the complete, flaccid lesion, however, neither erections nor ejaculations were possible.

Athelston, G. T., Scarlett, S., Thury, C., and Zupan, I. *Psychological, sexual, social and vocational aspects of spinal cord injury: A selected bibliography*. Minnesota Medical Rehabilitation Research and Training Center, No. 2, 1976.

The authors note that the purpose of this comprehensive publication is to provide a complete, up-to-date, indexed bibliography of references dealing with the psychosocial, vocational, and sexual aspects of spinal-cord injury. Author index and a list of sources of information consulted are also provided.

Baum, W. Neurogenic vesical and sexual dysfunction attendant on trauma to the spinal cord. *Michigan Medicine*, 1962, *61*, 574–584.

Sexual functioning in paraplegic and quadriplegic patients is discussed in light of the author's clinical experience and of data obtained from the research literature. The author indicates that about two-thirds of paraplegics and quadriplegics are capable of erections, and some two-thirds of these are capable of sexual intercourse.

Berger, S. The role of sexual impotence in the concept of self in male paraplegics. *Dissertation Abstracts*, 1952, *12b*, 533 (Unpublished Ph.D. Thesis, New York Univ., 1951).

The purpose of this study was to examine the role of sexual impotence in the concept of self of paraplegic males (n=30). The sample in this study was divided into two groups, one with subjects who were sexually impotent and the other with patients who were sexually potent. The subjects were 18 to 45 years of age. Rorshach tests, Thematic Apperception tests, Sentence Completion tests, and Draw-a-Person tests were administered. It was found that impotent subjects have, superimposed upon the difficulties inherent in their paraplegia, problems of sexual self-concept. Their concept of physical self includes marked feelings of body degeneration and distortion. Also, their concept of sexual self includes preoccupation with their own genitalia, which many of them regarded as a mutilated or castrated organ. The impotent patient's concept of emotional self included strong feelings of depression and anxiety and little drive or vitality. They also showed marked difficulties in establishing warm and satisfying interpersonal relationships, and manifested feelings of hostility and aggression.

Blanchard, M. G. Sex education for spinal cord injury patients and their nurses. *Supervisor Nurse*, 1976, *7*(2), 20–26, 28.

This article presents and discusses detailed information about setting up a program for the sexual rehabilitation of spinal-cord-injured patients. The author recognizes the importance of sexual adjustment for the disabled person, and the significant role of the nurse in facilitating this process. The author suggests that for the nurse to be effective in assisting patients in their sexual rehabilitation, she must learn about her own sexuality and be comfortable with the subject.

Bors, E. The challenge of quadriplegia. *Bulletin of the Los Angeles Neurological Society*, 1956, *21*(3), 105–123.

Sexual functioning was examined in a group of 84 quadriplegic patients as part of an extensive and comprehensive study conducted by the author. Results relating to the patients' ability to obtain erections, ejaculate, and have intercourse are presented and discussed.

Bors, E. Sexual function in patients with spinal cord injury. Proceedings of a Symposium of the Royal College of Surgeons held at Edinburgh, June 1963.

This was an oral presentation of the same material covered by this author and A. E. Comarr on the neurological disturbances of sexual function with special reference to 529 patients with spinal-cord injury (published in 1960 in the *Urological Survey*, Vol. 10, pp. 191–222).

Bors, E. Spinal cord-injuries. *Veterans' Administration Technical Bulletin*, December 15, 1948.

Sexual functioning following spinal-cord injury is one of the aspects studied and presented in this comprehensive report. One study reported shows that 86.6 percent of a group of 157 discharged patients with 90 incomplete and 67 complete lesions at various levels were capable of having erections. In another study it was found that of 200 patients, 63.5 percent had had erections while the remainder were unable to have erections; among the patients with erections, 42.5 percent responded to local reflex stimulation, intercourse was possible in 23 percent, and 12 percent had ejaculations. Yet another study showed that sexual dreams were reported by 60 percent of 157 spinal-cord patients. In this group, almost equal distributions of "complete wet," "complete dry," and "incomplete" dreams were reported by patients. The first two categories refer to a sexual dream with orgasmic feelings, with or without emission; in the last category, climax was not reached by the dreaming patients. The author also presents a physiological explanation for sexual functioning in spinal-cord-injured patients.

Bors, E., and Comarr, A. E. Neurological disturbances of sexual function with special reference to 529 patients with spinal cord injury. *Urological Survey*, 1960, *10*, 191–222.

The authors present the results of an extensive study aimed at the examination of sexual functioning in patients with spinal-cord injury (n=529). It was found that erections were maintained in 63.5 to 94 percent of the patients, and intercourse was possible in 23 to 33 percent. Ejaculation was found less likely to occur than erection. Other specific results are discussed and conclusions are presented.

Braverman, M., Hacker, F. J., and Shor, J. Psychotraumatic sexual response. *Journal of Forensic Medicine*, 1971, *18*(1), 24–29.

This paper presents an analysis of reactions to trauma in males. The authors identify four phases in the sexual reaction: (1) the most regressive phase, which is revealed by the patient's conviction that any sexual activity would harm the already injured body; (2) projected hostility and rage against the sexual partner, as if she was intent on harming the husband; (3) premature ejaculation or impotence occurs in this phase, which is characterized by the conviction that the genital organs have been affected by the trauma; and (4) acceptance of passive genital stimulation by manipulation and oral-genital practice. The authors conclude that the study of sexual response to injury provides an opportunity to examine the avenues by which sexual instinct is expressed. A patient's sexual response also "provides clinical landmarks to follow the effect of therapeutic intervention."

Bregman, S. Sexuality and the spinal cord injured woman. Minneapolis: Sister Kenny Institute, 1975.

This booklet reports the findings of a study examining sexuality in spinal-cord-injured women (n=31). Subjects were interviewed on a wide range of topics related to their sex life. The study material was organized and presented in five sections: (1) the importance of clear communication of feelings and needs between sexual partners, and various steps that can be used in setting the atmosphere for sexual intimacy; (2) suggestions made by subjects which relate to various sexual techniques and sexual stimulation practices; (3) orgasms experienced by subjects and the realization that an orgasm is a highly individual experience; (4) methods used in dealing with bowel and bladder problems faced by subjects; and (5) social techniques and skills that are essential for the initiation and development of sexual relationships. It is the author's hope that the information provided by her subjects will be helpful in assisting other disabled women in their rehabilitation process.

Bregman, S. Sexuality and the spinal-cord injured woman. Paper read at the Thirteenth World Congress of Rehabilitation International, Tel Aviv, Israel, June 13–18, 1976.

This project compiled data describing ways in which spinal-cord-injured women (n=31) cope with the effects of their disabilities as they relate to sexual and social adjustment. Subjects' ages ranged from 18 to 51 years, and each woman had had at least one sexual experience after injury. The correlation between sexual adjustment scores and time since injury was near zero (.053), suggesting that time alone is not enough for sexual adjustment after injury. Participants reporting good sexual adjustment were able to compensate for lack of sensation or mobility. If a woman had a very high injury, and could not move or feel below her shoulders, she frequently enjoyed sexual stimulation to her ears, mouth, or any other part of her body where she had partial feeling. Women provided descriptions of orgasms ranging from psychological sensations to physical experiences. Information related to bowel and bladder programs affecting sexual adjustment was provided. Two major conclusions were drawn: (1) despite the severity of some disabilities, the women were still able to live extremely fulfilling lives; and (2) many aspects of sexuality and social relationships are the same for spinal-cord-injured women as they are for able-bodied women.

Bregman, S., and Hadley, R. G. Sexual adjustment and feminine attractiveness among spinal cord injured women. *Archives of Physical Medicine and Rehabilitation*, 1976, *57*, 21–23.

This study examines ways in which spinal-cord-injured women cope with the effects of their disability on feminine attractiveness and sexual adjustment. Responses to semistructured interviews with 31 patients yielded sexual adjustment scores and material concerning sexual compensation, orgasm, bowel and bladder programs, and methods of enhancing attractiveness.

Cole, T. M. Sexual problems of paraplegic women. *Medical Aspects of Human Sexuality*, 1976, *10*(6), 105.

In this Answers to Questions section of the journal, Cole discusses the question: "Can a female paraplegic experience an orgasm, and can she conceive and then maintain a normal pregnancy?" He limits the discussion to the subjective sensation of orgasm, not its muscular-vascular responses.

Cole, T. M. Sexuality and the spinal cord injured. In R. Green (Ed.), *Human sexuality: A health practitioner's text*. Baltimore: Williams and Wilkins, 1975.

The importance of sexual adjustment for the physically disabled person, myths and misconceptions surrounding the disabled person's sexuality, the impact of spinal-cord injury on the sexuality of both male and female patients, and considerations for counseling with this population are thoroughly discussed in view of research and clinical data. Also presented are the male and female sexual response cycles for both the spinal-cord-injured and the able-bodied. Various inadequate approaches of rehabilitation workers in dealing with the sexuality of the disabled person are systematically analyzed, the reasons and possible undesirable effects of these approaches are outlined, and alternate approaches are suggested. The author concludes that given adequate counseling, "almost all physically disabled adults can expect to enjoy an active sex life."

Cole, T. M. Spinal cord injury patients and sexual dysfunction. Paper read at the Thirty-fifth Annual Assembly of the American Academy of Physical Medicine and Rehabilitation, Washington, D.C., October 24, 1973.

Sexual function in both male and female spinal-cord-injured patients is the main topic discussed in this presentation. Also presented are some specific suggestions concerning effective approaches to counseling the disabled person about his or her sexuality.

Cole, T. M., and Stevens, M. R. Rehabilitation professionals and sexual counseling for spinal cord injured adults. *Archives of Sexual Behavior*, *4*(6), 631–633.

Psychosexual adjustment difficulties in rehabilitation clients are problems with which counselors must deal. Recognizing the counselor's need for special sex education, the Michigan Rehabilitation Association and the Program in Human Sexuality of the University of Minnesota Medical School collaborated to conduct and evaluate a one-day seminar on sexuality in spinal-cord-injured persons. The seminar consisted of a combination of audio-visual presentations, lectures, and small group discussions of sexual topics such as nudity, masturbation, and sexual function in the disabled. Evaluation was made by a questionnaire developed specifically for the study. Results of the evaluation show that this program was beneficial for most of the participants and harmful for only a few. Most participants indicate that such a program should be a part of the formal training for rehabilitation counselors.

Cole, T. M., Chilgren, R., and Rosenberg, P. A new programme of sex education and counseling for spinal cord injured adults and health care professionals. *Paraplegia*, 1973, *11*(2), 111–124.

The authors describe an experimental two-day intensive sex education program for adult paraplegics and quadriplegics and for health professionals who counsel physically disabled persons. The program was developed by the University of Minnesota Medical School. Adapted from a training program in human sexuality that has recently been added to the medical school curriculum, the desensitization-resensitization program emphasized exposure to a variety of explicit slides and films of sexual activity, with periodic small group discussions under trained group leaders. It is suggested that the inadequate sex counseling given by many health professionals may contribute to a sense of disability on the part of the spinal-cord-injured adult.

Comarr, A. E. Marriage and divorce among patients with spinal cord injury: I. Proceedings of the Clinical Spinal Cord Injury Conference, U.S. Veterans' Administration, October 1962, *11*, 163–169.

The statistical data presented in this paper are based on a study of 858 spinal-cord-injured patients. The purpose of the study was to examine marriage and divorce rates in these subjects, who were chosen for the study randomly over a six-year period. Data show that 26 percent of this population remained bachelors before and after injury, 48 percent were married before injury, and 26 percent had never been married before injury but married for the first time after injury. Other aspects discussed are marriage, divorce, and widowhood among patients who married before injury and in those who married after injury. The author concludes that the divorce rate of any of the groups in his study was far less than that in California and Los Angeles County. It was also confirmed that the divorce rate was greater among patients who were married at the time of injury than among those who married after the injury, 31 percent and 21 percent respectively. The ability of the patient to perform sexual coitus did not play as great a role as one might anticipate.

Comarr, A. E. Marriage and divorce among patients with spinal cord injury: II. Proceedings of the Clinical Spinal Cord Injury Conference, U.S. Veterans' Administration, October 1962, *11*, 169–181.

This paper presents statistical data examining marriage and divorce rates of patients with service-connected spinal-cord injuries compared to patients whose injuries were not service-connected. In this study, 858 patients were interviewed, 54 percent of whom were veterans with service-connected (SC) injuries (injuries incurred during military duty), and 46 percent were veterans with non-service-connected (NSC) injuries. In both study groups, the percentage of patients who remained bachelors before and after injury was essentially similar. Thirty-five percent of the SC patients and 63 percent of the NSC patients were married before injury. Other data show statistics of marriage, divorce, and widowers among patients married before and those married after injury in both study groups. The author concludes that "sexual disability is undoubtedly not the sole reason for divorce" among the spinal-cord-injured patients studied.

Comarr, A. E. Marriage and divorce among patients with spinal cord injury: III. Proceedings of the Clinical Spinal Cord Injury Conference, U.S. Veterans' Administration, October 1962, *11*, 181–194.

This is a presentation of detailed statistical data of the marriage and divorce rates of paraplegic patients (n=623) and quadriplegic patients (n=235). The similar divorce rates in both groups after injury, 31 percent of the paraplegic patients and 34 percent of the quadriplegic patients, show that the level of the spinal-cord injury does not play a significant role in the marital adjustment of patients. It was also found that 46 percent of the paraplegic patients and 43 percent of the quadriplegic patients could have sexual coitus. The author concludes, however, that the data showed that potentially more quadriplegics can perform the act of coitus than paraplegics, since 26 percent of the quadriplegics and 11 percent of the paraplegics had made no attempt at sexual intercourse. These findings "can be further substantiated when one realizes that all quadriplegics have upper motor neuron lesions in regard to their spinal erection centers, whereas many paraplegic patients have lower motor neuron lesions in this respect."

Comarr, A. E. Marriage and divorce among patients with spinal cord injury: IV. Proceedings of the Clinical Spinal Cord Injury Conference, U.S. Veterans' Administration, October 1962, *11*, 195–208.

This study examined the marriage and divorce rates of spinal-cord-injured patients with complete neurological lesions (n=593) compared to those with incomplete neurological lesions (n=265). Results show that of those who were married before injury, 68 percent of the patients with complete lesions and 66 percent of those with incomplete lesions were still married after injury. The divorce rate after the onset of injury was also very similar in both groups. This suggests that the extent of the injury does not play a major role in the divorce rate of patients. However, other data suggest that for subjects who were married for the first time only after the onset of injury, those with complete lesions had a lower rate of divorce. While 56 percent of those with incomplete lesions could perform sexual coitus, only 39 percent of patients with complete lesions could do so. Finally, of those patients who were divorced at the final stages of this study, 41 percent with complete lesions and 53 percent with incomplete lesions could have sexual intercourse. The author suggests therefore "that the sexual disability is undoubtedly not the sole reason for divorce" among these patients.

Comarr, A. E. Marriage and divorce among patients with spinal cord injury: V. Proceedings of the Clinical Spinal Cord Injury

Conference, U.S. Veterans' Administration, October 1962, *11*, 208–215.

This is a summary of statistical data presented in the four preceding papers by the same author regarding the rates of marriage and divorce among 858 patients with spinal-cord injuries. Statistics discussed relate to overall marriage and divorce rates before and after the onset of injury, percent of married patients who had children before injury, adoptions after injury, artificial insemination by a donor, coitus ability after injury, and relationship of coitus ability to marriage and divorce.

Comarr, A. E. Sex among patients with spinal cord and/or cauda equina injuries. *Medical Aspects of Human Sexuality*, 1973, 7(3), 222–238.

The author asserts that "sufficient statistical data have been accumulated to aid the physician in attempting to prognosticate what sexual potentials a patient will have who has sustained injury to the spinal cord and/or cauda equina." In this article, the author examines sexual functioning in patients following spinal-cord injury in light of clinical and research findings. Also discussed are some practical suggestions for counseling patients regarding their sexuality. Some discussion is devoted to the female paraplegic and her sexuality.

Comarr, A. E. Sexual concepts in traumatic cord and cauda equina lesions. *Journal of Urology*, 1971, *106*, 375–378.

The level and extent of spinal-cord injury are most significant when evaluating the patient's sexual potential and functioning. The author examines the differences in sexual functioning among patients with spinal-cord injuries resulting from complete or incomplete upper and lower motor neuron lesions. It was found that the majority of patients with a complete upper motor neuron lesion are able to achieve reflexogenic erections. About 75 percent of them can have sexual coitus. Most patients with incomplete upper motor neuron lesions have erections, and 85 percent are successful at coitus. Other results are discussed.

Comarr, A. E. Sexual function among patients with spinal cord injury. *Urologia Internationalis*, 1970, *25*(2), 134–168.

This article presents and discusses the results of a study aimed at the examination of sexual functioning in patients following spinal-cord injury. Spinal cord injury patients (n = 150) were interviewed concerning erections, sexual intercourse, ejaculation, and orgasm. Results show that 82 percent were able to attain erections. In general, patients with complete upper motor neuron lesions have a higher percentage (96.4) of erections than do patients with complete lower motor neuron lesions (24.2), but they experience fewer ejaculations. As expected, patients with incomplete upper or lower motor neuron lesions have a better chance of erection, ejaculation, and orgasm than have patients with complete lesions. Many other findings and the neurologic aspects of sexual functioning are presented and discussed.

Comarr, A. E., and Gunderson, B. B. Sexual function in traumatic paraplegia and quadriplegia. *American Journal of Nursing*, 1975, *75*(2), 250–255.

The authors assert that "determining the extent of the patient's spinal lesion is the all important first step in helping both patient and partner gradually achieve a satisfactory sexual adjustment." In this paper, the authors discuss the sexual aspects of spinal-cord injuries and the role of the health-care practitioner in assisting the patient to achieve some level of sexual adjustment. Nine case studies are presented for illustration.

Comarr, A. E., Hohman, G. W., and Tempio, C. The sexual function of the spinal cord injured patient. In a source book: *Rehabilitating the person with spinal cord injury*. Washington, D.C.: Veterans' Administration, Department of Medicine and Surgery, 1972.

Among the first things a newly injured spinal-cord-injury patient will wonder about is his future sexual functioning. In this chapter, the authors discuss sexuality following a spinal-cord injury in male patients. Specific topics covered include classification and examination of sexual functioning, erections, coitus, ejaculations, and orgasms in these patients.

Cooper, I. S., Rynearson, E. A., Bailey, A. A., and MacCarty, C. S. The relation of spinal cord diseases to gynecomastia and testicular atrophy. *Mayo Clinic Proceedings*, 1950, *25*, 320–326.

The authors report at length on two patients with spinal-cord injuries who had gynecomastia and testicular atrophy. In addition to traumatic injury of the spinal cord, it seems that other lesions of the spinal cord of males may result in a tendency toward "demasculinization." The authors consider the occurrence of gynecomastia and testicular atrophy in males with degenerative lesions of the spinal cord significant for various reasons which they discuss.

Cottrell, T. L. C. Sexual problems of the paraplegic. *Medical Aspects of Human Sexuality*, 1975, *9*(5), 167–168.

In this brief guide to office counseling aimed at physicians, the author discusses psychosocial and sexual aspects and difficulties in paraplegics. Suggestions for sex counseling with this population are also presented.

Crigler, L. Sexual concerns of the spinal cord injured. *Nursing Clinics of North America*, 1974, *9*(4), 703–717.

This article discusses the sexual concerns of the spinal-cord-injured patient and the effects of injury on the self-concept. Information is given to show how medical personnel can be more sensitive in assisting the patient in restoring his self-image, beginning by dealing with the patient's sexual concerns.

Dahart, A. Assisting the patient with a spinal cord injury to maintain his or her sensual sexual identity. In *Nursing management of spinal cord injuries.* National Paraplegia Foundation, 1974, 118–120.

The author discusses sexual concerns and difficulties associated with spinal-cord injuries and makes suggestions for assisting patients in achieving an acceptable level of sexual adjustment.

David, A., Gur, S., and Rozin, R. Survival in marriage of the paraplegic couple. Paper read at the Thirteenth World Congress of Rehabilitation International, Tel Aviv, Israel, June 13–18, 1976.

The purpose of this study was to examine the motivation of women marrying paraplegic patients (n=20). A questionnaire was developed which included questions on sexual development and sex education of the spouse. Also included were questions relating to what the wife expected from marriage and the extent to which she succeeded in achieving her goals.

Deyoe, S. F. Marriage and family patterns with long-term spinal cord injury. *Paraplegia*, 1972, *10*, 219–227.

Although there have been numerous reports on education, vocations, and physical functional skills of the long-term spinal-cord injured, little has been described about the marriage and family patterns of this group. The purpose of this study was to offer a description of marriage and family patterns based on a study that involved 219 male subjects with long-term spinal-cord injury who had completed a rehabilitation program and had been living outside of the hospital for periods of 2 to 30 years. The subjects were from 21 to 75 years of age. An interview was held with each subject in which marital status, environment, and home situation were discussed. It was found that at the time of the interview, 72 percent of the "paras" and 55 percent of the "quads" were married. The results also indicated that the divorce rate among spinal-cord-injury persons was lower than that among the general population. In fact, combining both groups, the paraplegics and the quadriplegics, one finds a ratio of 1 in 6.7 marriages being terminated—well below the national ratio. The author concludes that, given the proper rehabilitation program, the spinal-cord-injured person can maintain a successful marriage and family life.

Disher, C. J., and Gilmore, L. S. Physical therapists knowledge of sexual functions in the spinal cord injured. Unpublished master's research project, Indiana University School of Nursing, 1976.

The purpose of this study was to examine the level of knowledge held by physical therapists (n=30) concerning sexual functioning in spinal-cord-injured persons. Results and conclusions are presented.

Eisenberg, M. G., and Rustad, L. C. Sex and the spinal cord injured: Some questions and answers. Veterans' Administration Hospital, Cleveland, Ohio, 1974.

Previously published to supply information of interest to the spinal-cord-injured person, this booklet in the second edition has been expanded to include information on the sexual potential of the spinal-cord-injured woman. Different topics discussed are male and female sexual anatomy (illustrated), the sexual responses, and problems concerning marriage, divorce, contraception, and the adoption of children. A glossary and lists of recommended readings and references are included.

Eisenberg, M. G., and Rustad, L. C. Sex education and counseling program on a spinal cord injury service. *Archives of Physical Medicine and Rehabilitation*, 1976, 135–140.

The authors describe a program for sex education and counseling developed at the Spinal-Cord-Injury Service of the Veterans' Administration Hospital in Cleveland, Ohio. The program consists of a series of eight weekly meetings of 90 minutes each. Although materials were a valuable part of the sessions, active sharing of experiences and feelings of the participants was considered of central importance. The authors further discuss the content of eight meetings of this program.

Engstrad, J. L. Psychosexual adjustment of spinal man and the multidisciplinary approach to patient care. *Association of Rehabilitation Nurses Journal*, 1975, *1*(1), 5–7.

The importance of sexual adjustment in facilitating the rehabilitation process and the role of the rehabilitationist in assisting the disabled person in achieving sexual adjustment are the main issues discussed in this paper. Also presented is a multidisciplinary approach to spinal-cord-injured patient care developed at the University of Alabama Spain Rehabilitation Center. Results of a survey conducted at this center indicate that all professional staff members who interact with patients must be prepared and willing to discuss with patients the sexual issues and concerns that they might have.

Evans, R. L., Halar, E. M., DeFreece, A. B., and Larsen, G. L. Multidisciplinary approach to sex education of spinal cord-injured patients. *Physical Therapy*, 1976, *56*(5), 541–545.

The need for sex education of spinal-cord-injured patients is recognized and discussed, along with an interdisciplinary approach to evaluating and treating sexual dysfunction in this population. The program provides information to spinal-cord-injured patients and their families about sexual disorders, and offers counseling services to patients experiencing difficulties in their altered sex relations. Physiological and psychological aspects of sexuality as they are integrated into this multidisciplinary sex education and treatment program are identified and discussed. Specific recommendations for content which should be included in the information-giving sex counseling process are presented.

Fitzpatrick, W. F. Sexual function in the paraplegic patient. *Archives of Physical Medicine and Rehabilitation*, 1974, *55*, 221–227.

The results of a study aimed at the examination of sexual functioning in paraplegic patients (n = 14) are discussed and conclusions are presented. Some forms of therapy are recommended and the importance of supportive counseling by the physician is stressed.

Gregory, M. F. Sexual adjustment: A guide for the spinal cord injured. Bloomington, Ill.: Accent on Living, Inc., 1974.

The paralysis that results from spinal-cord injury causes medical complications beyond the mere loss of motion. This guide discusses the various physical and psychological aspects of paraplegia, with particular emphasis on the sexual adjustment of the paraplegic. The ability to perform coitus, the ability to procreate, and the continued ability of the paralyzed male to maintain a positive self-image are treated in theory. The role of the rehabilitation counselor is seen as important in sexual, family, and marital adjustment for the paraplegic. Research in these sexual areas is summarized and projections concerning the future role of the rehabilitation counselor are made.

Griffith, E. R., and Trieschmann, R. B. Sexual functioning in women with spinal cord injury. *Archives of Physical Medicine and Rehabilitation*, 1975, *56*, 18–21.

This review of the literature was conducted to gather and evaluate information relating to sexual functioning in women following spinal-cord injury. While studies on males were related to sexual functioning, i.e., erection, ejaculation, and orgasm, the studies conducted with female patients deal primarily with the factors of hormonal function, fertility, and delivery. Information is limited concerning issues which are relevant to the total sexual functioning of these women. Sociocultural restrictions on women's sexual responsivity, responsibility, and willingness to discuss sexual issues are considered, along with areas for future research. The authors emphasize the need to consider sexuality in its totality in future research, and the need for women to join research teams on this topic.

Griffith, E. R., Tomko, M. A., and Timms, R. J. Sexual function in spinal cord-injured patients: A review. *Archives of Physical Medicine and Rehabilitation*, 1973, *54*(12), 539–543.

In this review of the medical literature pertaining to sexual function in spinal-cord-injured patients, some deficiencies in the literature are identified. In clinical surveys, such variables as sex, age, marital status, hospital status, time or duration of study in relation to onset of injury, types and degree of neurological lesion, medications, ablative procedures, and genitourinary complications are not always clearly defined or controlled. Highlights of nine surveys of male patients are presented in terms of frequencies of erection, coitus, fertility, and libido.

The relationship of these functions to degree of completeness and site of cord lesion is noted. Human sexuality is considered in terms of psychic, hormonal, biologic, and neuromuscular components. Information on female subjects is primarily restricted to clinical observations of menstruation, pregnancy, and labor.

Areas requiring further study are suggested; these include attitudes of both sexual partners toward their relationship and its physical expressions, mechanical aspects of sexual activities, accurate endocrinological information, measures of counseling effectiveness, and systems of analyzing methods of evaluation and treatment.

Guttman, L. The married life of paraplegics and tetraplegics. *Paraplegia*, 1964, *2*, 182–188.

This paper presents a comprehensive survey on the marital status of 1,505 paraplegics and tetraplegics of marriageable age treated at Stoke Mandevill Hospital in England. It has been proven that the subjects studied make very satisfactory partners in marriage. This applies to marriages both before and after the onset of the disability. The divorce rate among these patients was not significantly higher than the rate found in the general population.

Hanlon, K. Maintaining sexuality after spinal cord injury. *Nursing*, 1975, *5*, 58–62.

The author is a nurse addressing nurses on various aspects of psychosexual adjustment to spinal-cord injury. She questions the feasibility of nurses facing honest acceptance of the sexuality of spinal-cord patients. Discussed in this paper are the nurses' anxieties in dealing with this human need and their lack of understanding of human sexual response in the para- or quadriplegic person. The nurse's moral judgments and the repressed sexuality of the patient are reviewed as being obstacles to attaining sexual rehabilitation. Steps in providing sex counseling for the spinal-cord-injured patient are also given. Also presented is a review of the anatomy and physiology of normal human sexual response, including in-depth explanations of the spinal cord and of the modified sexual response of the paralyzed patient.

Hanson, R. W., and Franklin, M. R. Sexual loss in relation to other functional losses for spinal cord injured males. *Archives of Physical Medicine and Rehabilitation*, 1976, *57*, 291–293.

The major purpose of this study was to examine the relative importance of sexual loss in spinal-cord-injured patients as compared to other functional losses, i.e., legs, arms, and bowel and bladder. Subjects were 54 paraplegics 18 to 58 years of age and 74 quadriplegics ranging in age from 18 to 67 years. Subjects were asked to rank-order these functional losses to indicate the relative importance they attached to each. In addition, staff members of the rehabilitation team working with these patients were asked to predict the relative importance of these functional losses to the patients studied. Results showed that compared to subjects' ranking, staff predictions tended to overemphasize the relative importance of sexual functioning. Both paraplegics and quadriplegics ranked sexual functioning to be the least important of the functional losses. More than 80 percent of the paraplegics ranked their legs' function higher than sex, and more than 70 percent ranked control of bowel and bladder as being more important than sex. These findings were consistent regardless of the age of the patient, time since onset of disability, and marital status.

Held, J., Cole, T., Held, C., Anderson, C., and Chilgren, R. Sexual attitude reassessment workshop: Effect on spinal cord injured adults, their partners and rehabilitation professionals. *Archives of Physical Medicine and Rehabilitation*, 1975, *56*, 14–18.

The authors describe a program in human sexuality for spinal-cord-injured patients offered at the University of Minnesota Medical School. The objectives of this program are to help the disabled person to be more self-sufficient, and to assist health-care professionals to become more effective in dealing with the sexuality of the patient. Evaluation data show that 96 percent of the participants reported that the program is important and that they benefited from it.

Hetric, W. R. Sexuality following functional transection of the spinal cord. *Dissertation Abstracts*, 1968, *28B*, 5206–5207.

The purpose of this study was to examine various aspects of the sexual attitudes, functioning, and behavior of persons with functionally complete transection of the spinal cord. Two hypotheses were examined: 1) sex role identification is negatively related to the degree of physical disability; and 2) sex role identification of disabled males is weaker than that of disabled females with respect to their non-disabled peers. Subjects were 35 male and 8 female spinal-cord-injured patients in a rehabilitation center, and their spouses. Various psychological tests and questionnaires were used to examine study variables. Results revealed that sexual role identification appeared to be uninfluenced by the consequences of the injury. In spite of physical limitations in sexual functioning, the psychosexuality of subjects was quite active. Sexual concerns of subjects showed a shift from behavioral to intellectual and interpersonal activities, possibly as an adjustment to the sexual difficulties and limitations they experience as a result of the injury. Sexuality seems to be a vital aspect of the disabled person's rehabilitation process.

Hohmann, G. W. Considerations in management of psychosexual readjustment in the cord injured male. *Rehabilitation Psychology*, 1972, *19*(2), 50–58.

The physiological and psychosocial aspects of sexual function of men with spinal-cord injury are discussed. Guidelines are provided as to who should provide sex counseling for patients and their spouses, what should be told to them, what techniques are available to those who lack normal genital functioning, and some of the emotional and sexual rewards which the cord-injured person can achieve from his sexual functioning. A list of precautions for persons engaging in sex counseling with such men is presented.

Hohmann, G. W. Psychological aspects of treatment and rehabilitation of the spinal cord injured person. *Clinical Orthopaedics and Related Research*, 1975, *112*, 81–88.

The author discusses various phases in the adjustment process following a spinal-cord injury. The phases identified include: denial, withdrawal, internalized hostility, externalized hostility, and reaction against dependence. Preexisting psychopathology and its impact on the rehabilitation process of the spinal-cord-injured person is also discussed. One of the most threatening implications of this disabling condition is the patient's anxiety about his sexual functioning. The rehabilitation worker should be knowledgeable regarding the effects of the injury on sexuality. There is need for an organized program in sexuality as part of the rehabilitation process. Considerable information should be gathered before any attempt to undertake the sex re-education and counseling of the disabled.

Hohmann, G. W. Sex and the spinal cord injured male. *Accent on Living*, Summer 1973, 15–24.

The information presented in this comprehensive paper has been the result of the author's extensive clinical experience in working with thousands of spinal-cord-injured persons and their spouses. The article is aimed primarily at rehabilitationists working with spinal-cord-injured populations. Topics discussed include information to be given to patients, the sexual activities that are open to the spinal-cord injured, sexual gratifications reported by patients, statistical data on the sexual functioning of patients, and some precautions in the process of sex counseling with the disabled. Some of these precautions are: not to interfere with the person's moral and religious convictions about sexuality; not to impose one's own morality on the patient; not to force the patient to discuss his or her sexuality; not to threaten the patient with one's own sexuality; and not to make sex an all-or-none experience. Sexuality must be a topic continually open to counseling.

Hohmann, G. W. Sex and the spinal cord injured male. In N. Little, L. Stewart, G. Simmins, and B. Nobles (Eds.), *Rehabilitation of the spinal cord injured.* Fayetteville: Arkansas Rehabilitation Research and Training Center, University of Arkansas, 1974.

The author discusses the importance of sexuality in the rehabilitation of spinal-cord-injured males. The rehabilitation counselor has a responsibility to develop and maintain an effective and comfortable relationship with clients so that sexual matters can be discussed adequately. The author also presents alternative viewpoints in defining sexual relationships for spinal-cord-injured patients and their partners, their sexual capabilities and the meaning of sexual gratification, and some important precautions to be kept in mind by counselors in dealing with the client's sexuality.

Isaacson, J., and Delgado, H. E. Sex counseling for those with spinal cord injuries. *Social Casework*, 1974, *55*(10), 622–627.

In an effort to understand the specific problems and needs of the spinal-cord-injured patient, the authors of this article conducted a series of structured interviews with a sample of 30 outpatients at Rancho Los Amigos Hospital, a regional rehabilitation center for spinal-cord injuries on the West Coast. The major focus of the research interview included the following factors: areas of principal concern to the patient after injury; attitudes about the importance of sex to the individual; sources and kinds of sexual help received after injury; sexual adjustment; sexual problems after injury; nature and extent of need for sex education and a counseling program; and suggestions for sex education and counseling programs. Results indicate the need for a program of lectures, films, individual and group counseling sessions, and inclusion of the partners.

Jackson, R. W. Sexual rehabilitation after cord injury. *Paraplegia*, 1972, *10*, 181–186.

Many articles have been written on the altered physiology of sexual function after cord injury, but very little has been written on the practical aspects of sex. The purpose of this paper was to review and summarize the pertinent literature on sexual rehabilitation after cord injury. In addition, the author surveyed a small sample of tetraplegic and paraplegic athletes. The sample consisted of twenty male athletes surveyed by questionnaire and interviewed during the Canadian National Wheelchair Games. Results of this survey are discussed, along with topics such as erections, positions of intercourse, urinary considerations, frequency of intercourse, sexual satisfaction, female paraplegics, and artificial insemination.

Jockheim, K. A., and Wahle, H. A study on sexual function in 56 male patients with complete irreversible lesions of the spinal cord and cauda equina. *Paraplegia*, 1970, *8*, 166–172.

The purpose of this study was to examine the sexual function of males with complete irreversible lesions of the spinal cord (n=56). All subjects exhibited complete paralysis of motor sensory functions as well as loss of bladder control, bowel control, and sexual function. Extensive personal interviews were conducted, the wives being interviewed when possible. Of the 35 men with spastic paralysis who had just completed rehabilitation, 26 could achieve erection, 2 had libido, none could ejaculate or achieve orgasm. Of the 21 men with flaccid paralysis, 1 achieved erection, none had libido or achieved ejaculation or orgasm. Of 29 men with spastic paralysis who were in later stages of rehabilitation, 22 achieved erection, 6 had libido, 2 could ejaculate, 1 achieved orgasm. Of 19 men with flaccid paralysis who had just completed rehabilitation, 6 achieved erection, 1 had libido, 2 could ejaculate, none achieved orgasm. The authors concluded that their study only confirms past data collected and they draw no conclusions of their own.

Kirby, A. R. Sexual function in the spinal cord injured person. *Rehabilitation Digest*, 1974, *6*(2), 3–6.

The physiology of sexual function in the male and in the female is discussed in detail. Psychic, gonadal, and neuromuscular involvement in sexual functioning are investigated in particular. The importance of, and guidelines for, sex counseling are discussed. Also presented is a review of studies dealing with sexuality following spinal-cord injury. Sexual function does present a very real problem and concern in those who have suffered a transection of the spinal cord. In all cases sexual function is impaired, but much depends upon the level of the spinal-cord injury and whether or not the lesion is complete.

Knorr, N. J., and Bull, J. C., Jr. Spinal cord injury: Psychiatric considerations. *Maryland State Medical Journal*, 1970, *19*, 105–108.

The psychosocial aspects of spinal-cord injury are common to many other disabling conditions. However, the relative youth of many patients, the severity and limitations imposed by the disability, the duration of rehabilitation, and the physical complications make the spinal-cord-injured person one for special care and consideration. Among the psychosocial manifestations of spinal-cord injuries discussed in this paper, the sexual aspects seem to be of great importance. Following the loss of sexual function, the patient experiences high anxiety concerning his loss of "manliness." "Rather than leaving the patient confused and with unrealistic expectations," a frank and open discussion concerning the sexuality of the patient and his future functioning is suggested and can be very helpful. The authors stress that the quality of sexual adjustment made by the disabled person depends on his level of maturity and a cooperative relationship with his sexual partner.

Kuhn, R. A. Functional capacity of the isolated human spinal cord. *Brain*, 1950, *73*(1), 1–51.

This study was conducted in an attempt to estimate the functional capacity of the isolated cord in spinal-cord-injured patients. Reflex patterns elicitable below the level of cord transection were examined in 29 patients with total transection of the cord. This extensive report presents the results of this comprehensive study. Of special interest in this report is a section discussing the results of the examination of penile erection and ejaculation achieved by subjects. Examinations show that there was a sharply circumscribed reflexogenous area for the elicitation of penile erection which included the corona of the glans and the penile frenulum. Ejaculation was not observed in the subjects, and, with two exceptions, none had noted its occurrence since time of injury.

Lassen, P. L. Sex and the spinal cord injured: A selected bibliography. Washington, D.C.: Paralyzed Veterans of America, 1973.

This bibliography is presented to promote increased understanding of the sexual problems of the spinal-cord-injured person. There are 134 entries, dating as far back as 1917.

Lovitt, R. Sexual adjustment of spinal cord injury patients. *Rehabilitation Research and Practice Review*, 1970, *1*(3), 25–29.

In this article the author discusses several guidelines that can aid rehabilitation personnel in working with spinal-cord-injury patients regarding sexuality. It is noted that rehabilitation personnel need to consider a person's sexual functioning within the overall context of the personality. It is important to know how the patient views his sexual functioning. Persons who view sex as a biological release instead of as a part of a total relationship may have difficulties adjusting psychologically and socially. The author also points out that rehabilitation of sexual functioning should be integrated within the total treatment program and not treated as an end in itself. The most successful psychosexual adjustment is usually made only after major physical problems are under control.

Masham, B. The psychological and practical aspects of sex and marriage for the paraplegic. *Royal Society of Medicine*, 1973, *66*, 133–136.

Paraplegics and tetraplegics need much understanding from others like themselves with the same problems, and also from a professional staff so that they can adjust to their disability and learn to cope with their new problems, especially sexual problems. Many more doctors are becoming interested in sex and the paraplegic and the author feels that it is the doctor who should take personal responsibility for the sexual adjustment of the paraplegic. Some of the issues involved in this area are presented and discussed. The author asserts that both partners in a marriage involving a paraplegic must become totally involved. Women paraplegics are usually found to have better sexual adjustment than men paraplegics. When a male paraplegic loses both erection and ejaculation he must remain relatively passive, and this causes psychological problems. Many paraplegics and tetraplegics marry, and some have children. For those unable to have children, adoption is usually an adequate answer.

Miller, D. K. Sexual counseling with spinal cord-injured clients. *Journal of Sex & Marital Therapy*, 1975, *1*(4), 312–318.

This article is written specifically for the education of social workers, but can be helpful to all involved in the rehabilitation process. Various aspects of sexuality and sex counseling with the spinal-cord-injured person are discussed. The author suggests that it is important that the person doing sex counseling be aware of his own sexual attitudes and values and not let these interfere with the therapeutic process. An adequate knowledge of the sexual problems facing one's client is essential.

Money, J. Phantom orgasm in the dreams of paraplegic men and women. *Archives of General Psychiatry*, 1960, *3*, 373–382.

The purpose of this study was to assemble verbatim data on cognitional eroticism of paraplegic patients in both imagery and dreams. Subjects were 14 males and 7 females, all with complete spinal interruption. Patients were thoroughly interviewed about their sexual functioning and erotic imagery and dreams. The article presents two detailed case reports for illustration, one taken from a male subject and the other from a female. Also included is a table summarizing the data collected, including age of subject, duration of disability, spinal site of injury, sexual functioning before and after injury, sexual eroticism, and daydreams and sleep dreams. The study data show that although there were individual variations, patients in general "did not have the subjective feelings of sexual urge and gratification they formerly could experience." Despite complete lack of somesthetic sensation from the genitopelvic area in patients, they still had the capacity for vivid orgasm imagery to occur in dreams. The author concludes that "the imagery of orgasms in [a] paraplegic's dreams may be regarded as a special example of the phantom phenomenon."

Money, J. Phantom orgasm in paraplegics. *Medical Aspects of Human Sexuality*, 1970, *4*(1), 90–99.

This article presents the results of a study aimed at the examination of cognitional eroticism in both waking imagery and sleeping dreams of paraplegic patients. The subjects were 14 men and 7 women suffering complete spinal cord interruption who were interviewed extensively regarding their sexual functioning and erotic imagery and dreams. Results showed a wide range of individual differences and variations. However, a general finding was noted. Patients had lost their pre-injury subjective feelings of sexual urge and gratification. Subjects had the ability for vivid orgasm imagery to occur in their dreams.

Mooney, T. O., Cole, T. M., and Chilgren, R. A. *Sexual options for paraplegics and quadriplegics*. Boston: Little, Brown, 1975.

The authors have explicitly and graphically described and illustrated means by which the disabled person can give and receive sexual pleasure. They discuss attitudes toward sexuality and explore preparatory measures, arousal techniques, intercourse, and oral-genital or manual stimulation for the spinal-cord-injured person and his or her partner. Sixty-five full-page photographs and a detailed glossary augment the discussions.

Mueller, A. Psychological factors in rehabilitation of paraplegic patients. *Archives of Physical Medicine and Rehabilitation*, 1962, *43*, 151–159.

A comprehensive review of the psychological and social aspects in the rehabilitation process of paraplegic patients is presented. Sexual functioning and adjustment in these patients is one of the topics included in this report. The author indicates that "in the light of present knowledge optimism regarding the sex function of paraplegic patients has increased." He added that study results seem to indicate that the paraplegic patient can have a successful and happy marriage.

Munro, D., Horne, H. W., and Paull, D. P. The effect of injury to the spinal cord and cauda equina on the sexual potency of men. *New England Journal of Medicine*, 1948, *239*, 903–911.

The authors conducted an extensive examination of sexual potency in 84 spinal-cord-injured patients. Results of this study are presented and discussed.

Myers, J. S. The effect of testosterone upon certain aspects of personality in male paraplegics. *Dissertation Abstracts*, 1954, *14*, 397–398.

The purpose of this study was to examine the effect of testosterone on the personality of male paraplegics (n=21). To control the effects of such factors as suggestion and attention, a placebo was used half of the time. Subjects were given daily intramuscular injections of one cubic centimeter of testosterone propionate for a period of fourteen days, followed by daily injections of a placebo for fourteen days. Subjects were interviewed and given a battery of psychological tests prior to all injections, following the testosterone injections, and following the injections of placebo. The psychopersonality variables measured were mental efficiency, fatigue, sense of bodily well-being, basic personality structure, anxiety, depression, assertiveness, and drive. Data showed that none of the results following testosterone treatment were significantly higher than those obtained following the placebo or the initial tests. Subjects were classified as sexually impotent, potent on a reflex basis, or potent on a psychic basis. Subjects who were potent on a reflex basis showed statistically significant improvement in muscular efficiency scores as a result of testosterone treatment.

National Paraplegia Foundation. Programs of sexuality with the spinal cord injured. Proceedings of a workshop on Sex: Rehabilitation's Stepchild, Indianapolis, June 23, 1973.

This publication includes numerous presentations made in a workshop titled Sex: Rehabilitation's Stepchild, organized by the Allied Health Profession Advisory Committee of the National Paraplegia Foundation. Among the topics discussed are the role of the rehabilitation professional in sexual counseling and adjustment of the spinal-cord-injured person, the sexual alternatives open to the patient, the role of rehabilitation facilities in promoting sexual adjustment, and religion and sex.

National Paraplegia Foundation. Paraplegics discuss their sexual problems. Proceedings of the Conference on Continuing Education in the Treatment of Spinal Cord Injuries, Milwaukee, Wisconsin, June 28–29, 1972.

The main purpose of this conference was to provide for an exchange of pertinent information regarding total care and development of the spinal-cord-injured person. In response to growing demand for information on sexuality and spinal-cord injuries, a special feature of the conference included a session that was devoted to this topic. A panel of three married couples of whom the husbands were spinal-cord-injured discussed their sexual experiences. Couples also described sexual techniques they enjoy, including penile-vaginal intercourse and oral-genital sex. A direct and frank approach to the discussion of sexuality between rehabilitationists and their spinal-cord-injured patients is recommended.

Piera, J. B. The establishment of a prognosis for genito-sexual function in the paraplegic and tetraplegic male. *Paraplegia*, 1973, *10*, 271–278.

This article presents and discusses the results of a study aimed at the assessment of genital and sexual functioning in paraplegic and tetraplegic male patients (n = 100). Subjects were grouped according to four types of lesion: complete spastic, complete flaccid, incomplete spastic, and incomplete flaccid. Information was gathered through personal interviews and medical examination. Results show that, generally, erections were more frequent than ejaculations in all groups. Of the 52 patients with complete spastic lesions, 49 had erections, 22 were able to ejaculate, and 21 were able to have intercourse. Among the 15 patients with complete flaccid lesions, no erection, ejaculation, or coitus ability was recorded. Among the 20 patients with incomplete spastic lesions, 19 had erections, 13 were able to ejaculate, and 12 were able to have coitus. Finally, among the 13 patients with incomplete flaccid lesions, 11 had erections, 9 were able to ejaculate, and 6 were able to have sexual intercourse.

The author concludes that the prognosis for genital and sexual function in paraplegic patients is closely tied to the neurological characteristics of the lesion in the lumbosacral spinal cord, which contains the ejaculation and erection centers. It was found that generally the prognosis was not as good for patients suffering a complete lesion as it was for those with incomplete lesions. In complete spastic lesions, erection is possible but only as a mechanical reflex. The quality of spermatozoa was found to vary, but was, on the average, mediocre. In patients with complete flaccid lesions, neither erection nor ejaculation was possible. In incomplete lesions, however, erection and ejaculation were often possible. The author suggests that the physician not establish a sexual prognosis too soon following injury. There is need to wait for neurological stabilization of the spinal lesion, a satisfactory trophic state, and complete bladder control.

Purdy, S. Assisting the patient with a spinal cord injury to maintain his or her sensual sexual identity. In *Nursing management of spinal cord injuries.* National Paraplegia Foundation, 1974, 115–117.

The author places great emphasis on the importance of the nurse becoming an adequate sex counselor, which is a gradual accomplishment. Having an adequate background of knowledge and knowing her own comfort level in discussing the topic with the patient are essential. To become even more effective she must remember not to project her value system on the patient. The nurse can also use herself as a therapeutic tool in interrelationships with the patient. Personal greetings, casual conversation about his positive qualities, and touching are ways to communicate. Because the nurse has a one-to-one relationship with the patient, she can be sensitive to his readiness to be counseled in sexual matters. His readiness might be indicated by his checking the genital area for feeling, by erections, by jokes (sexual), and by masturbation.

Romano, M., and Lassiter, R. Sexual counseling with the spinal cord injured. *Archives of Physical Medicine and Rehabilitation*, 1972, *53*, 568–572.

A follow-up of discharged spinal-cord-injured patients revealed a high incidence of marital and sex-related conflicts and difficulties in patients and their spouses. To improve this situation, the authors developed a sex education program for these patients. The program was developed at the Department of Physical Medicine and Rehabilitation of the University of Michigan Medical School. This article describes the program and presents evaluation observations made by the authors.

Rossier, A. B., Ziegler, W. H., Duchosal, P. W., and Meylan, J. Sexual function and dysreflexia. *Paraplegia*, 1971, *9*, 51–63.

This paper presents a case history of a tetraplegic patient with complete cord transection at C7–C8 who ejaculated after intrathecal injections of neostigmine. A close relationship was found between ejaculations, blood pressure, cardiac rate, and cardiac rhythm. Results of other examinations are presented.

Rozin, R. Sexual dysfunction in spinal cord injury. Paper presented at the Thirteenth World Congress of Rehabilitation International, Tel Aviv, Israel, June 13–18, 1976.

Injury to the spinal cord may cause a disturbance in sexual function, depending upon the nature, extent, and site of the lesion. The various difficulties in sexual function that may arise are presented, as well as the associated problems of sphincter control and spermatogenesis. The implications in terms of patient-staff, male-female, and patient-family relationships are discussed.

Rusk, H. A. Roundtable: Sex problems in paraplegia. *Medical Aspects of Human Sexuality*, 1967, *1*(12), 46–50.

Moderated by Howard A. Rusk, a panel of experts discussed sexuality in spinal-cord-injury patients. Some of the topics raised and discussed by panel members were marriage, neurophysiology of coitus, effects of therapeutic nerve destruction, methods of stimulating an erection in patients, and fertility in paraplegics.

Ryan, J. H. Dreams of paraplegics. *Archives of General Psychiatry*, 1961, *5*, 286–291.

A series of 29 dreams was studied in an attempt to examine and demonstrate the underlying psychodynamic conflicts in paraplegic patients. Several sexual wish-fulfillment dreams are presented, showing the patient's anxieties, feelings of inadequacy, and sexual frustration. The content of dreams revealed that the patients are reluctant to give up their former body image, and that they deny their present incapacity and inadequacies. The patient's low level of self-esteem is also revealed in dreams. The reduction in self-concept seems to alter the patient's awareness of himself, as well as of his surroundings. He perceives the world as hostile and threatening, and himself as powerless and inadequate. It has been observed that these symptoms can interfere with the rehabilitation process of the paraplegic patient.

Sandowski, C. L. Sexuality and the paraplegic. *Rehabilitation Literature*, 1976, *37*(11–12), 322–325.

The author discusses various aspects of sexuality and sexual functioning in male and female paraplegics. She indicates that "in the process of rehabilitating the paraplegic, it is important that the area of sexuality not be overlooked." The paraplegic must be assisted by rehabilitation personnel to achieve sexual adjustment. The author also discusses specific sexual techniques and surgical procedures aimed at helping the paraplegic toward a satisfying sex life. A recent surgical procedure enables patients to "have an erection that is 85 percent of a normal erection." Suggestions for nongenital sexual activities for patients who are unable to achieve an erection or sexual intercourse are presented. Also discussed are the ability of paraplegic patients to ejaculate, fertility and sterility in this population, the sensation of orgasm, pregnancy in paraplegic women, and the need for birth control information and counseling.

Sex and the Paraplegic. *Medical World News*, 1972, *13*, 35–38.

A program aimed at reassessing sexual attitudes in both rehabilitation and medical personnel as well as in physically disabled persons is presented and discussed. This is a three-day program involving a combination of lectures, films on sexual material, and small group discussions. Through these presentations an attempt is made to desensationalize and desensitize sexuality, and to allow participants to express freely their thoughts, feelings, and attitudes regarding their sexuality.

Sexual interviewing with the spinal cord injured and their sexual partners. Proceedings of a special seminar, Indiana University Medical School, Indianapolis, May 8–9, 1976.

This publication presents the proceedings of a seminar aimed at training participants in the techniques of sexual interviewing with spinal-cord-injured persons and their sexual partners. Papers presented were: male and female sexual response; sexual myths and fallacies; anatomy and neurophysiology of spinal-cord injury and sexual functioning; and sexual interview procedures.

Silver, J. R., and Owens, E. Sexual problems in disorders of the nervous system. II. Psychological reactions. *British Medical Journal*, 1975, *3*, 532–533.

The authors argue that the aim of sexual rehabilitation of paraplegics is not necessarily to achieve full conventionally accepted sexual function, "but to enable the patients to compensate for their disability by using their remaining faculties to satisfy their partners and thus, secondarily, themselves." In this paper, the authors present and discuss sexual concerns and difficulties faced by the paraplegic person, psychological reactions to the disability, counseling and treatment procedures, and some practical advice to facilitate sexual adjustment.

Singh, S. P., and Magner, T. Sex and self: The spinal cord injured. *Rehabilitation Literature*, 1975, *36*, 2–10.

Injuries to the spinal cord frequently cause partial or complete loss of sensory and motor function below the lesion. The impact of these injuries on the sexual functioning of patients is the main subject discussed in this paper. Presented are statistics on the level of sexual functioning in accordance with the location and completeness of the lesion, psychosocial aspects of the disability—emphasizing the self-concept—and findings of various research studies dealing with sexuality in spinal-cord injuries.

Talbot, H. S. Psycho-social aspects of sexuality in spinal cord injury patients. *Paraplegia*, 1971, *9*, 37–39.

Sexual function of the spinal-cord-injury patient has been a topic that in the past has been either totally ignored and avoided or inadequately dealt with by the medical profession. In this article, the author discusses the psychosexual aspects of spinal-cord injury. He asserts that sexuality can no longer be dealt with as solely a physiological function. Sexuality may be expressed in a variety of forms and behavior patterns and needs to be incorporated into the total rehabilitation program. Rehabilitation should focus on that potential for sexual expression that remains after injury and develop its utmost utilization. The author concludes that research on sexual function must continue if total rehabilitation of spinal-cord-injury patients is to be achieved.

Talbot, H. S. A report on sexual function in paraplegics. *Journal of Urology*, 1949, *61*, 265–270.

The main purpose of this study was to examine the sexual responsiveness of paraplegics with complete and incomplete cord lesions, at various levels, and to relate this to psychogenic and reflexive erections and ejaculations. The sample included 200 male paraplegic patients, all with spinal-cord lesions of more than four months' duration. Three distinct groups were recognized: those experiencing no erections since the onset of lesion (n=73), those having reflex erections only (n=85), and those who were able to experience psychogenic erections (n=42). All subjects showed dysfunction of bladder and bowel. Each subject was interviewed in order to assess various dimensions of his sexual functioning. Results show that psychogenic erection and ejaculation are possible only when lesion of the spinal cord is incomplete. When lesion is complete, erection and ejaculation are still possible by reflex in response to direct local stimulation. In these cases 75 percent of those with lesions at or above the dorsal 11 level retained the erectile reflex. Lesions at lower levels are more likely to interrupt the reflex arc involved in erection. If nerve roots of sacral 2 level are intact, a mechanism for reflexive erection may remain. Sexual function appears to return following recovery from spinal shock. This shock period varies from individual to individual. Ejaculation was more prevalent in those with incomplete lesions; however, it was also observed, with less frequency, among those with only reflex erection capabilities. A sense of sexual gratification was experienced both by those who ejaculated and by those who did not.

Talbot, H. S. Sexual function in paraplegics. *Journal of Urology*, 1949, *61*(2), 265–270.

This paper presents the results of a study that examined sexual function and behavior in a group of 200 paraplegic males. Results show that 46 patients were able to have intercourse with intromission, 20 had ejaculations, and 12 patients reported gratification without ejaculation. The author notes that in regard to sexual function one can anticipate certain types of alterations after spinal-cord injury: a) destruction of either reflex or cortical centers and their fibers, resulting in absence of their mediated responses; b) complete transection of the cord above the centers, with remaining reflex activity but no cortical control; c) incomplete transection of the cord, with persistent reflex function and different levels of cortical control.

Talbot, H. S. The sexual function in paraplegics. *American Medical Association Archives of Neurology and Psychiatry*, 1951, *66*, 650–651.

It is probable that the psychical and gonadal activities involved in sexual functioning are not significantly altered as a result of spinal-cord injury. The present study examined sexual functioning in 408 paraplegic and quadriplegic patients. Results showed that of these patients, 46 percent had erections in response to local stimulation, and 20 percent in response to psychical, as well as local, stimulation; 34 percent of the patients had no erections at all. One third of the patients who had erections were able to have sexual intercourse, and 7 percent of these were fertile. The recovery of sexual functioning in this population usually occurred within six months after injury. The author concludes that the common belief that all spinal-cord-injury patients are sexually impotent is unjustified, and that restoring in patients a satisfying level of sexual readjustment contributes significantly to their rehabilitation.

Talbot, H. S. Sexual function in paraplegia. *Journal of Urology*, 1955, *73*, 91–100.

This investigation is an extension of an earlier study on sexual function in paraplegics conducted by the author in 1954. In addition to the 200 patients studied in the original study, 208 patients provided data for this paper. Data were collected by questionnaires. Results show that the psychic aspect of sexuality in the spinal-cord-injury patient remains unchanged. There is inadequate data to support the previously accepted theory that testicular atrophy is directly related to a neurogenic cause. In some studies, testicular changes, as revealed through histological examination, have been found to be reversible, while in other studies they have been found to be irreversible. The varying degrees of change in sperm productivity which have been commonly found may be the result of a hormonal imbalance or a generalized systemic debilitation. The author thus concludes that the endocrine aspect may also remain unchanged if general good health is maintained, with satisfactory adjustment to the patient's altered way of life. Results also show that approximately two-thirds of the patients in the study were able to have erections. Of those men who had erections, about one-third had intercourse, with more than half of them reporting gratification. Only about 5 percent of the group were reported to be fertile. The author concludes that the significance of developing the sexual potential in the spinal-cord-injury patient cannot be overemphasized.

Tarabulcy, E. Sexual function in the normal and in paraplegia. *Paraplegia*, 1972, *10*(11), 201–209.

The physiological aspects of sexual function and responsivity both in paraplegics and in able-bodied persons are presented and discussed.

The author notes that in the spinal-cord-injury person, the ability to have an erection and ejaculation is determined by the level and extent of the lesion. Erection is possible for 77 percent of paraplegics, while only 10 percent are able to ejaculate.

Teal, J. C., and Athelston, G. T. Sexuality and spinal cord injury: Some psychosocial implications. *Archives of Physical Medicine and Rehabilitation*, 1975, *56*(6), 264–268.

There have been numerous studies of both physiological and psychological aspects of sexual functioning, but only the physiological part of this literature has been organized in a systematic fashion. This paper reviews 33 articles that deal mainly or exclusively with psychosocial aspects of sexuality. It is observed that the psychosocial literature in this area is relatively diffuse, dealing with concepts that are inadequately specified and validated.

Tjajkovski-Svensson, D. The possible use of erotic movies in the sexual rehabilitation of males with spinal cord injury. Paper read at the Thirteenth World Congress of Rehabilitation International, Tel Aviv, Israel, June 13–18, 1976.

An exploratory study has been carried out over the past five years in Sweden with regard to the sexual rehabilitation of males with spinal-cord injuries. Erotic films were used to establish whether they could be useful as a diagnostic instrument when testing physiological and psychological sexual status in males with spinal-cord injuries. Also studied was whether erotic psychological stimulation could have an effect and could be useful in sex therapy. Results of this study were presented and discussed in the context of the many social and psychological barriers that exist, both in the disabled themselves and in the general public—even in a so-called "sex liberated" country such as Sweden—to hinder sexual rehabilitation.

Tomko, M. A., Timms, R. J., and Griffith, E. R. Sexual adjustment counseling with the spinal-cord-injured male. *Journal of Applied Rehabilitation Counseling*, 1972, *3*(3), 167–172.

Both biological and psychological facets of sexual functioning in the spinal-cord-injured male are reviewed in order to acquaint counselors and therapists with accurate scientific information concerning sexual functioning in general and in these specific cases. Rehabilitation personnel are urged to take the initiative in discussing sexual problems with such patients and to encourage the patient toward experimentation and reeducation to help him achieve the maximum possible degree of sexual satisfaction.

Tsuji, I., Makajima, F., Morimoto, J., and Mounaka, Y. The sexual function in patients with spinal cord injury. *Urologia Internationalis*, 1961, *12*, 270–280.

Two studies conducted in Japan involving sexual functioning in patients following spinal-cord injury are presented. The first study examined sexual behavior and function in 638 male and 17 female patients, and the second study involved an analysis of testicular biopsy, seminal vesiculography, 24-hour urine K's, and chromatographic fraction in 62 patients. Results of these studies are discussed, along with some conclusions.

Von Werssowetz, D. F. Mental and emotional readjustment of the hemiplegic patient. *Psychiatric Digest*, 1966, *27*, 25–37.

Psychosocial aspects of hemiplegic patients are discussed in this paper. Among the specific implications of this disability, changes in sexual behavior and attitudes are markedly noticed. Many hemiplegic patients, especially males, feel an increase in sexual desire. Patients attempt to have sexual coitus more frequently, often disregarding the time, the place, and the partner's needs. This behavior often poses a major problem for the patient's spouse. In severe cases, a patient may cause damage to the partner's genitals through extremely active and vigorous sexual behavior. The author indicates that "management of this problem is difficult; sedatives, tranquilizers, and muscle relaxants are the treatment of choice." He suggests that estrogen therapy should be used with great caution.

Wada, M. A., and Brodwin, M. G. Attitudes of society toward sexual functioning of male individuals with spinal cord injuries. *Psychology*, 1975, *12*(4), 18–22.

This study was an attempt to evaluate the general public's attitude and knowledge concerning sexual functioning of males with spinal-cord injuries. Subjects for this study were taken randomly from the general population of a large western metropolitan city. A small sampling was also taken from the staff of a rehabilitation center to see if those who work directly with the disabled had similar attitudes. The individuals filled out a questionnaire that included an attitude survey and items on sexuality interspersed with questions relating to psychological, social, educational, and vocational information. Items on sexuality dealt with both the functioning of and attitudes toward the disabled. Results are presented.

Wahle, H., and Jochheim, K. A. Studies on neurogenic disorders of sexual function in 56 paraplegic men with complete irreversible injuries of the spinal cord. *Archives of Sexual Behavior*, 1971, *1*, 184–188.

The authors report the results of a study they conducted to examine the impact of a complete spinal-cord lesion on erection ability, ejaculation, orgasm, and sexual libido in 56 spinal-cord-injury male patients. Lower motor and sensory dysfunction was complete in all subjects. Interviews were conducted with patients at intervals of 7.5 months and 15 months from the onset of the injury. Results of these two sets of interviews are discussed and conclusions are drawn.

Walker, M. L., Clark, R. P., and Sawyer, H. Sexual rehabilitation of the spinal cord injured: A program for counselor education. *Rehabilitation Counseling Bulletin*, 1975, *18*(4), 279–285.

Due to the importance of sexual adjustment in the total rehabilitation process of severely disabled persons, rehabilitation educators have recognized the need to include sexual instruction in the training of rehabilitation counselors. An instructional plan and sequence in human sexuality and disabilities is specified in this article. The plan includes film presentations and small group discussions to assist students in reassessing and restructuring their attitudes toward sexuality. The films used are "Just What Can You Do" and "Touching." The authors suggest that a follow-up to this plan would be the opportunity for participants to discuss sexuality with a disabled person.

Walsh, J. J. *Understanding paraplegia.* Philadelphia: J. B. Lippincott, 1964.

Sexual implications of spinal-cord injuries in both male and female patients are discussed in one of the chapters of this book. Also discussed are aspects of marriage and parenthood in these patients.

Weber, D. K., and Wessman, H. C. A review of sexual function following spinal cord trauma. *Physical Therapy*, 1971, *51*(3), 290–294.

For the purpose of making the physical therapist aware of the complications involved and their effects on the patient, the authors review some of the sexual problems encountered by patients following spinal-cord trauma. The psychological factors, physiological factors, and fertility of the patients are discussed.

Williams, J. G. P. Sex and the paralyzed. *Sexology*, 1965, *31*, 453–456.

Although the spinal-cord-injury person may lose some of his physical capacity for sex, he still has sexual drives and needs. This article discusses the sexual response in both males and females with spinal-cord injuries. The effects of the injury on sexual functioning vary from patient to patient depending on the location, severity, and completeness of the injury. A physiological explanation of how paralysis affects erection and ejaculation is also presented.

Zeitlin, A. B., Cottrell, T. L., and Lloyd, F. A. Sexology of the paraplegic male. *Fertility and Sterility*, 1957, *8*, 337–344.

The purpose of this study was to examine psychosocial difficulties and sexual functioning associated with spinal-cord injury in males (n= 100). Patients were grouped into four categories according to the level of their spinal lesion. These categories were (a) cervical, (b) upper thoracic, (c) lower thoracic, and (d) lumbar, which also included cauda equina lesions. The variables studied were type of erection (complete, incomplete, or none), and presence of conception after injury. Correlations between the ability to have an erection and the level of the spinal lesion were found. It seemed that reflex erections can occur with any lesion above the sacral level. The higher the spinal lesion, the greater the probability that a satisfactory erection may be obtained. Sixty-four percent of the men had complete erections, while fourteen percent experienced no erections. Thirty-eight percent had attempted intercourse, while twenty-six percent indicated that intercourse was successful. Other findings show that five percent of the males could experience orgasm and only three percent reported ejaculation.

Brain Injury

Dengrove, E. Sexual disorder in posttraumatic and postconcussional states. *Medical Trial Technique Quarterly*, 1964, *10*, 213–216.

Posttraumatic and postconcussional states are accompanied by anxiety and depression. The effect of these conditions on sexual activity and functioning is the focus of this paper.

Kalliomake, J. L., Markkanen, T. K., and Mustonen, V. A. Sexual behavior after cerebral vascular accident: A study of patients below the age of 60 years. *Fertility and Sterility*, 1961, *12*, 156–158.

The main purpose of this study was to examine the impact of cerebrovascular accident on sexual functioning and behavior. Interviews were conducted with 105 patients, age 20 to 60 years, who had suffered such an accident. Results show that a cerebrovascular accident tends largely to diminish libido and the frequency of active coitus. The decrease in libido seems to be more common after a right-side paralysis than a left-side one. Other findings and conclusions are presented.

Walker, A. E., and Jablon, S. A follow-up study of head wounds in World War II. *Veterans' Administration Medical Monograph*, 1961.

Among 739 World War II veterans with head injuries seen for follow-up medical examinations, 87 percent reported they had no sexual dysfunctions, and only 8 percent complained of impotence and decrease in sexual libido.

Weinstein, E. A. Sexual disturbances after brain injury. *Medical Aspects of Human Sexuality*, 1974, *8*, 10–31.

The author identifies and discusses psychological and sexual implications of brain injuries. Lesions of the limbic system contribute the most overt disturbances in sexual behavior. Electroconvulsive shock therapy and ruptured aneurysms at the base of the brain also may result in altered sexual behavior. Brain dysfunction (as evidenced by an abnormal EEG), premorbid personality, individual adaptive ability, and the doctor-patient relationship are factors to be considered in evaluation of the dysfunction. Alterations in sexual behavior may be demonstrated by delusions, breast and genitalia exposure, masturbation, verbal and physical advances, and repeated joking regarding sex. Behavior disorders, including violence, changes in mood and psychomotor activity, and disorientation, are frequently seen. Further review of relevant studies is followed by a discussion of other psychosexual manifestations in brain-injured patients.

Weinstein, E. A., and Kahn, R. L. Patterns of sexual behavior following brain injury. *Psychiatry*, 1961, *24*, 69–78.

Although changes in sexual behavior have frequently been cited among individuals suffering from brain disease, no serious attempt has been made to analyze these behaviors and their significance. The purpose of this article was to describe these behaviors and their relationship to other changes, and to consider other influencing factors, such as motivation and social interaction. The material described is based on a study conducted by the authors. Neurological patients of two general hospitals were studied, during hospitalization and after discharge (n = 196). Observations by staff were made of any altered sexual behaviors which persisted for at least one week. Results show that 36 patients, 19 women and 17 men, showed altered sexual behaviors of more than one week's duration. Most patients with altered sexual behaviors manifested them by verbal references to sexuality. Physical advances were less common than verbal ones. Exposure and masturbation were prominent in 12 patients. Delusions which contained primarily sexual material were reported in 20 patients. Other findings are presented and conclusions are drawn.

Epilepsy

Bandler, B., Kaufman, I. C., Dykens, J. W., Arico, J. T., and Geller, H. The role of the psychologic factors related to the menstrual cycle and the sexual life of women in the production of epileptic seizures. *Journal of Nervous and Mental Disease*, 1953, *117*, 162.

This study of epileptic women was designed to investigate the role of the patient's sexual life (sexuality, menstruation, pregnancy) in the production of seizures. It consisted of an integrated approach to various aspects of the problem, along psychologic and physiologic paths but with a unitary point of view. Effective diagnosis, including the use of electroencephalograms, and effective treatment, including antiepileptic drugs and intensive psychotherapy, were central to this work. The psychiatric interviews also served the purpose of psychologic investigation. Rorschach and thematic apperception tests, including specially devised cards, were used to gain an understanding of each patient's personality structure and fantasies. The various phases of each patient's menstrual cycle were charted through the use of daily vaginal smears and daily basal temperatures. The state of fluid balance was determined by daily weighing.

Bandler, B., Kaufman, I. C., Dykens, J. W., Schleifer, M., and Shapiro, L. N. Seizures and the menstrual cycle. *American Journal of Psychiatry*, 1957, *113*, 704–708.

The idea that there is a relationship between the epileptic seizure and the female patient's sexual life is well known. This study examined the normality of the menstrual cycle of epileptic women with respect to length and ovulation. Also studied was the hypothesis that sexuality plays an important etiological role in the occurrence of seizures in epileptic women between the menarche and the menopause. Results and conclusions are presented and discussed.

Bandler, B., Kaufman, I. C., Dykens, J. W., Shapiro, L. N., and Arico, J. Role of sexuality in epilepsy. *Psychosomatic Medicine*, 1958, *20*, 227–234.

The purpose of this paper was to present some evidence in support of the authors' theory regarding the etiology of epileptic seizures. The authors' experience in a combined psychiatric and psychologic investigation of 30 epileptic women leads them to conclude that the dynamic activity which leads to epileptic seizures is a sexual conflict. They present selected case material describing an epileptic seizure and automatism episode. The material shows that epileptic seizures occur in relationship to current sexual conflicts and to the sexual transference the patient experiences. However, "aggression is mainly intelligible as either a response to the sexual conflicts or as an attempted solution of them."

Bandler, B., Kaufman, I. C., Dykens, J. W., Shapiro, L. N., and Schleifer, M. The role of sexuality in seizures. Paper presented at the Annual Meeting of the American Psychosomatic Society, Boston, Mass., March 24–25, 1956. (Abstract, *Psychosomatic Medicine*, 1956, *18*, 512.)

This paper presents the authors' attempt to support their hypothesis that sexual conflicts are the main etiology in the occurrence of epileptic seizures in women. They discuss selected excerpts from an extensive psychiatric and psychological investigation of an epileptic woman. Material shows that epileptic attacks occur in relationship to the patient's current sexual conflicts. Material also shows the role of other types of conflicts, such as aggression, in the occurrence of seizures. However, aggression appears to represent only a response to the more basic, core conflicts of sexuality.

Bhaskaran, K. Psycho-sexual identification in the epilepsies. *Journal of Nervous and Mental Disease*, 1955, *121*, 230–235.

This paper presents two case histories of epileptic patients with a focus on their psychosexual misidentification, which is believed to contribute to their epileptic attacks. The first case is that of a 27-year-old unmarried male with both major and minor epileptic seizures. The other case study describes the history of a 37-year-old married male with atypical psychomotor attacks. The author, using a psychoanalytic approach, analyzes both cases to show that both patients had difficulties in normal heterosexual intercourse and identification. He also notes that the situations precipitating the epileptic attacks in both patients were psychodynamically similar.

Blumer, D. Hypersexual episodes in temporal lobe epilepsy. *American Journal of Psychiatry*, 1970, *126*(8), 83–90.

The sexual histories of 50 temporal lobe epileptic patients were carefully examined. Of these, 58 percent were found to be hyposexual prior to unilateral temporal lobectomy, and 14 percent had distinct episodes of hypersexuality. In 6 patients the hypersexual episodes followed the abrupt cessation of temporal lobe seizure activity. The author asserts that his findings "document the role of the temporal limbic structures in the regulation of sexual arousal." Several case histories of patients are presented and analyzed.

Blumer, D. Transsexualism, sexual dysfunction, and temporal lobe disorder. In R. Green and J. Money (Eds.), *Transsexualism and sex reassignment*. Baltimore: The Johns Hopkins University Press, 1969.

In this chapter, the author reviews the research and clinical literature on temporal lobe dysfunction and sexual aberrations. This extensive review reveals "good evidence for an occasional close relationship between sexual aberrations (transvestism in particular) and paroxysmal temporal lobe disorders." Erectial problems were found in all patients in whom transvestism was associated with temporal lobe epilepsy. The treatment of sexual aberration and temporal lobe epilepsy in transsexual patients is discussed. Hyposexuality associated with temporal lobe disturbances is also discussed.

Blumer, D., and Walker, A. E. Sexual behavior in temporal lobe epilepsy. *Archives of Neurology*, 1976, *16*, 37–43.

The main purpose of this study was to document sexual changes which occur in the course of temporal lobe epilepsy and following unilateral temporal lobectomy (n=21). The authors also made an attempt to clarify the role of temporal lobe functions in human sexual behavior. The average age of the patients at the time of the operation was 33. Information was obtained on a wide range of sexual issues and activity, including frequency and satisfaction of intercourse and masturbation, sexual fantasies, libidinous feelings, and the like. Findings confirmed the results of previous studies by showing marked hyposexual reaction in 50 percent of the patients prior to unilateral temporal lobectomy. A total or a substantial lack of sexual interest, drive, and feelings had developed in patients following the onset of temporal lobe epileptic attacks. This correlation between seizure activity and hyposexuality was further confirmed after operation took place. Four patients in whom seizure activity was diminished became very active sexually. Postoperative hypersexual activity terminated in two subjects with recurrence of epileptic attacks. The authors assert that changes in sexual activity are not to be attributed to anticonvulsant drugs. The postoperative increase in sexual activities reported in some of the patients took place in spite of continued medication.

Davis, B., and Morgenstern, F. A case of cysticercosis, temporal lobe epilepsy and transvestism. *Journal of Neurology, Neurosurgery and Psychiatry*, 1960, *23*, 247–249.

The author reports and discusses four case histories of transvestism associated with epileptic foci in the temporal lobe; three of the patients described had overt seizures. In one patient, the desire to transvest would be preceded by an aura of epigastric sensations, but later the desire to transvest occurred without the aura and became more persistent.

Epstein, A. W. Disordered human sexual behavior associated with temporal lobe dysfunction. *Medical Aspects of Human Sexuality*, 1969, *3*(2), 62–68.

Temporal lobe disorder often may be a significant factor in cases of sexually deviant behavior, altered libido, and disturbed gender identity. This article discusses the relationships between temporal lobe dysfunctions and disordered sexual behavior.

Epstein, A. W. Relationship of fetishism and transvestism to brain and particularly to temporal lobe dysfunction. *Journal of Nervous and Mental Disease*, 1961, *133*, 247–253.

The author presents and discusses a case of fetishism, two cases of fetishism-transvestism, and a case of transvestism, all with epileptic foci in the temporal lobe. One of the four cases reported had overt seizures.

Erickson, T. C. Erotomania (nymphomania) as an expression of cortical epileptiform discharge. *Archives of Neurology and Psychiatry*, 1945, *53*, 226–231.

The author presents a detailed case report of a female patient who "began to manifest nymphomania, which occurred in paroxysms of short duration, at the age of 43 years." This condition was found to be associated with Jacksonian seizures she was having. Examination of this patient "revealed the presence of a neoplasm, causing excitation of the topical projection of the genital structures in the right paracentral lobule." A year after the removal of the neoplasm, the patient no longer exhibited "nymphomania."

Freeman, W. Sexual behavior and fertility after frontal lobotomy. *Biological Psychiatry*, 1973, *6*, 97–104.

Following an extensive review of relevant literature, the author presents his clinical findings regarding sexuality in patients following frontal lobotomy. Promiscuity, homosexual behavior, marriage and divorce, pregnancy and delivery, and child birth are the specific variables discussed. In his conclusions the author notes that frontal lobotomy is often followed by an increased sexual libido; promiscuity is only seldom noted, and illegitimate pregnancy among lobotomy patients is no more frequent than in the general population.

Greenson, R. R. On genuine epilepsy. *Psychoanalytic Quarterly*, 1944, *13*, 139–159.

This is a detailed case study of an epileptic patient who was undergoing psychoanalytic treatment. The role of the patient's sexuality and exhibitionistic impulses and tendencies in relation to his epileptic seizure is identified and analyzed. The author found that the exhibitionistic tendencies and their reaction formations were interwoven with the patient's epileptic attacks.

Hierons, R., and Saunders, M. Impotence in patients with temporal-lobe lesions. *Lancet*, 1966 (October), 761–763.

The authors examined fifteen patients with temporal lobe disorders who were sexually impotent. In this report they describe some of these patients and discuss the evidence implicating the temporal lobe in the control of sexual functioning. The fifteen patients examined were all married men who were between the ages of 31 and 48 at the onset of their sexual dysfunction. Twelve patients had temporal lobe epileptic attacks at some time while they were impotent, and one patient had general convulsions only.

Hill, D. H., Pond, D. A., Mitchel, W., and Falconer, M. A. Personality changes following temporal lobectomy for epilepsy. *Journal of Mental Science*, 1957, *103*, 18–27.

The authors report clinical observations made on patients following temporal lobectomy for epilepsy. Of particular interest is the increase in sexual drive and potency found in thirteen of twenty-seven patients. It was also noted that three patients who formerly had a tendency toward "perverse" sexual behavior acquired "normal libidinal interest" and activity after the operation.

Hoeng, J., and Hamilton, C. M. Epilepsy and sexual orgasm. *Acta Psychiatrica et Neurologica Scandinavica*, 1960, *35*, 448–456.

This article presents a case study report on a rare incidence of epilepsy induced by sexual orgasm in a 32-year-old housewife. To induce her epilepsy for the study, the patient was placed under hypnosis and it was suggested to her that she was having intercourse. After three minutes she became pale, lost consciousness, and twitching of the left arm and leg occurred. Discussion in this article centered around reviewing possible factors that may have stimulated the seizure. These include changes in body chemistry, peripheral neuronal mechanisms, and psychological factors. A cortical element is suspected of playing a part in orgasmo-epilepsy. In this woman's case it was suggested that orgasm lowered the threshold of the localized epileptic lesion. Different parts of the brain where the lesion may have been located were reviewed. In this woman's case the lesion was found in the right temporal area.

Hooshmand, H., and Brawley, B. W. Temporal lobe seizures and exhibitionism. *Neurology*, 1969, *19*, 1119–1124.

The authors' intent in this report was to demonstrate that "a form of automatic behavior seen in temporal lobe seizures can be almost identical with, and mistaken for, the psychiatric problem of exhibitionism." Two cases of patients suffering from temporal lobe epilepsy and having automatisms simulating exhibitionism are presented. In the first case, the scalp EEG showed a left temporal spike focus, and in the second case, the patient had a right temporal lobe astrocytoma. Both cases were involved in legal suits for exhibitionism. Major points of differentiation between true exhibitionism syndrome and ictal indecent exposure are also discussed.

Hunter, R., Logue, V., and McMenemy, W. H. Temporal lobe epilepsy supervening on longstanding transvestism and fetishism. *Epilepsia*, 1963, 60–65.

The purpose of this paper was to present and discuss a case history of a patient with transvestism and fetishism present since age nine, in whom epileptic foci in the temporal lobe developed at age twenty-nine. Exacerbation of deviant sexual behavior of this patient coincided with a considerable increase in the epileptic seizures. Both the epilepsy and the abnormal sexual behavior were at first temporarily improved by anticonvulsant drugs, and then eliminated by left temporal lobectomy performed on the patient at age thirty-nine.

Johnson, J. Sexual impotence and the limbic system. *British Journal of Psychiatry*, 1965, *111*, 300–303.

The author presents and discusses two case histories of impotent patients who were found to have intracerebral tumors. In the first patient, the tumor was limited to the temporal lobe, and in the second patient it was situated in the posterior part of the frontal lobe. The clinical and neurophysiological evidence supporting the relation of the limbic system to sexual functioning is discussed in light of a thorough review of the literature. The author recommends that "inquiry into the sexual function should form part of the routine clinical history taking of patients suspected of organic cerebral disease."

Lennox, W. G., and Cobb, S. Sex and seizures. *Transactions of the American Neurological Association*, 1941, *67*, 233–234.

This article presents results of a comparative study of medical histories of 200 male and female epilepsy patients. It was concluded that the hereditary factor in the etiology of epilepsy is more prominent in female than in male patients, and it is especially marked in female patients who have only petit mal seizures or who display mental deterioration.

Levine, J., and Albert, H. Sexual behavior after lobotomy. *Journal of Nervous and Mental Disease*, 1950, *111*, 166–168.

Forty patients were interviewed from six months to four years after each underwent a prefrontal lobotomy. The purpose of the interviews was to determine postoperative changes in the preoperative patterns of sexual behavior. Subjects were questioned about their sex drive, inhibitions, fantasies, types of sexual activity, subjective responses, and moral and religious attitudes. An attempt was made to correlate these variables with the subject's clinical condition and work adjustment. Results showed that, in general, sexual expression remained primarily the same after as before the lobotomy. There was a striking decrease in feelings of anxiety, guilt, and modesty concerning sexual activity. Preoperative religious, moral, and social attitudes were maintained after lobotomy, but there was a reduction in modesty, embarrassment, and guilt in association with sexual activity. It was felt that making generalizations such as these was dangerous because not enough evidence exists concerning postlobotomy patients.

Levine, J., and Albert, H. Sexual behavior after lobotomy. *Journal of Nervous and Mental Disease*, 1951, *113*, 332–341.

This article reports and discusses the results of a study that was done to answer questions concerning sexual drives, guilt, morals, and anxieties of people who had undergone frontal lobe lobotomies (n=40). Information concerning each patient's sexual drives, fantasies, sexual activities, inhibitory forces, social problems, and other variables was gathered. The authors conclude that the evaluation was difficult because of the unknown effects of long hospitalizations and long duration of illness. They did feel in general that homosexuality was decreased after the lobotomies, and fantasies were practically nonexistent. Religious, moral, and social attitudes were maintained after lobotomy; however, there was a reduction in modesty, embarrassment, and guilt in association with sexual activity. Sexual expression remained primarily the same after as before the lobotomy.

Mitchell, W., Falconer, M. A., and Hill, D. Epilepsy with fetishism relieved by temporal lobectomy. *Lancet*, 1954, *2*, 626–630.

The authors present and discuss the case history of a patient in whom fetishism was believed to be associated with temporal lobe epilepsy. The patient's viewing of a fetish object became the invariable trigger of temporal lobe seizures at some time between the ages of eight and eleven years. During postictal confusional states, the patient used to dress himself in his wife's clothing. A left temporal lobectomy, at age thirty-eight, relieved both the epilepsy and the fetishism. The patient acquired normal libidinal interests and sexual activity.

Money, J., and Hosta, G. Laughing seizures with sexual precocity: Report of two cases. *Johns Hopkins Medical Journal*, 1967, *120*, 326–336.

Two case histories of patients exhibiting both sexual precocity and laughing seizures are presented and discussed in light of a review of the literature. Both patients were seen and examined at the Johns Hopkins Hospital.

Savard, R., and Walker, E. Changes in social functioning after surgical treatment for temporal lobe epilepsy. *Social Work*, 1965, *10*, 87–95.

This paper discusses changes in social functioning and behavior observed in temporal lobe epilepsy patients following surgical treatment. One specific aspect of postoperative behavior studied was sexual functioning. It was found that hyposexuality in patients was relieved following successful surgical treatment of temporal lobe epilepsy.

Sha'ked, A. Sexuality and the person with epilepsy: Rehabilitation practice applications. Paper read at the Third Annual Indiana Epilepsy Conference, Indianapolis, November 4–6, 1976.

The psychosexual aspects of disabilities in general, with a focus on epilepsy in particular, were presented. The impact of psychosexual adjustment on the total rehabilitation process was discussed in light of concepts of normalization and social integration. Finally, the unique role of the rehabilitationist in promoting sexual adjustment within the rehabilitation process was outlined.

Taylor, D. C. Sexual behavior in temporal lobe epilepsy. *Archives of Neurology*, 1969, *21*, 510–516.

This paper presents the results of an investigation of the sexual behavior of 100 patients with temporal lobe epilepsy. This study was a part of a broader evaluation of the outcomes of temporal lobectomy for epilepsy. Pre- and postoperative sexual behavior and functioning were examined and recorded. The results of this study are discussed in light of the findings of other studies reported in the literature. Results showed that 22 patients had improved their sexuality, but in 14 it had worsened, largely as a function of age. Patients in the former group were the most relieved of epilepsy. Adjustment varied with age, age at onset of epilepsy, and general social adjustment. Adjustment was found to be better among female patients than males. The most common sexual dysfunction was loss of sexual drive, rather than erectial or ejaculation problems. Heterosexual hypersexual behavior was rare.

Terzin, H. Observations on the clinical symptomatology of bilateral partial or total removal of the temporal lobes in man. In M. Baldwin (Ed.), *Temporal lobe epilepsy*. Springfield, Illinois: Charles C. Thomas, 1958.

The role of the temporal lobes in regulating sexual behavior is one of the topics of this chapter. It was found that bilateral temporal lobectomy results in hypersexual behavior in men.

Thompson, G. N. Relationship of sexual psychopathy to psychomotor epilepsy and its variants. *Journal of Nervous and Mental Disease*, 1955, *121*, 374–377.

The purpose of this study was to compare the psychopathic personality and the psychomotor epileptic. The author believes these two disorders are variations of the same fundamental cerebral disturbance. By using electroencephalograms of a patient with sexual psychopathic behavior and a patient with psychomotor seizures, he shows a striking similarity between the wave patterns. Overt actions of the patients were also observed to be similar.

Walker, A. E., and Blumer, D. Long-term effects of temporal lobe lesions on sexual behavior and aggressivity. In W. S. Fields and W. H. Sweet (Eds.), *Neural bases of violence and aggression*. St. Louis: Warren H. Green, 1975.

In the course of a long-term follow-up of 50 patients who underwent unilateral anterior temporal lobectomy for epilepsy, the authors studied changes in aggressivity and sexual functioning and activity. Before the operation, the majority of patients showed evidence of global hyposexuality, while after the operation most patients showed a very significant increase in sexual activity.

Parkinson's Disease

Barbeau, A. L-dopa therapy in Parkinson's disease: A critical review of nine years experience. *Canadian Medical Association Journal*, 1969, *101*, 791.

The impact of L-dopa therapy on the sexual function of 86 Parkinson's disease patients is one of the aspects discussed in this article. Increased libido was reported by only 5 percent of the patients studied.

Bowers, M. B., and Van Woert, M. H. Sexual behavior during L-dopa treatment of Parkinson's disease. *Medical Aspects of Human Sexuality*, 1972, *6*(7), 88–98.

A number of observations pertaining to sexual behavior and functioning have been made by physicians treating parkinsonian patients with L-dopa. Results of these observations are presented and discussed. Also presented are the results of a study conducted by the authors examining the sexual effects of L-dopa treatment on 19 parkinsonian patients.

Hyyppa, M., Rinne, U. K., and Sonninen, V. The activating effect of L-dopa treatment on sexual functions and its experimental background. *Acta Neurologica Scandinavica*, 1970, *46*, Suppl., 223.

The results of a study examining the sexual effect of L-dopa therapy in 41 Parkinson's disease patients are presented. Increased sexual libido was reported by 24 percent of the patients.

Jenkins, R. B., and Groh, R. H. Mental symptoms in parkinsonian patients treated with L-dopa. *Lancet*, 1970, *2*, 177.

The sexual effect of L-dopa therapy in a group of 90 Parkinson's disease patients was one of the variables studied and discussed in this article. Increased libido was reported in only 2 percent of the patients.

Mawdsley, C. Treatment of parkinsonism with Laevo dopa. *British Medical Journal*, 1970, *1*, 331.

The effect of L-dopa on sexual function in 32 Parkinson's disease patients was one of the variables observed in this study. Increased sexual libido was reported by 9 percent of the patients.

Mones, R. J., Elizan, T. S., and Siegel, G. J. Evaluation of L-dopa therapy in Parkinson's disease. *New York State Journal of Medicine*, 1970, *70*, 2309.

The sexual effect of L-dopa therapy in a group of 152 Parkinson's disease patients is one of the aspects examined in this study. Increased libido was reported in only 3 percent of the sample.

Muenter, M. D. Double-blind, placebo controlled study of laevodopa therapy in Parkinson's disease. *Neurology*, 1970, *20*, 6.

The impact of L-dopa therapy on the sexual function of Parkinson's disease patients (n=32) is one of the variables examined in this study. Increased sexual libido was reported in 6 percent of the sample.

Cerebral Palsy

Freedman, R. D. Psychiatric problems in adolescents with cerebral palsy. *Developmental Medicine and Child Neurology*, 1970, *12*(1), 64–70.

Based on six years of clinical experience with handicapped children and adolescents, the author discusses the causes of psychiatric disorders. Special attention is given to sexual impulses among the handicapped, and to psychiatric referral and treatment in a society where the changing picture of adolescent behavior makes it difficult to establish any rigid criteria of normality. The pitfalls in work with handicapped adolescents that may be relevant to the prevention of emotional disability are identified.

Geiger, R. C., and Knight, S. E. Sexuality of people with cerebral palsy. *Medical Aspects of Human Sexuality*, 1975, *9*(2), 70–83.

Cerebral palsied individuals have been for the most part misunderstood, misinterpreted, and avoided in the area of sexuality. When asked, these people almost invariably state that they received no significant sex education. One major reason for this is that society often views them as asexual or as too vulnerable to sexual advances. The authors present these and other sexual and interpersonal relationship problems and concerns faced by persons with cerebral palsy. They stress that these persons should be given adequate sex education and help in developing social skills.

Richardson, S. A. People with cerebral palsy talk for themselves. *Developmental Medicine and Child Neurology*, 1972, *14*, 524–535.

This paper presents a panel discussion conducted at the 1971 meeting of the American Academy of Cerebral Palsy. The panel included three persons with cerebral palsy and a mother of a cerebral palsied child. The discussion covers various topics such as social experiences, education, parents' reactions, communication problems, and the like. At several points during this discussion, the participants spoke of their lack of preparation in sexual matters and in understanding their own sexuality. They expressed the feeling that nonhandicapped people usually think that physically disabled persons are nonsexual beings. This is contrary to what they really are.

Steinbock, E. A., and Zeiss, A. M. Sexual counseling for cerebral palsied adults: Case report and further suggestions. *Archives of Sexual Behavior*, 1977, *6*(1), 77–83.

The authors present a multidisciplinary sex counseling modality with severely disabled adults. For illustrative purposes, a detailed case study of a cerebral palsied woman who received premarital sex and genetic counseling is discussed. Childbirth, pregnancy, sexual intercourse positions, and other topics should be included in counseling of this nature.

Multiple Sclerosis

Ivers, R. R., and Goldstein, N. P. Multiple sclerosis: A current appraisal of symptoms and signs. *Mayo Clinic Proceedings*, 1963, *38*, 457.

This article presents the results of a study conducted at Mayo Clinic and aimed at the examination of symptoms and signs of multiple sclerosis. Results show that 14 of the 54 male patients examined (26 percent) mentioned impotence as a presenting symptom of their condition. Whether the impotence described by patients was absolute, partial, or variable is not clear from this article.

Lilius, H. G., Valtonen, E. J., and Wikstrom, J. Sexual problems in patients suffering from multiple sclerosis. *Journal of Chronic Diseases*, 1976, *29*(10), 643–647.

A questionnaire was sent to 302 patients suffering from multiple sclerosis. The questionnaire asked, among other things, about the patient's sex life. Results show that sexuality was altered in 91 percent of the males and in 72 percent of the females. About half the patients reported either having an unsatisfactory sex life or having ceased sexual activity altogether. In males erection was normal in only 20 percent of the patients. In females there was a lack of orgasmic response in 33 percent and loss of libido in 27 percent. There was no correlation between the incidence of sexual dysfunctions and the duration of the disease. Some compensatory methods of maintaining sexual intercourse are discussed.

Smith, B. H. Multiple sclerosis and sexual dysfunction. *Medical Aspects of Human Sexuality*, 1976, *10*(1), 103–104.

It is expected, depending on the site of the lesion, that multiple sclerosis may affect sexual functioning in different ways in different individuals. In this brief communication, the author identifies and discusses the sexual aspects of multiple sclerosis and presents specific suggestions for counseling. He notes that disorders of sexual function in patients with multiple sclerosis are likely to affect the upper rather than the lower motor-sensory neurons. In the male patient, impaired potency is common, while in female patients there may be a lack of feeling in the vagina and clitoris. At times, increased libido or hypersexuality is a feature of the disease, perhaps more in female than in male patients.

Vas, C. J. Sexual impotence and some autonomic disturbances in men with multiple sclerosis. *Acta Neurologica Scandinavica*, 1969, *45*, 166–182.

Patients with multiple sclerosis have a long-standing history of sexual impotence. This research study was conducted with 37 male patients who had multiple sclerosis. Different aspects of the patients' testicular and autonomic functions were investigated. Results indicated that 47 percent of the 37 men examined had an impairment of erection, while neurological disability was not marked. Sudomotor function was examined in a controlled clinical setting where sweating was stimulated. Totally impotent patients perspired normally down to the waist but not below. Men classified as partially impotent had perspiration in all areas with the exception of the lower limbs. When the testing was repeated at a later date, changes in potency status correlated with sweating patterns. Another feature investigated was excretion of gonadatrophins. These levels were found to be elevated in all of the totally impotent men and in about one-third of the partially impotent men. Other results are presented and discussed in light of previous research findings.

Chapter Five

Muscular and Joint Pain

Arthritis / Low-Back Syndrome

Arthritis

Cobb, S., Miller, M., and Wieland, M. On the relationship between divorce and rheumatoid arthritis. *Arthritis and Rheumatism*, 1959, *2*, 414–418.

The hypothesis of suppressed hostility as a factor in rheumatoid arthritis was supported by the finding that these patients are more liable to divorce, but hold on to an unsuccessful marriage longer than persons free of the disease.

Ehrlich, G. E. Arthritis management: Treating rheumatoid arthritis with behavioral and clinical strategy. *Nursing Digest*, 1976, *4*(5), 24–26.

Among the problem areas discussed in this article are the sexual aspects of arthritis, and the management of this disease and its implications through behavioral methods.

Halstead, L. S. Aiding arthritic patients to adjust sexually. *Medical Aspects of Human Sexuality*, 1977, *11*(4), 85–86.

There is evidence to suggest that sexual interest and activity continue to remain important for arthritic patients, even for those with severe movement impairment. This article presents a step-by-step guide to counseling patients for sexual adjustment. The author stresses the importance of providing patients with basic information about the disease and about the anatomy and physiology of sexual functioning. This can prevent unnecessary apprehension and fears.

Hamilton, A. The problems of the arthritic patient. *Nursing Mirror and Midwives Journal*, 1976, *142*, 54–55.

The adverse effects which arthritis often has upon sexual functioning and activity are discussed. The basic problem from which other difficulties may stem is the limitation and the pain that the disability produces in the physical expression of sex. Arthritis of the hip is the disability most likely to affect sexual activity. Counseling and treatment aspects in dealing with sexual difficulties of arthritic patients are also discussed.

Hamilton, A. Sexual problems of arthritis and allied conditions. Paper read at the Thirteenth World Congress of Rehabilitation International, Tel Aviv, Israel, June 13–18, 1976.

The adverse effects of arthritis and its treatment on sexual function are more common and more severe than is generally recognized, since any condition leading to joint dysfunction, with resulting stiffness, fixation, pain, or instability of one or more joints, may reduce the ability of a patient to pursue unimpeded the conventional expression of sexual feeling. Many of the problems experienced by arthritic patients could be alleviated by a greater willingness on their part to use less conventional modes of sexual expression, and by adequate counseling and medical and surgical treatment from those who give care. The need for a greater appreciation of the disability and the various types of joint dysfunction is stressed, so that an increased readiness to inquire for possible difficulties may lead to the realization of their presence and their implications. An account is given of an attempt to solve the domestic and sexual problems of seriously disabled arthritic patients attending Mary Marlborough Lodge, a Disabled Living Unit within the Muffield Orthopaedic Centre complex in Oxford.

Hellgren, L. Marital status in rheumatoid arthritis. *Acta Rheumatologica Scandinavica*, 1969. *15*, 271–276.

This study examines the marital status of persons with rheumatoid arthritis. Subjects were 102 male and 282 female patients. The marital status of these subjects was compared with that of matched healthy controls. No significant differences were found.

Jivoff, L. Rehabilitation and rheumatoid arthritis. *Bulletin on the Rheumatic Diseases*, 1975–76, *26*(6), 838–841.

Among a variety of topics presented in this article, the author discusses sexual aspects and the need for sex counseling with rheumatoid arthritis patients.

Medsger, A. R., and Robinson, H. A comparative study of divorce in rheumatoid arthritis and other rheumatic diseases. *Journal of Chronic Diseases*, 1972, *25*, 269–275.

Divorce statistics for rheumatoid arthritis presented in various studies and sources have shown conflicting results. The major goal of this study was to examine the marital history of 100 rheumatoid arthritis patients in comparison with 100 subjects of similar biographical characteristics but having other types of rheumatic disorders. Marital status was analyzed as an indicator of psychopersonal adjustment in patients. Results attest to a significantly greater than expected number of divorced rheumatoid arthritis female patients compared to subjects with other rheumatic disorders. Educational achievement discrepancy between spouses was significantly greater in marriages that terminated in divorce among patients with rheumatoid arthritis than in the control group.

Todd, R. C., Lightowler, C. D. R., and Harris, J. Low friction arthroplasty of the hip joint and sexual activity. *Acta Orthopaedica Scandinavica*, 1973, *44*(6), 690–693.

This article deals with problems in sexual function for people with severe conditions of arthritis of the hip, which includes pain. The purpose of the study was to find the influence on sexual function of surgery to replace the hip. The subjects were selected from 292 patients who had undergone this particular hip replacement. Only 123 patients (49 men and 74 women), who had active sexual relationships at the time of the onset of hip problems, were used in the study. To obtain information, personal interviews were conducted and written questionnaires were provided for those who were unable to attend an interview. Of those interviewed, 11 men (22 percent) and 36 women (49 percent) had experienced severe sexual problems which they attributed to the pain of their hip disease. Following hip replacement, only 6 men (12 percent) and 19 women (26 percent) continued to have severe problems. Although the number of people studied was too few to come to any definite conclusions, the study does show that surgery was effective in relieving problems in nearly half of those who had had sexual difficulties due to pain. In some cases, although the surgery was somewhat successful in restoring sexual function, the patients did continue to have some pain. The authors advocate the use of this surgical procedure. They suggest that it be done early before sexual relationships deteriorate or stop.

Low-Back Syndrome

Amelar, R. D., and Dubin, L. Impotence in low-back syndrome. *Journal of the American Medical Association*, 1971, *216*(3), 530.

In this letter to the editor, the authors report on their clinical findings relating to impotence in lumbar disk disease. They indicate that the cause for impotence is organic and not psychologic. Impotence was found to be a presenting complaint in patients with occult lumbar disease, and can be completely relieved following surgical correction of the herniated disk.

Friedman, L. W. Sexual adjustment in patients with acute and chronic back pain. *Medical Aspects of Human Sexuality*, 1977, *11*(11), 65–66.

Sex during acute and chronic back pain, and the role of the physician in assisting the patient to arrive at sexual adjustment, are the topics discussed in this brief communication.

Kraus, H. Backache and sex. *Medical Aspects of Human Sexuality*, 1974, *8*(12), 78–86.

Sex-related psychopersonal problems are frequent causes of back pain in both males and females. Sexual maladjustment and dysfunction can cause tension, often followed by pain in the affected muscles. Pregnancy and endocrine dysfunction and deficiency are other causes of back pain. The author evaluates these factors and discusses the management of pain, as well as its relation to sexuality. The author's presentation is followed by commentaries by two medical authorities.

LaBan, M. M., Burk, R. D., and Johnson, E. W. Sexual impotence in men having low-back syndrome. *Archives of Physical Medicine and Rehabilitation*, 1966, *47*, 715–723.

The purpose of this study was to examine the patient's social, psychological, and vocational status and organic factors in low back disability patients (n=43) as a means of identifying those elements playing a significant role in sexual impotence. The sample consisted of 16 potent and 27 impotent male patients. Incidence of impotence was related to the onset of low-back pain. A detailed clinical history was obtained from each patient, including psychological testing and family interviews. A comparison between the two groups shows that the majority of statistically significant differences were those of a social and emotional nature, such as a working wife with patient managing the home, patient being the first-born or only child, and showing overconcern with physical symptoms. A high correlation between predicted vocational success and the presence or absence of impotence was also found; the impotent patient was more likely to be unsuccessful in vocational adjustment.

Rubin, D. Sex in patients with neck, back, and radicular pain syndromes. *Medical Aspects of Human Sexuality*, 1972, *6*(12), 15–27.

Sexual function and behavior in patients with neck, back, and radicular pain is discussed in light of numerous case studies.

Chapter Six

Sensory Disabilities

Blindness / Deafness

Blindness

Bidgood, F. E. A study of sex education programs for visually handicapped persons. *New Outlook for the Blind*, 1971, *65*, 318–323.

This survey was conducted as an initial phase of a project aimed at producing a resource guide of programs and materials in sex education for the blind. The purpose of the survey was to study the extent and nature of existing programs, the use of special educational materials, and the willingness of institutions for the blind to include sex education programs. Public schools (n=44), residential schools for the blind (n=32), and multiservice agencies serving the blind (n=42) were identified and surveyed. Of these 118 institutions, 81 percent indicated that sex education was viewed as the responsibility of the institution. Fewer agencies (47.6 percent) than public schools (61.4 percent) and residential schools (78.1 percent) were offering some form of sex education program for visually handicapped persons. In conclusion, the author notes that public school sex education programs appear to be best planned and developed in content. However, being developed primarily for sighted children, they are not very effective for visually handicapped children, who need adequate audio and tactile teaching aids.

Burleson, D. C. Starting a sex education program: Guidelines for the administrator. *New Outlook for the Blind*, 1974, *68*(5), 216–218.

The author asserts that school and rehabilitation agency administrators bear the primary responsibility for the adequate development and implementation of sex education programs for the blind. A guideline describing what is required of administrators in this matter is presented. This includes the development of an advisory committee, appropriate publicity to promote positive public reaction, staff development, the provision of specialized training for staff, careful selection of teaching staff, and careful budget planning.

Cataruzolo, M. J., and Enis, C. A. Sex education and/or family living in the residential school for the blind. *Journal of School Health*, 1971, *41*(10), 563–566.

The blind child's acquisition of necessary knowledge about his physiological and psychological development is hampered by his visual impairment, although his physical development takes place at the same rate as that of his normal peers. After summarizing existing sex education programs for the blind, the authors suggest a model curriculum of family living and sex education to be included in every school for the blind, beginning in the primary grades and continuing through high school. This includes progressive information disseminated by various auditory and tactile techniques, along with a structured health education program in the schools.

Cowan, M. K. Sex role typing in the blind child as measured by play activity choices. *American Journal of Occupational Therapy*, 1972, *26*(2), 85–87.

The purpose of this study was to compare and discover differences in sex role typing between blind and sighted children. Subjects were 21 blind and 21 sighted children in the second through eighth grades who were given the Rosenberg and Sutton Smith list of game preferences. There were no significant differences between the two groups in preference.

Dickman, I. R. Sex education and family life for visually handicapped children and youth: A resource guide. New York: Sex Information and Education Council of the United States, 1975.

This resource guide is a result of work conducted by a task force composed of authorities in sex education from the Sex Information and Education Council of the United States (SIECUS), and of experts from the American Foundation for the Blind. The guide is intended for teachers, parents, and counselors who work with visually handicapped persons. The guide can be used in a variety of ways, including in-service training and workshops, curriculum development, individual counseling, and general orientation meetings. The author indicates that this guide attempts to "sensitize persons to the need for responsible education in human sexuality and to the special problems which visual impairment imposes in this area." The guide provides a broad view of sex education and concepts of family life and offers suggestions for learning activities appropriate for visually handicapped students. Also provided are general guidelines for administrators in the area of planning and developing a curriculum in these subjects.

Emerson, R., Uhde, T. Do blind children need sex education? *New Outlook for the Blind.* 1974, *68*(5), 193–200, 209.

Recognizing the fact that there has been no systematic research examining sexual knowledge among blind individuals, the authors conducted a comprehensive study with two major objectives: (1) to examine, by interviewing blind persons, the extent of their knowledge of sexual anatomy and the manner of its involvement in sexual behavior, and to obtain expressions of their attitudes toward sexuality and its regulation; (2) to examine attitudes toward sex education held by parents of blind children. This paper is a preliminary report of this study. Interviews with 18 males and 3 females regarding sources of sex education, sex-related expressions, sources of advice about sexual problems, masturbation, and other aspects are described. Also presented is a Human Sexuality Opinion Survey, a questionnaire developed specifically for this study. This questionnaire was mailed to some 2,000 parents, teachers, houseparents, and others involved in the education of blind children. The questionnaire was designed to gather information regarding attitudes toward sex education programs for blind children, and about the preferred methods and content of such programs.

Enis, C. A., and Cataruzolo, M. Sex education in the residential school for the blind. *Education of the Visually Handicapped,* 1972, *4,* 61–64.

A questionnaire seeking information about programs in sex education in residential schools for the blind was sent to 44 schools in the United States. A summary of the information acquired, with conclusions and recommendations, is presented and discussed.

Foulke, E., and Uhde, T. Do blind children need sex education? *New Outlook for the Blind,* 1974, 132–140.

The objective of this study was the examination of the level of sexual knowledge held by blind children and of their attitudes concerning sexuality. Also studied were the attitudes toward sex education held by parents of blind children. The results indicate that the subjects with some formal type of sex education were better informed about the anatomy and the function of sex than the subjects with no formal sex education. Other aspects of the study and its results are further analyzed and discussed.

Foulke, E., and Uhde, T. W. Sex education and counseling for the blind. *Medical Aspects of Human Sexuality*, 1976, *10*(4), 51–52.

Problems in psychosexual development and possible difficulties and concerns in sexual activity and behavior in the blind are discussed, and specific suggestions for sex counseling and education are made.

Gillman, A. E., and Gordon, A. R. Sexual behavior in the blind. *Medical Aspects of Human Sexuality*, 1973, *7*(6), 48–60.

The authors made clinical observations of sexual behavior in the blind. First, preschool and school-age individuals were observed to see if there were any deviations in the development of their gender role. No deviations were found, since the children that were observed demonstrated an age-appropriate notion of their sex and correctly identified with their playmates. Also studied were blind teenagers. It was found that the more intelligent blind teenagers with fewer signs of disturbed behavior demonstrated a realistic knowledge of sexual anatomy and function, while more disturbed and less intelligent teenagers did not. It was concluded that development of sexual knowledge in the blind takes place through the use of language and that the degree of sexual sophistication of the congenitally blind child seems to be related to his general intelligence, psychological status, and opportunity for instruction. Finally, the psychological reactions to adventitious blindness and their effects on sexuality were studied. The various reactions to blindness were categorized as denial, acceptance, or depression. It was found that individuals who accept their blindness may not report any sexual problems. On the other hand, the individual who denies his blindness may reflect this in his sexual behavior by perhaps becoming sexually aggressive.

Haj, F. On intermarriage among the blind. *New Outlook for the Blind,* 1967, *61*(5), 137–141.

Reflecting upon his personal experiences and a review of relevant literature, the author discusses intermarriage among the blind. Factors enhancing intermarriage are identified and discussed.

Holmes, R. B. The planning and implementation of a sex education program for visually handicapped children in a residential setting. *New Outlook for the Blind*, 1974, *68*(5), 219–225.

A sex education curriculum developed at the Illinois Braille and Sight Saving School is introduced and described. The premise was that sex education needs to take place constantly from infancy to maturity. Thus, different levels of instruction were developed and implemented. Detailed criteria for the selection of effective instructors for the program are outlined. Teachers need to have wide knowledge of the subject, to be sensitive to the unique needs of the visually handicapped student, to have the ability to relate to students and to communicate the subject comfortably, and to have the ability to develop effective rapport with students. Experience shows that careful planning is necessary to develop and maintain a high quality sex education program for blind students which is designed to inform and guide, yet is flexible enough to recognize and meet individual needs.

Holmes, R. B. A sex education program for the visually impaired in a residential school. *SIECUS Report*, Special Issue on the Handicapped, 1976.

The author asserts that the residential school provides "a unique opportunity to develop a sex education program that is comprehensive and has continuity." She describes the development and outcomes of a sex education program at the Illinois Braille and Sight Saving School. Students' evaluation of the program proved it was a successful experience.

Hooft, F. van't, and Heslinga, K. Sex education of blind-born children. *New Outlook for the Blind*, 1968, *62*(1), 15–21.

While the sexual development of a blind child is essentially similar to that of a sighted child, some special problems and unique implications of blindness arise when one considers sex education for blind-born children. This article identifies and discusses the difficulties and the special considerations involved in the planning, development, and implementation of a sex education program with blind-born children. Some of the authors' recommendations are: (1) blind children should be grouped in a manner as similar as possible to normal family structure, with a mixed staff; (2) learning about sexual anatomy should start at an early stage, long before the children have sexual feelings; (3) there is a need to use effective physical models for demonstrations; (4) male and female nudes are needed as teaching model aids; and (5) individual counseling is to be offered along with group sex education programs.

Karpen, M. L., and Lipke, L. A. Sex education as part of an agency's four-week summer workshop for visually impaired young people. *New Outlook for the Blind*, 1974, *68*(6), 260–267.

A sex education program for the visually impaired was developed by agency staff, parents, and resource persons in Grand Rapids, Michigan. Curriculum content, which included the physical, emotional, and social aspects of sexual maturation, grooming and hygiene, cosmetics, and drug use and abuse, was based on the expressed interests of the students. Aiming for the development of personal growth in awareness, self-expression, and individual responsibility, the teaching strategies were student-oriented and included group discussion, group activities, problem-solving, and demonstration/participation. The over-all goal of the program is to help youngsters who are visually impaired "cross the bridge" from childhood to adulthood. Multimedia learning resources are suggested.

Knappe, H. K., and Wagner, N. N. Sex education and the blind. *Education of the Visually Handicapped*, Spring 1976, 1–5.

This extensive and comprehensive review of the literature shows that sex education is highly important for the visually handicapped person. Due primarily to negative attitudes toward the disability and sex education, it has only been in recent years that sex education has been seriously considered as part of the curriculum for blind students. The authors describe some of the problems associated with sex education for the blind and offer some solutions. They conclude that "positive changes in the attitude of society toward sex education of the blind is largely dependent upon changes in the view that society takes of sexuality in general."

Langdon, J. N. Sex education: A study of the reported opinions of parents and former pupils. *Teacher of the Blind*, 1970, *59*(1), 30–35.

The opinions of parents and former students were obtained through a comprehensive survey of services for blind children and young persons. Parents were asked whether their children had received sex education from their schools appropriate to their age and whether they thought that the education received had been adequate or not. About half the parents had no idea as to whether their children had received sex education at school. About 25 percent reported that their children had received adequate sex education at the secondary stage. About 90 percent were in favor of sex education's being offered at the secondary stage. These findings were roughly in agreement with the opinions and reports of former pupils. The survey was supported by the Nuffield Foundation at the School of Education, University of Birmingham (England).

Moore, D. D. Sex education for blind high school students. *Education of the Visually Handicapped*, 1969, *1*, 22–25.

This article describes and discusses a course in sex education for blind students. The course is designed "to confront the students with basic considerations of the fundamental aspect of marriage and family life, including the vital area of sex education." Thirty visually handicapped students of a residential high school were tested with a premarital opinionnaire and a Sex Knowledge Inventory at the beginning and at the end of a six-weeks' course. The class utilizes a "talking book," a series of tape recordings on sexual issues, an opportunity to bring prepared questions to class anonymously, and life-size male and female urogenital models. Results of the evaluation indicate that the students showed significant gains in knowledge regardless of race or sex. There was high interest in the subject matter. The author suggests that research is needed because of the small sample of this study.

Noff, J. Behavior objectives and learning activities in sex education for the visually handicapped: Suggestions for a curriculum. In *Sex education for the visually handicapped in schools and agencies*. New York: American Foundation for the Blind, 1975.

The goals of this behavior objectives guideline for the development of a sex education curriculum are to increase sexual knowledge and understanding of self, and to eliminate fears, anxieties, and misconceptions regarding the individual's sexuality. The guideline suggests that the curriculum be designed to work toward the achievement of behavioral objectives through a series of sequential experiences. The areas of development to be achieved are (1) self-understanding and emotional development, (2) social and cultural development, and (3) biological development. Separate behavior objectives and learning sequential objectives are given for different developmental levels, i.e., primary, intermediate, early adolescence, and later adolescence. Also presented is a list of materials and resources for teaching aids.

Scholl, G. T. The psychosocial effects of blindness: Implications for program planning in sex education. *New Outlook for the Blind*, 1974, *68*(5), 201–208.

The initiation, design, and development of sex education programs for blind persons require that serious consideration be given to the unique psychosocial aspects of blindness and to their impact on the individual's development. Selected variables in the physical, psychosocial, educational, and mental developmental processes are identified and related to specific aspects of sex education. A distinction is made between factors related to the blindness per se and those related to characteristics of the blind person or his immediate environment. Some of the variables related to the impact of blindness on the individual are the nature and extent of blindness, family characteristics, physical and motor development, restricted mobility resulting from blindness, impact of blindness on physical appearance, and the mental and educational aspects of the disability.

Sex education for the visually handicapped in schools and agencies: Selected papers. New York: American Foundation for the Blind, 1975.

This selection includes the following topics: (1) sex education of blind children; (2) do blind children need sex education? (3) starting a sex education program: guideline for the administrator; (4) the psychological effects of blindness: implications for program planning in sex education; (5) a humanistic and futuristic approach to sex education for blind children; (6) sex education as part of an agency's four-week summer workshop for visually impaired young people; (7) the planning and implication of a sex education program for visually handicapped children in a residential setting; and (8) behavior objectives and learning activities in sex education for the visually handicapped: suggestions for a curriculum.

Special issue: Planning sex education programs for visually handicapped children and youth. *New Outlook for the Blind*, 1974, *68*(5).

Contents: Do blind children need sex education? by Emerson Foulke and Thomas Uhde, p. 193–209. The psychosocial effects of blindness: implications for program planning in sex education, by Geraldine T. Scholl, p. 201–209. A humanistic and futuristic approach to sex education for blind children, by David S. Torbett, p. 201–215. Starting a sex education program: guidelines for the administrator, by Derek L. Burleson, p. 216–218. The planning and implementation of a sex education program for visually handicapped children in a residential setting, by Ruth V. Holmes, p. 219–225.

Torbett, D. S. A humanistic and futuristic approach to sex education for blind children. *New Outlook for the Blind*, 1974, *68*(5), 210–215.

The author discusses the importance of adequate sex education for the blind in light of the existing sexual negativism and mythological orientation in American culture. He stresses that sex education must "work to overcome resistance to the use of touch so necessary to learning by blind children." He also suggests greater access to sexual material by blind children. Educators and parents must become aware of their own sexuality so that they can comfortably incorporate sex education in the overall developmental process of the blind child. Finally, there is a need to develop special educational equipment to facilitate sex education with blind children, who experience their world tactually.

Vogel, D. S., and Muxen, M. J. A sex education program for congenitally blind adults in a rehabilitation center setting. *New Outlook for the Blind*, March 1976, 104–108.

After realizing the lack of sex education programs for congenitally blind adults, the authors developed a curriculum to meet this important need. The program includes various units of instruction, such as male and female sexual anatomy and bodily function, and the understanding of and attitudes toward sexual intercourse, childbirth, masturbation, homosexuality, contraception, and premarital sex. The course's most recognized weakness was the lack of an adequate model of the human body. The authors suggest that in their opinion only live models can accurately teach the concepts of sexuality. They felt that, based on reactions and observations, the course was successful in meeting original goals.

Deafness

Blish, S. C. Problems involved in sex education in a residential school for the deaf. *Volta Review*, 1940, *42*, 133–138.

The importance of sex education in residential schools for the deaf, and some problems involved in this process, are discussed.

Chaplin, J. W. Sex education of deaf children. *Volta Review*, 1957, *59*, 201–203.

The author discusses some unique problems and difficulties experienced by parents and teachers of deaf children in relation to sex education. Because of communication difficulties, parents of deaf children sometimes feel at a loss when trying to explain sex to their children. As a result, they avoid the subject whenever possible. Some suggestions for sex education programs for deaf students are presented.

Chigier, E. Sex education for the deaf. Paper read at the Thirteenth World Congress of Rehabilitation International, Tel Aviv, Israel, June 13–18, 1976.

The deaf adolescent poses particular problems in communication and in social relationships, especially with regard to contacts with the hearing population. The tendency toward integration of the deaf in society intensifies the basic requirement for sex education for adolescents in general, when physical and psychosocial development leads to sex arousal and tensions. For the past eight years, exploratory and somewhat sporadic programs of sex education have been provided at the Niv School for the Deaf and in the Youth Section at the Helen Keller Center, both in Tel Aviv. This paper describes the nature of the problem, some of the techniques employed, and the unanswered questions that exist with regard to planning better educational programs in the future.

Cook, L., and Rossett, A. The sex role attitudes of deaf adolescent women and their implications for vocational choices. *American Annals of the Deaf*, 1975, *120*(3), 341–345.

The sex role attitudes of deaf and hearing adolescent women were investigated and compared. A Likert scale was used as an attitude survey; the deaf women were found to be significantly more traditional in their perception of sex role attitudes than were their hearing peers. The implications of sex role attitudes as they influence vocational choices are discussed. Suggestions for learning opportunities designed to effect a less traditional sex role attitude in deaf women are made.

Craig, N. W., and Anderson, E. P. The role of residential schools in preparing deaf teen-agers for marriage. *American Annals of the Deaf*, 1966, *3*, 488–498.

The purpose of this study was to examine existing residential school policies and programs aimed at preparing deaf teenagers for marriage. A questionnaire was mailed to the administrators of 66 public residential schools for the deaf throughout the country. Results showing the extent of the schools' involvement in sex education and marriage preparation programs are presented.

Enterline, M. Sex education for the deaf adolescent. *SIECUS Report*, Special Issue on the Handicapped, 1976.

The author developed, conducted, and evaluated a special curriculum in the area of sex education for deaf adolescents. The goal of the program was to provide students accurate information on physiological changes and to explore with them the various emotional issues associated with these changes. Based on this experience, the author made the following recommendations for improvements: (1) there is a need for an expansion of coordination and cooperation between parents and teachers; (2) filmstrips allowing a pace control are preferred to motion picture films; (3) curricula should be developed for all deaf children on a developmental basis; and (4) the method of instruction needs to be based on total communication, including speech, lipreading, signing, finger spelling, and hearing aids. Sex education must be accepted as an integral part of the deaf child's education.

Fitz-Gerald, D., and Fitz-Gerald, M. Sex education in residential facilities for the deaf. *American Annals of the Deaf*, 1976, *121*, 480–483.

In order to better determine the kinds of formal sex education programs within residential facilities for the deaf, a sex education survey was conducted during the winter of 1974. This 24-item survey was sent to the 112 public and private residential institutions for the deaf in the United States. Of these facilities, 88 percent responded to the survey, and of this group, 66 percent reported the existence of a formal sex education program. According to these respondents, very little programming was coordinated at the primary level. Furthermore, sex education was offered as a separate course in 60 percent of the facilities. In 54 percent of the institutions, the academic department was responsible for the sex education instruction, although 46 percent of the public facilities and 25 percent of the private facilities offered sex education through the dormitories as well. The amount of time devoted to instruction varied from one hour to 720 hours per year. Seventy percent of the facilities reported that classroom teachers conducted the sex education program within the school and 45 percent of all the instructors involved in sex education had received special training for this position. Many of these programs seemed to be crisis oriented, but it is hoped that the development of ongoing, long-range, and more comprehensive programming will be forthcoming in the area of sex education.

Hill, A. Some guidelines for sex education for the deaf child. *Volta Review*, 1971, *73*(2), 120–124.

The author identifies and discusses several positive steps parents can take to educate a deaf child about sex and to help him adjust to his developing personality and bodily changes. She describes the various stages of development of sexual feeling in children, appropriate vocabulary for communication about sex, and the general awareness that parents must have regarding nonverbal communication through which their deaf child learns.

Kline, L. F. A social hygiene program in a residential school for deaf children. *Volta Review*, 1968, *70*, 509–512.

A social hygiene program that was incorporated into the curriculum of the Illinois School for the Deaf is presented and its effectiveness is evaluated. The program includes sex education for deaf children.

Miller, A. S. The "growing up" program at Clarke School. *Volta Review*, 1969, *71*(7), 472–482.

The author describes a sex education program developed for preadolescent and adolescent students at Clarke School for the Deaf in Northampton, Massachusetts. The basic philosophy developed in preadolescent students is that "satisfactory adulthood results only when an individual can demonstrate a sense of responsibility, personal self-control, and consideration for others." Physical changes at puberty and maturation are discussed in accordance with the student's developmental level. An attempt is made to develop in students the realization that there is much more to sexuality than the physical aspects. The program includes discussions and instruction on personal hygiene, menstruation, the management of sexual urges, dating, homosexuality, pregnancy, heredity, venereal diseases, birth control, and other related areas.

Miller, A. S. "If I have a daughter . . ."; The sex education program for teen-agers at Clarke School. *Volta Review*, 1973, *75*(8), 493–503.

Clarke School for the Deaf, in Northampton, Massachusetts, has had a program of personal hygiene and sex education for many years. Since the students range in age from 10 to about 17 years, the program is divided into various levels appropriate to different age groups. Sessions are held separately for boys and girls except for general topics such as drug abuse or heredity. A conscious effort is made to keep the program up-to-date. Excerpts from older students' responses to questions about what sex and hygiene mean to them and how the hygiene program has helped them indicate the effectiveness of the program. A bibliography of references on sex education that have been used by the program staff is included. It covers publications for adults, publications to read to young children, materials for teen-agers, transparencies and charts, films, and miscellany. Appropriate age levels are noted for the films, and films with captions, suitable for use with deaf students, are listed.

Miller, A. S. Personal hygiene for teenagers. *Volta Review*, 1964, *66*, 179–183.

This article describes a special personal hygiene curriculum developed at Clarke School for the Deaf. Sex education is an integral part of this program.

Smith, M. S. The deaf. In H. L. Gochros and J. S. Gochros (Eds.), *The sexually oppressed*. New York: Association Press, 1977.

Problems encountered by the deaf person that have an impact on his or her sexual development and behavior are discussed in this chapter.

Steinmar, H. Hearing impaired marriage: A counseling challenge. *Journal of Rehabilitation*, 1973, *39*(3), 12–13, 40.

The need for marriage counseling with hearing impaired couples is rapidly increasing due to a mounting divorce rate in this population. This article shows how marriage counselors who work with hearing impaired couples can chart their progress on marital problems, help in solving them, and facilitate further work and research in this field.

Work, M., Noble, C., and Burney, E. Sex education for the deaf: Three parents reply to suggestions from schools. *Volta Review*, 1940, *42*(9), 501–505, 550.

This article presents the response of three parents of deaf children to previous articles on sex education for deaf children that appeared in *The Volta Review*.

Chapter Seven

Miscellaneous Medical Conditions

Biskind, M. S. The relation of nutritional deficiency to impaired libido and potency in the male. *Journal of Gerontology*, 1947, *2*, 303–314.

Results of this study show that of 143 patients with nutritional deficiency, definite impairment of libido and potency occurred in two thirds. Of the 76 patients who were observed subsequently, nutritional therapy alone led to alleviation of the avitaminotic lesions in all and to definite improvement in libido and potency in 62 patients. Seven case histories of patients are discussed in detail, along with the various therapeutic modalities used.

Blaue, S. P., and Blaue, B. Sex and systemic lupus erythematosus. *Medical Aspects of Human Sexuality*, 1976, *10*(11), 93–94.

Systemic lupus erythematosus is an inflammatory connective tissue disease accompanied by fever, joint pain or arthritis, fatigue, visceral lesions, skin eruptions, and other symptoms. This article outlines and discusses various symptoms and drugs used for the treatment of lupus which can affect the patient's sexual functioning and relationship.

Cummings, V. Amputees and sexual dysfunction. Paper read at the Thirty-fifth Annual Assembly of the American Academy of Physical Medicine and Rehabilitation, Washington, D.C., October 24, 1973.

Sexual concerns and difficulties associated with a major limb amputation are discussed in this presentation. Sexual problems of amputees may be related to emotional trauma such as depression and distortion of body image. Additionally, phantom sensations, difficulties in balance and positioning, and associated diseases may alter sexual activity and behavior.

Currey, H. L. F. Osteoarthrosis of the hip joint and sexual activity. *Annals of the Rheumatic Diseases*, 1970, *29*, 488–493.

The goal of this study was to examine the impact of osteoarthrosis of the hip on the sexual relationship of married couples. A questionnaire on sexual difficulties was sent to 230 patients aged 60 years or younger who had undergone surgical treatment for osteoarthrosis of one or both hip joints. One hundred and twenty one questionnaires were adequately completed and returned (73 women and 48 men). Results show that 60 percent of the subjects had sexual difficulties. Difficulties were experienced more severely among women than men. Stiffness was the most common cause of difficulty, which included painful intercourse in 74 percent of the patients and loss of libido in 22 percent. One fourth of the respondents said these difficulties caused unhappiness in marriage. Surgery helped the pain, but not the sexual difficulties. Sexual counseling was needed and wanted by and with both spouses by 64 percent of the respondents.

Davidson, P. W. Transsexualism in Klinefelter's syndrome. *Psychosomatics*, 1966, *7*, 94–98.

A case of transsexualism and transvestitism in a patient with Klinefelter's syndrome (the XXY syndrome) is presented and discussed.

Edwards, W. H. Abdominal aortic aneurysmectomy and impaired sexual function. *Medical Aspects of Human Sexuality*, 1977, *11*(11), 67–68.

Various considerations in the diagnosis and treatment of sexual dysfunctions associated with aortic aneurysms are discussed in this brief article. The patient and his partner should be willing to explore alternative methods of sexual stimulation, if satisfactory sexual adjustment is to be achieved.

Feldman, J. M. Effects of tuberculosis on sexual functioning. *Medical Aspects of Human Sexuality*, 1977, *11*(5), 29–30.

The author asserts that tuberculosis can alter sexual functioning by its general debilitating effect or by its destructive effect on the genitourinary system. This article discusses the effects of tuberculosis on the libido, sexual potency, the sexual partner, and family members. Decreased libido and sexual potency are common problems in persons with this disease. The author also makes some suggestions for diagnosis and therapy.

Gruner, O. P. N., Naas, R., Fretheim, B., and Gjone, E. Marital status and sexual adjustment after colectomy: Results in 178 patients operated on for ulcerative colitis. *Scandinavian Journal of Gastroenterology*, 1977, *12*(2), 193–197.

Marital status and sexual adjustment were surveyed in 178 patients operated on for ulcerative colitis. Results show that frequency of intercourse practiced by married patients did not differ from that of the general population. However, the frequency of premarital sexual activity seemed low in patients of either sex. Other results are reported and discussed.

Haggan, M. Sexual desire in tuberculous women. *American Review of Respiratory Diseases*, 1944, *49*, 53–57.

This study examined sexual feelings and desire in a group of 50 female tuberculous patients who were married and of "a sexually active age." Results of interviews revealed that: (1) 25 subjects recognized sexual desire at some time during their hospitalization; (2) desire was not correlated with the degree of illness; (3) sexual desire was correlated with the attitude toward coitus but not with the success of the subject's marriage or the use of contraceptives; and (4) libido was increased in 3 cases, decreased in 11, and unchanged in 36 subjects.

Hallbrook, T., and Holmquist, B. Sexual disturbances following dissection of the aorta and the common iliac arteries. *Journal of Cardiovascular Surgery*, 1970, *11*, 255–260.

The purpose of this study was to examine the effects on sexual functioning of dissecting either the aorta or the common iliac arteries. Thirty-one male patients between 44 and 73 years of age who had similar operations involving the aorta or the common iliac arteries were interviewed. Results show that of these thirty-one patients, fifteen reported no decrease in sexual functioning, two reported impotency experienced before as well as after surgery, and the remaining fourteen reported some sexual disturbances following surgery. Ten of the fourteen patients reporting change could still achieve erections, whereas the remaining four could not. A comparison was then made between the type of operation and the extent of dissection of these arteries. The authors assert that because the erection mechanism is so complex, it is difficult to understand why some of these patients suffered total impotency while others had no change. In two out of ten patients, orgasms were diminished and became less intense. The authors discuss some possible explanations for these changes. Apparently, injury to the hypogastric nerve often results in retrograde ejaculation (where the sperm go back into the bladder), making sterility inevitable.

Hanna, M. K., and Williams, D. I. Genital function in males with vesical exstrophy and epispadias. *British Journal of Urology*, 1972, *44*, 169–174.

The purpose of this study was to examine the sexual functioning and potential fertility of males with vesical exstrophy, and to assist in planning surgery that would obtain optimal urinary and sexual function for men with these conditions. In this study, 16 males with exstrophy and 15 with epispadias were studied. Clinical examinations, semen analyses, blood chemistries, IVPs, and urethral explorations were performed. Results show that in the exstrophy patients all 16 achieved erection, 10 were able to complete intercourse, 12 ejaculated normally; 5 of the 16 had normal sperm counts, 7 had lowered counts, 3 had total absence of sperm, and 1 could not ejaculate. Following surgery in the epispadias cases, all 15 achieved erection, 11 copulated satisfactorily, 9 produced normal sperm counts, and 4 had subnormal sperm counts. The authors stress that in order to achieve erection without chordee (often absent in exstrophy and epispadias) surgical correction is necessary. The chief dangers to fertility in reconstructive surgery lie in damage to the ejaculatory tract. The authors conclude that there is need for greater emphasis on sexual function following surgery.

Herman, M. Role of somesthetic stimuli in the development of sexual excitation in man. *American Medical Association Archives of Neurology and Psychiatry*, 1950, *65*, 42–56.

In the normal male, sexual excitation can occur as a result of mental stimulation, endocrine stimulation, or somesthetic stimuli. The purpose of this study was to evaluate the role of somesthetic disturbance in sexual function. The subjects were 19 men, 12 with complete transections, 7 with partial. Their ages ranged from 19 to 42, the average age being in the late 20s. These patients were chosen because their somesthetic brain tracts had been transected, but their endocrine and mental systems were intact. The study was conducted by obtaining case studies, four of which are presented in detail. It is from these four cases that conclusions in this paper are stated. Of these four men, none had sexual excitation, which led the author to conclude there was some defect in the interrelation of the three factors of mental, endocrine, and somesthetic stimuli.

Huffman, J. W. Sex and endometriosis. *Medical Aspects of Human Sexuality*, 1971, *5*(9), 150–204.

Women with pelvic endometriosis are likely to report a change in sexual behavior because acquired dyspareunia is a common symptom of endometriosis. This and other sexual aspects of endometriosis are discussed and suggestions for treatment are given. Several case histories are presented for illustration.

Johnson, S. A. M. Sexual problems associated with dermatologic conditions. *Medical Aspects of Human Sexuality*, 1976, *10*(9), 157–158.

Sexual problems are often associated with nonvenereal dermatological conditions such as hirsutism, unsightly skin, baldness, and atrophic changes of the genitourinary tract. The effects of these and other conditions on sexual functioning and behavior are discussed and a brief guide to office counseling by physicians is provided.

Kass, I., Updegraff, K., and Muffly, R. B. Sex in chronic obstructive pulmonary disease. *Medical Aspects of Human Sexuality*, 1972, *6*(2), 33–42.

Sexual aspects of chronic obstructive pulmonary disease are discussed in light of numerous case histories. The authors, based on their clinical experience, assert that "even with quite advanced disease, many male patients are capable of continuing an active and gratifying sexual relationship."

Luparello, T. J. Asthma and sex. *Medical Aspects of Human Sexuality*, 1970, *4*(3), 97–107.

Sexual conflicts may be among the emotional factors involved in asthma. In this article, the author discusses the interrelationship between asthma and sexuality. A case report of a patient is presented for illustration, and some suggestions for management are outlined.

Lyons, H. A. Sexual relations for male patients with chronic obstructive lung disease. *Medical Aspects of Human Sexuality*, 1977, *11*(4), 119–120.

Chronic obstructive lung disease hinders the patient's physical activity, including sexual activity. Oxygen consumption, cardiovascular function, and the respiratory work load during sexual intercourse are considerable. Oppressive dyspnea in patients with obstructive lung disease can prevent satisfactory sexual intercourse. This article presents a guide to sex counseling with these patients. It is suggested that the male patient should adopt a passive position during sexual intercourse.

Martin, M. J. Postcoital headaches. *Medical Aspects of Human Sexuality*, 1976, *10*(8), 101–102.

The relationship between headaches and sexual activity and behavior is discussed. Specific types of headaches identified are muscle-contraction, vascular, hypertensive, and angina pectoris.

Mason, I. A. A study of headaches and vertigo and their correlations to the derangement of the sexual function. *Ohio State Medical Journal*, 1945, *41*, 131–136.

A review of the literature shows little correlation between headaches and vertigo and derangement of sexual function. The article reports the results of a study aimed at the examination of these variables. Premature ejaculation was the most common sexual dysfunction.

May, A. G., DeWeese, J. A., and Rob, C. G. Sexual function in men after abdominal aortic surgery. *Medical Aspects of Human Sexuality*, 1971, *5*(4), 181–195.

Results of a study examining sexual functioning in patients (n=44) following abdominal aortic surgery are discussed and a case study is presented. Ninety-two percent of aneurysm patients, and 51 percent of those with aortoiliac occlusive disease, were sexually potent prior to surgery. In these patients, aneurysmectomy and reconstruction for aortoiliac occlusive disease resulted in impairment of erection in 21 percent and 34 percent respectively. Other results and some suggestions for treatment are presented.

Melman, A. Experience with implantation of the Small-Carrion penile implant for organic impotence. *Journal of Urology*, 1976, *116*, 49–59.

This article describes the author's experience with various techniques of implantation of penile prostheses in 13 patients who were impotent due to organic reasons. Eight of the patients had diabetes mellitus.

Money, J. Cytogenetic and psychosexual incongruities with a note on space-form blindness. *American Journal of Psychiatry*, 1963, *119*(9), 820–827.

The author discusses his observations and examination of 21 patients with the XXY syndrome (Klinefelter's syndrome). Patients were found to be low-powered in sexual drive and frequency of erections and orgasms. Other aspects of genitopelvic eroticism, sexual activity, and psychosexual development in these patients are discussed.

Mourad, M., and Chiu, V. S. Marital-sexual adjustment of amputees. *Medical Aspects of Human Sexuality*. 1974, *8*(2), 47–51.

This article discusses the results of a study conducted with 12,000 amputees. The results showed that 58 percent of the amputations were due to disease (usually diabetes mellitus and/or arteriosclerosis) and 32 percent of the amputations were from traumatic injuries. The rest of the amputations were related to congenital conditions. The authors present five cases to illustrate conflicts regarding sexual adjustment. It is noted that amputees who have lost a limb due to trauma are initially desperate and depressed. Once the patient has been rehabilitated and discharged there may be some sexual dysfunction, which usually subsides within a month. Persons who require an amputation because of disease processes are usually 50 years of age and older. The psychological shock experienced by this group of patients is most profound. Comfort and reassurance from the rehabilitation team can facilitate the patient's coping with his amputation. Persons who have had amputations as children adjust relatively well. If, as adults, there is any sexual dysfunction, it is not significantly different from sexual dysfunction in the general population. The importance of sexual counseling for amputees is stressed.

Novicki, D. E. Ejaculatory pain: Diagnosis and management. *Medical Aspects of Human Sexuality*, 1977, *11*(7), 97–98.

This brief article provides a review of the physiology of ejaculation, followed by a discussion of causes and clinical approaches to patients with painful ejaculation. The author concludes that "to correctly diagnose and treat a patient complaining of ejaculatory pain, the physician must carefully determine the cause, utilizing a thorough history, physical examination, and laboratory testing."

Oliver, H. Sexual counseling following disfiguring surgery. *Medical Aspects of Human Sexuality*, 1977, *11*(10), 55–56.

The need for sex counseling with women following disfiguring surgery of the face or the breast is discussed. Some suggestions for counseling of this nature are offered. Joint counseling, including the patient and her spouse, is recommended.

Paulson, G. W. Headaches associated with orgasm. *Medical Aspects of Human Sexuality*, 1975, *9*(5), 7–16.

Sexual headaches, especially those associated with orgasm, are usually benign and have many etiologies. The author discusses this medical phenomenon and asserts that "for some people sexual headaches are intense, severe, and incapacitating, occurring abruptly in an otherwise enthusiastic sexual participant." Although these headaches are often occipital, they can be bitemporal, and are usually nonthrobbing. They are not relieved by routine analgesics. The role of the physician, and some medical procedures to be taken with these patients, are further discussed.

Retief, P. J. M. Physiology of micturition and ejaculation. *South African Medical Journal*, 1950, *24*, 509.

The author reports that seven of eleven male patients who underwent lumbar sympathectomy experienced retrograde ejaculation. In retrograde ejaculation, an orgasm occurs and the semen reaches the prostatic urethra, but it then passes into the bladder rather than to the outside. This condition results from failure of the vesical neck to close during orgasm.

Rose, S. S. An investigation into sterility after lumbar ganglionectomy. *British Medical Journal*, 1953, *1*, 247.

The author reports that 4 of 38 patients who underwent lumbar sympathectomy developed retrograde ejaculation complications. In retrograde ejaculation, an orgasm occurs and the semen reaches the prostatic urethra, but it then passes into the bladder rather than to the outside. This condition results from failure of the vesical neck to close during orgasm. Inasmuch as closure of the vesical neck is under control of the sympathetic nervous system, the development of retrograde ejaculation after removal of the lumbar sympathetic ganglia is understandable.

Scheig, R. Changes in sexual performance due to liver disease. *Medical Aspects of Human Sexuality,* 1975, *9*(4), 67–79.

According to the author, most patients with chronic liver disease suffer from problems in sexual functioning. This paper discusses the common physical characteristics and sexual dysfunctions associated with liver disease. Three case histories of patients are presented for illustration.

Scheig, R. Sexual sequelae of liver disease. *Medical Aspects of Human Sexuality*, 1969, *3*(10), 137–145.

The author discusses various sexual implications of liver disease. Although endocrine changes resulting from a chronic liver disease are not completely discovered and understood, there are many clinical features that suggest disturbed endocrine function associated with this disease. These include changes in sexual functioning and behavior, e.g., loss of libido, impotence. Other changes in male patients may include oligospermia, female distribution of pubic hair, and testicular atrophy. In female patients, dysmenorrhea, cystic mastitis, acne, and sterility may be found.

Sohval, A. R. Klinefelter's syndrome. *Medical Aspects of Human Sexuality*, 1969, *3*(8), 69–86.

Clinicopathological, psychosocial, and sexual aspects of Klinefelter's syndrome are discussed. An illustrative case study is presented.

Stahlgren, L. H., and Ferguson, L. K. Influence on sexual function of abdominoperineal resection of ulcerative colitis. *New England Journal of Medicine*, 1958, *259*(18), 873–875.

Changes in sexual functioning in patients undergoing abdominoperineal resection for ulcerative colitis were examined. Of the 25 male patients studied, 18 reported that there has been no alteration in sexual function, while only 5 patients indicated some impairment. In none of the patients has there been a complete loss of the physical ability of sexual functioning. Of the 26 female patients followed up, 23 reported no change, 1 claimed improvement, and 2 have noted some difficulties.

Stewart, B. L. Inflammatory causes of impotence. *Medical Aspects of Human Sexuality*, 1973, *7*(6), 158–170.

The purpose of this article is to demonstrate some of the complexities of treating impotence associated with inflammatory disease. Several case histories are presented to illustrate that "inflammation of the genital tract per se is rarely the primary cause of impotence." Specific inflammations discussed include urethritis, stricture, prostatitis, seminal vesiculitis, verumontanitis, and other conditions.

Straus, S., and Dudley, D. L. Sexual activity for asthmatics: A psychiatric perspective. *Medical Aspects of Human Sexuality*, 1976, *10*(11), 63–64.

Sexual activity puts increased demands on the person's respiratory system. It may be too exhausting to accomplish sexual responsivity and orgasm during even a mild asthmatic episode. The purpose of this brief guide to office counseling is to discuss sexual difficulties associated with asthma and to present some therapeutic and counseling techniques and suggestions to alleviate these difficulties.

Tauber, E. S. Effects of castration upon sexuality of adult males. *Psychosomatic Medicine*, 1940, *2*, 76–87.

The effects of castration upon sexual libido and functioning is the theme of this article. Castration can be a result of various things, such as religion, physical trauma, or medical condition. The information on traumatic injuries has been so superficial that it is of little value. The author presents two case histories of men castrated for medical reasons. The attitudes of the castrated patient, and some psychosocial problems and implications, are discussed at length, and conflicts that influence sexual functioning are outlined. Results of some studies in this area are also presented.

Tyler, E. A. Disfigurement and sexual behavior. *Medical Aspects of Human Sexuality*, 1975, *9*(7), 77–78.

Disfigurement can be perceived as a handicap to the person's ability to attract a sexual partner. In this guide to office counseling, the author discusses the psychosexual and social aspects of disfigurement, and outlines some treatment and counseling ideas, e.g., correcting the physical disability, improving the patient's overall health, and increasing the patient's self-esteem. The physician's role is to provide needed sex education and counseling to the patient.

Van Thiel, D. H. Liver disease and sexual functioning. *Medical Aspects of Human Sexuality*, 1976, *10*(3), 117–118.

Based on his clinical experience, the author asserts that questions about sexual functioning in patients with liver disease range from concerns about transmitting the disease to concerns about adequacy and performance. This brief guide to office counseling outlines and discusses some of the sexual problems associated with liver disease, and presents suggestions for treatment and counseling.

Weiss, A. J., and Diamond, M.D. Sexual adjustment, identification and attitudes of patients with myelopathy. *Archives of Physical Medicine and Rehabilitation*, 1966, *47*, 245–250.

The purpose of this study was to gain information regarding sexual adjustment, identification, and general sexual attitudes of patients with myelopathy of various forms. The sample consisted of 50 men and 40 women, all suffering from illness-induced myelopathy, the majority of whom were paraplegics. Ages ranged from 22 to 65. Subjects were given the Wechsler Work Interest Inventory, the Sexual Adjustment Schedule, and the Weiss Sex Role Associated Noun Test. Results were used to draw conclusions about sexuality and myelopathy. Results revealed that the subjects had continued sexual activity, despite their disability. Men exhibited significantly more sex role function and identity impairment as a result of the disability than did women. There was a "convergence effect" noticed involving the psychosocial, sexual personalities of both men and women in the postdisability period, as contrasted with the predisability period.

Whitelow, G. P., and Smithwick, R. H. Some secondary effects of sympathectomy with particular reference to disturbance of sexual function. *New England Journal of Medicine*, 1951, *245*(4), 121–130.

This study is an effort to obtain knowledge regarding the effect of sympathectomy upon sexual function, i.e., potency, erection, sterility, and ejaculation. Subjects were 183 patients, aged 20 to 69, who had sympathectomies of various types, at various times. Results show that 42.8 percent of the patients reported decrease of sexual functioning, 27 percent experienced disturbance of erection, 19.8 percent reported permanent loss of ejaculation, and 7.6 percent had temporary loss of ejaculation. Only 7 percent reported an increase in sexual ability. Other findings and conclusions are discussed.

Chapter Eight

Substance Abuse

Alcoholism / Drug Addiction

Alcoholism

Al-Anon Family Group. *The dilemma of the alcoholic marriage.* New York: Al-Anon Family Group Headquarters, Inc., 1971.

This book was written by members of the Al-Anon Family Group for the purpose of helping alcoholic persons and their spouses overcome marital problems associated with alcoholism. Spouses of compulsive drinkers find it difficult to adjust to the personal characteristics, attitudes, and behavior of the alcoholic. This book presents a step-by-step program designed to alleviate marital difficulties. Of special interest is a chapter discussing sexual problems in the alcoholic marriage and some suggestions for improvement.

Belfer, M. L., Shader, R. I., Carroll, M., and Harmatz, J. S. Alcoholism in women. *Archives of General Psychiatry*, 1971, *25*, 540–544.

Premenstrual function, depression, anxiety, femininity, and other psychopersonality variables were evaluated in 34 alcoholic women, and in 10 nonalcoholic women who accompanied their alcoholic husbands to an alcoholic treatment clinic. Results showed that 67 percent of menstruating women and 46 percent of nonmenstruating women in the alcoholic sample related drinking to their menstrual cycles. These women indicated that their drinking began or increased in the premenstruum. Results relating to other aspects of alcoholism in women, and the relation between alcoholism and sexuality, are further discussed.

Carver, A. E. The interrelationship of sex and alcohol. *International Journal of Sexology*, 1948, *2*, 78–81.

The author discusses the interrelationships between sexuality and alcoholism. The role of alcoholism in homosexuality is also examined.

Ewing, J. A. Alcohol, sex, and marriage. *Medical Aspects of Human Sexuality*, 1968, *2*(6), 43–50.

The effect of alcohol abuse on sexual functioning and marriage is discussed, and suggestions for treatment and counseling are given. The unilateral treatment of the nonalcoholic spouse is also discussed.

Ewing, J. A. How to help the alcoholic marriage. In D. W. Abse, E. M. Nash, and L. M. R. Louden (Eds.), *Marital and sexual counseling in medical practice* (2nd ed.). New York: Harper and Row, 1974.

In this chapter the author discusses marital conflicts and difficulties associated with alcoholism in light of alcoholic personality attributes and marriage dynamics. Various stages in counseling the alcoholic and his or her spouse are presented, along with a detailed outline for an adequate diagnosis. Diagnostic work includes items such as personal health, family health problems, interpersonal difficulties, work difficulties, and other aspects of the patient's evaluation. Psychotherapeutic principles in the treatment and counseling of marriage problems connected with alcoholism are further developed and discussed.

Ewing, J. A., Fox, R., Carstair, G. M., and Beauburn, M. H. Alcohol, drugs, and sex. *Medical Aspects of Human Sexuality*, 1970, *4*(2), 18–34.

In this round table, moderated by Dr. Ewing, the authors answer questions relating to the impact of various drugs and alcohol on sexual functioning and behavior and on marriage.

Gallant, D. M. The effect of alcohol and drug abuse on sexual behavior. *Medical Aspects of Human Sexuality*, 1968, *2*(1), 30–36.

The use of drugs and alcohol as aphrodisiacs in primitive and advanced societies, and the effects of these substances on human sexual functioning and behavior, are discussed in this article. The author suggests that most alleged aphrodisiacs are likely to produce the opposite effect.

Lemere, F. Alcohol-induced sexual impotence. *American Journal of Psychiatry*, 1973, *130*(2), 212–213.

Sexual impotence is a serious complication of prolonged alcohol abuse and may persist even after years of sobriety. The author believes that "this problem is neither a psychological nor a hormonal defect but is due to the destructive effect of alcohol on the neurogenic reflex arc that serves the process of erection." Based on many years of clinical experience in working with alcoholic patients, the author asserts that the damage in the erection process may be irreversible, and this may account for the inability of some alcoholics to reattain sexual potency.

Lemere, F. Sexual impairment in recovered alcoholics. *Medical Aspects of Human Sexuality*, 1976, *10*(10), 69–70.

This brief guide to office counseling concentrates on a discussion of the effect of alcohol abuse on sexual functioning in recovered alcoholics. There is evidence to show that recovered alcoholics continue to suffer from sexual impotence even after achieving sobriety. The causes of sexual dysfunctions in alcoholics, and treatment and counseling modalities, are identified and discussed.

Levine, J. The sexual adjustment of alcoholics: A clinical study of a selected sample. *Quarterly Journal of Studies on Alcohol*, 1955, *16*, 675.

This study was designed to examine the sexual behavior and attitudes of alcoholics. The author assumed that the prolonged excessive consumption of alcohol is associated with disturbances in heterosexual relations and adjustment. Sixty-three male and sixteen female alcoholic patients were the subjects of this investigation. Results showed that the majority of these patients showed a diminished interest in heterosexual relationships. A large proportion of the male subjects were raised in homes with an overpowering and controlling mother, upon whom they were very dependent. The fathers in these cases, toward whom the patients felt hostile, were described as passive distant.

Machover, S., Puzzo, F. S., Machover, K., and Plumeau, F. Clinical and objective studies of personality variables in alcoholism. III. An objective study of homosexuality in alcoholism. *Quarterly Journal of Studies on Alcohol*, 1959, *20*, 528–542.

This study tested two hypotheses: (1) that homosexual trends are more prevalent among male alcoholics than among nonalcoholic nonhomosexual control subjects, and (2) that homosexual trends are more in evidence among remitted than among unremitted alcoholics. The subjects were divided into two study groups, a group of 23 alcoholics in remission and a group of 23 alcoholics still drinking. The Rorschach-Content Male Homosexuality Scale and the MMPI were used as study measurement instruments. Results showed that the first hypothesis was not confirmed, and the second hypothesis was confirmed in that the group of alcoholics in remission had higher homosexuality scores on all tests used.

Paredes, A. Marital-sexual factors in alcoholism. *Medical Aspects of Human Sexuality*, 1973, *7*(4), 98–115.

In middle-aged men, impotence is most common in males who use alcohol excessively. However, alcohol may act as a facilitator in releasing the inhibitions of younger persons. In this article, the author discusses the impact of alcoholism on sexual functioning and marital relationships. Studies show that there is a high incidence of sexual dysfunction among alcoholics. Frigidity is commonly reported as a problem for women married to alcoholics. A general lack of interest in sex seems typical among alcoholics. Verbal-emotional sharing and sensitivity and the subtleties involved in foreplay are not present when the alcoholic husband has sex with his wife. Sexual gratification may become subordinated to the use of alcohol in the husband, whereas the wife may seek alternate means to satisfaction. The extent of responsibility that the wife shares in the alcoholic condition is discussed by the author. There is evidence to suggest that wives of many alcoholics are more likely to be women who had both an inadequate mother and an unhappy childhood. Some suggestions for therapy and counseling are presented.

Rada, R. Alcohol and rape. *Medical Aspects of Human Sexuality*, 1975, *9*(3), 48.

The relationship between alcohol abuse and sexual crimes, particularly rape, is the main focus of this paper. Studies are reviewed to show that there is evidence to suggest a high association between alcohol, alcoholism, and the commission of sexually aggressive behavior and crime. Several theories attempting to explain this association, and some therapeutic programs, are also presented and discussed.

Renshaw, D. C. Sexual problems of alcoholics. *Chicago Medicine*, 1975, *78*(10), 433–436.

The author reviews the literature regarding the impact of alcoholism on women's sexual interest and functioning and concludes that there is agreement "that the women alcoholics described have many sexual problems, often deeply rooted in a general dissatisfaction with life." She also presents several possible factors associated with sexual dysfunctions in alcoholics. These are: (1) the central cerebral depressant effect of alcohol; (2) the toxic chemical inhibitory effect on autonomic nerves associated with sexual functioning; (3) peripheral neuropathy;

(4) vascular factors; (5) endocrinological disturbances; and (6) physical concomitants, such as liver damage and diabetes mellitus, which have a higher incidence in alcoholics. The author concludes that "there are many unanswered questions and much yet to be studied in the field of alcoholic sexual dysfunctions."

Schuckit, M. A. Sexual disturbance in the woman alcoholic. *Medical Aspects of Human Sexuality*, 1972, *6*(9), 44–65.

In this paper the author discusses sexual functioning and disturbance in alcoholic women in light of research and clinical findings. The author concludes that contrary to common opinion, promiscuity is appropriate to only 5 percent of all women drinkers. Most of the remaining 95 percent seem to have a diminished interest in heterosexual activity. The average alcoholic woman has many sexual problems and difficulties. The author suggests that "sexual misbehavior in an alcoholic woman should raise the suspicion that sociopathic alcoholism, with its greater resistance to therapy, may be present." Therapy should be aimed at both the alcoholic woman and her husband and should evidence an awareness of the deep-seated and troublesome sexual problems usually encountered in the alcoholic woman's life.

Selling, L. S. Role of alcoholism in the commission of sex offenses. *Medical Record*, 1940, *151*, 289–291.

The relationships between alcoholism and the commission of sex offenses are examined and discussed.

Smith, J. W., Lemere, F., and Dunn, R. B. Impotence in alcoholism. *Northwest Medicine*, 1972, *71*, 523–524.

While the excessive use of alcohol has been recognized as a major contributing factor to impotence, it has not been recognized that some percentage of alcoholics become sexually impotent when alcohol consumption is discontinued. The authors present statistics from their long clinical experience to show that 8 percent of their male alcoholic patients experienced impotence once they were completely detoxified. Of this group, 50 percent "gradually returned to their previous level of competence." Of the remainder, 25 percent remained relatively impotent, and 25 percent were totally impotent. Possible psychological and physiological explanations of this phenomenon, and some suggestions for the treatment of impotence in these cases, are presented and discussed briefly.

Straus, R. Excessive drinking and its relationship to marriage. *Marriage and Family Living*, 1950, *12*, 79–82.

A three point thesis regarding excessive drinking and marriage is considered and comprehensively discussed. These points are: (1) the same characteristics which make the individual prone to excessive drinking also tend to preclude marriage; (2) married life and excessive drinking are incompatible; and (3) the destruction or disruption of the marital association frequently results in the onset of excessive drinking. Data dealing with marital status and excessive drinking are presented and examined against this three-point thesis.

Van Thiel, D. H. Testicular atrophy and other endocrine changes in alcoholic men. *Medical Aspects of Human Sexuality*, 1976, *10*(6), 153–154.

Sexual dysfunctions and endocrine abnormalities associated with alcohol abuse are presented and discussed in this brief guide to office counseling for practicing physicians. Gonadal abnormalities found linked to alcoholism include infertility, sterility, gonadal atrophy, hypoandrogenization, and feminization. Some suggestions for counseling are presented.

Van Thiel, D. H., and Lester, R. Sex and alcohol. *New England Journal of Medicine*, 1974, *291*, 251–253.

This article deals with the long-range effects of large quantities of alcohol over long periods of time on sexual function. The authors suggest that in view of the frequency of disturbances of sexual function in chronic alcoholics, alcoholism is almost certainly the most common cause of impotence and sterility in the United States. The authors also point out that sexual inadequacy further disturbs the already alcoholic person, and may exacerbate the need for alcohol, creating a vicious circle. Laboratory tests show that alcohol ingestion, particularly in great quantities, has direct and indirect metabolic effects. Initially there is diminished testosterone synthesis and diminished spermatogenesis as a consequence of metabolic alterations. Ultimately, hepatic and testicular tissue damage occurs, which is irreversible.

Viamontes, J. A. Alcohol abuse and sexual dysfunction. *Medical Aspects of Human Sexuality*, 1974, *8*(11), 185–186.

Marital and sexual difficulties associated with alcohol abuse are discussed in this brief communication. According to the author, alcoholism can be directly linked to a variety of sexual dysfunctions. The most common dysfunction is impotence in male alcoholics. Some specific suggestions for office counseling are presented.

Virkunon, M. Incest offenses and alcoholism. *Medical Science Law*, 1974, *14*, 124–128.

The relationship between alcoholism and incest behavior and offense is the topic of this paper.

Wood, H. P., and Duffy, E. L. Psychological factors in alcoholic women. *American Journal of Psychiatry*, 1966, *123*(3), 341–345.

Marital and sexual difficulties and adjustment were two of various other psychosocial variables examined in this study of 69 alcoholic women. Results and conclusions are presented and discussed.

Drug Addiction

Bell, D. S., and Trethowan, W. H. Amphetamine addiction and disturbed sexuality. *Archives of General Psychiatry*, 1961, *4*, 74–78.

The effect of amphetamine addiction on sexual functioning and activity is discussed in this article. Based on the examination of 14 cases, it was found that the effect bears a close relationship to the preaddiction sexual adjustment of the individual. Results of this examination, and some conclusions, are presented in detail.

Carter, C. S., and Davis, J. M. Effects of drugs on sexual arousal and performance. In J. K. Meyer (Ed.), *Clinical management of sexual disorders*. Baltimore: Williams and Wilkins, 1976.

This chapter reviews the effects of various drugs on sexual activities and functioning. The focus is on three drug-induced alterations of sexual functioning: (1) changes in sexual desire or in subjective pleasure obtained; (2) changes in sexual potency, with or without alterations in sexual desire; and (3) failure to ejaculate, with otherwise apparently normal subjective responses. The authors relied on two sources of information in compiling this review. These were case studies regarding side-effects of various medical drugs, and accounts of persons involved in the use of illicit drugs or purported aphrodisiacs. In conclusion, the authors state that increased sexual behavior was found to be related to moderate doses of drugs that are central nervous system stimulants. Decreased sexual desire seems to be associated with the use of depressants. The physician "should be particularly sensitive to the potential ability of a variety of medications to disrupt potency."

Cicero, T. J. Function of male sex organs in heroin and methadone users. *New England Journal of Medicine*, 1975, *292*, 882–886.

The purpose of this study was to examine the overall functioning of secondary sex organs in heroin users, in methadone maintenance patients, and in a control group of subjects who were not using any drug. Results show that heroin users were experiencing delayed ejaculation and impotence, and that both heroin users and methadone maintenance patients were occasionally experiencing failure to ejaculate. The methadone patients also complained about painful ejaculation. All subjects reported substantially fewer orgasms when on drugs. Other results show that the functioning of secondary sex organs is markedly disturbed in methadone maintenance clients as compared to heroin users or drug-free controls. In addition, sperm motility was markedly reduced in the methadone maintenance group, and sperm count was two times that of the control group, reflecting a lack of sperm dilution by secondary sex organ secretion.

Cushman, P. Sexual behavior in heroin addiction and methadone maintenance. *New York State Journal of Medicine*, 1972, *72*, 1261–1265.

Disturbances in sexual drive and functioning in heroin addicts were examined by interviewing four groups: controls, active heroin addicts, abstinent former addicts, and methadone-maintained former addicts. Results show a high incidence of sexual dysfunctions accompanying heroin use in the currently addicted and formerly addicted group of subjects. Dysfunctions were related to difficulties in erection and ejaculation and to decreased sexual libido. All subjects described normal sexuality before addiction. At the time of the study, all abstinent subjects indicated they were functioning adequately, and most methadone-maintained subjects reported improved or normal sexual performance and libido. The author concludes that "the sedative or euphoric effects of heroin itself may play a contributory role in what may be primarily a psychologic disturbance."

Dahlberg, C. C. Sexual behavior in the drug culture. *Medical Aspects of Human Sexuality*, 1971, *5*(4), 64–74.

The effects of various drugs on sexual functioning and behavior are discussed in this article. Specific substances discussed are marijuana, LSD, amphetamines, and heroin. The author concludes that "the acting out of sexual problems in the drug culture often leads to greater problems which require professional help."

De Leon, G., and Wexler, H. K. Heroin addiction: Its relation to sexual behavior and sexual experience. *Journal of Abnormal Psychology*, 1973, *81*(1), 36–38.

The aim of this investigation was to study the relationships between sexual behavior, sexual experience, and heroin addiction. Thirty-one male drug-free heroin addicts were questioned about several sexual variables, e.g., frequency of sexual intercourse, quality of orgasm. Results show that during addiction, "sexuality" was suppressed in that most subjects reported decreased frequencies of sexual activities. The proportion of orgasms achieved, ratings of sexual desire, and the quality of orgasm were also decreased. In the postaddiction period, sexuality recovered and resembled or was higher than that reported for preaddiction periods. Based on their results, the authors conclude that "a relationship between changes in sexuality and heroin addiction appears firmly established." A reinforcement hypothesis is discussed.

Densen-Gerber, J., Wiener, M., and Hochstedler, R. Sexual behavior, abortion, and birth control in heroin addicts: Legal and psychiatric considerations. *Contemporary Drug Problems*, 1972, *1*, 783–793.

Female residents of a drug-free therapeutic setting (n=57) were studied as to the nature of their past sexual activity, the use of birth control methods, and the incidence of abortion. Results show a high incidence of promiscuity and prostitution. The average age at first sexual intercourse was 14.5 years. Histories of five sexual contacts per day for a period of years were not uncommon. Other results relating to the availability of birth control information and to pregnancies and abortions are presented and discussed, along with some specific conclusions and recommendations.

Ellinwood, E. H., and Rockwell, W. J. K. Effect of drug use on sexual behavior. *Medical Aspects of Human Sexuality*, 1975, *9*(3), 10–23.

This discussion focuses on the effects of various drugs on sexual functioning and behavior. According to the authors, "chronic dependency on sedative and narcotic drugs is associated with decreased sexual desire and potency."

Espejo, R., Hogben, G., and Stimmel, B. Sexual performance of men on methadone maintenance. Proceedings of the National Conference on Methadone Treatment, New York, 1973, 490–493.

Interference with sexual function is considered one of the most aggravating side-effects of methadone maintenance. This paper presents the results of a study examining sexual potency in 266 men enrolled in a methadone maintenance treatment program.

Ewing, J. A. Students, sex, and marijuana. *Medical Aspects of Human Sexuality*, 1972, *6*(2), 101–117.

The relationship between marijuana use and sexual functioning and activity among students is discussed in light of the results of a research study and clinical interviews conducted by the author. The author concludes that marijuana is not a significant precipitant of sexual activity among youth.

Fort, J. Sex and drugs: The interaction of two disapproved behaviors. *Postgraduate Medicine*, 1975, *58*(1), 133–136.

According to the author, sex and drug problems often run concurrently. Recreational drug use generally affects sexual functioning adversely. This article examines the effects of various drugs on sexuality. This includes medicinal use of drugs as well as recreational drug consumption. The author concludes that both sex education and drug education "should begin in early childhood through parental example of naturalness about the body, concern and tolerance for others, and an ability to relate to others."

Freedman, A. M. Drugs and sexual behavior. *Medical Aspects of Human Sexuality*, 1967, *1*(3), 25–31.

The effects of opium-antagonist cyclazocine, marijuana, and the psychedelic drugs on sexual behavior and functioning are discussed. Five case histories of patients are presented for illustration.

Freedman, A. M. Drugs and sexual behavior. In A. M. Freedman, H. I. Kaplan, and B. J. Sadock (Eds.), *Comprehensive text-*

book of psychiatry (Vol. 2). Baltimore: Williams and Wilkins, 1975.

The diversity of the effects of various types of drugs on sexual function and behavior is identified. The specific sexual effects of alcohol, marijuana, LSD, amphetamines, heroin, psychotropic drugs, and other substances are discussed.

Freedman, A. M. Drugs and sexual behavior. In B. J. Sadock, H. I. Kaplan, and A. M. Freedman (Eds.), *The sexual experience*. Baltimore: Williams and Wilkins, 1976.

The author claims that "a person's current psychological status and his total personality makeup must be considered in evaluating the effects of drugs on his sexual behavior." Most drugs vary in their impact on sexual experience and behavior from person to person. The resulting effects of a certain drug on a person's sexuality depend on his expectations and needs and the current mythology surrounding the drug. The author discusses the effects of a wide variety of drugs on sexual function and behavior. These include marijuana, LSD and related drugs, amphetamines, heroin, cyclazocine, methaqualone, and psychotropic drugs. He concludes that most authorities agree that "the typical drug user has problems of socialization and little tolerance for frustration and is extremely immature sexually."

Gay, G. R., and Sheppard, C. W. Sex in the "drug culture." *Medical Aspects of Human Sexuality*, 1972, *6*(10), 28–47.

The purpose of the study reported in this article was to examine the relationships between marijuana and other commonly used drugs to human sexual function and behavior. Interviews were made with fifty persons, 18 to 30 years of age, who were selected randomly from patients seen at a heroin and drug detoxification clinic. The effects on sexuality of alcohol, marijuana, barbiturates, amphetamines, cocaine, heroin, LSD, and other substances were examined. Results and conclusions are presented and discussed.

Goode, E. Drug use and sexual activity on a college campus. *American Journal of Psychiatry*, 1972, *128*, 92–96.

This is a report on a questionnaire study aimed at examining drug and sexual activity on one college campus. Results reveal that drug users were significantly more likely to engage in sexual activity, to start it earlier in life, and to engage in it regularly and with a greater variety of partners.

Goode, E. Sex and marijuana. In L. Gross (Ed.), *Sexual behavior: Current issues.* New York: Spectrum Publications, 1974.

The effect of marijuana smoking on sexual responsivity, functioning, behavior, and morality is discussed in this chapter in light of contemporary research and clinical data. The author reports that results of his study show that marijuana renders sexual experience more pleasurable and exciting. The frequent users attributed significantly more sexual impact to the drug than the infrequent users did. Over half of the frequent users indicated that marijuana acted as an aphrodisiac, but less than a third of the infrequent users agreed.

Gossop, M. R., Stern, R., and Connell, P. H. Drug dependence and sexual dysfunction: A comparison of intravenous users of narcotics and oral users of amphetamines. *British Journal of Psychiatry*, 1974, *124*, 431–434.

Psychosexual histories were obtained from a group of 30 intravenous narcotics users and a group of 24 oral amphetamine users. Six items were selected for the assessment of sexual difficulties in subjects: (1) menstrual periods absent beyond three months; (2) lack of sexual desire; (3) difficulty in attaining orgasm; (4) lack of pleasure from sexual activity; (5) no sexual intercourse or masturbation; and (6) expressed disgust at the idea of sexual activity. Intravenous users of narcotics were found to have more sexual dysfunctions than oral users of amphetamines, and female subjects were found to be more dysfunctional than males. No correlation was found between the length of drug abuse and the severity of sexual disturbance. The authors discuss some implications of their study for diagnosis, education and public health, and treatment.

Greaves, G. Sexual disturbances among chronic amphetamine users. *Journal of Nervous and Mental Disease*, 1972, *155*(5), 363–365.

Sexual behavior and outlook were compared between a group of amphetamine users (n=25) and a matched sample of non-drug control subjects with similar personality disorders (n=25). Interviews covered the following areas of sexuality: (1) previous sexual intercourse activities; (2) sexual promiscuity; (3) attitude toward sexual activity; (4) satisfaction with sex; and (5) normative vs. non-normative sexual views. Results showed that the amphetamine users were more experienced sexually, more promiscuous, and held more negative views toward sex than the non-drug psychiatric group. In terms of overall sexual satisfaction, the amphetamine users tended to be less satisfied than the controls. Although these differences and others were found, data did not "clearly support the hypothesis that the use of drugs was either substitutive for sexual activity or contributory to sexual pathology."

Keeler, M. H. Drug abuse and marriage counseling. In D. W. Abse, E. M. Nash, and L. M. R. Louden (Eds.), *Marital and sexual counseling in medical practice* (2nd ed.). New York: Harper and Row, 1974.

The author outlines and discusses the special marital difficulties associated with drug abuse, and presents the unique problems faced by the marriage counselor who works with drug abusers.

Kolodny, R. C., Masters, W. H., Kolodner, R. M., and Toro, G. Depression of plasma testosterone levels after chronic intensive marihuana use. *New England Journal of Medicine*, 1974, *290*, 872–874.

The main purpose of this study was to examine the reproductive status of men using large amounts of marijuana. Subjects were twenty heterosexual men 18 to 28 years of age who used marijuana at least four days a week for a minimum of six months prior to this study. Subjects did not use any other drug during that time. Plasma testosterone was significantly lower in these subjects than in a control group. The authors report that with the exception of two subjects, sexual functioning was not impaired in the men studied. Impaired potency was noted in these two subjects. In one of these men, this problem reversed upon cessation of marijuana use.

Mathis, J. L. Sexual aspects of heroin addiction. *Medical Aspects of Human Sexuality*, 1970, *4*(9), 98–109.

The negative relationship of heroin to sexual behavior and functioning is discussed. Unlike alcohol, heroin "does not simply reduce inhibitions and allow the acting out of suppressed desire—it actually removes the desires." It appears that there is little or no time or energy for sexual activity in the life of the heroin addict.

Mintz, J., O'Hare, K., O'Brien, C. P., and Goldschmidt, J. Sexual problems of heroin addicts. *Archives of General Psychiatry*, 1974, *31*, 700–703.

The purpose of this study was to compare the occurrence of premature ejaculation, retarded ejaculation, and impotence of addicts when they are drug-free, when using heroin, when on high-dose (60 mg/day) methadone hydrochloride maintenance, when on low-dose (20-40 mg/day) methadone hydrochloride maintenance, and when on a detoxification program. Reports were obtained from 91 patients who were addicted to heroin at the time of application for out-patient treatment. Reports on the effects of methadone were obtained from 45 patients engaged in methadone treatment at the time of the survey; 15 patients were sampled from each of three methadone treatment groups. Results show that at the time the subjects were drug-free the sexual problems were premature ejaculation in 46 percent, retarded ejaculation in 20 percent, and impotence in 16 percent of the subjects. The results of the three methadone hydrochloride treatment groups were pooled as no significant differences were found. In the heroin use group, 43 percent were impotent, 62 percent suffered retarded ejaculation, and 35 percent had premature ejaculation. Methadone use was found to lessen premature and retarded ejaculation and to increase impotency. The authors believe there were too many uncontrolled variables to be certain of their results.

Rockwell, K., Ellinwood, E., Kantor, C., Maack, W., and Schrumpf, J. Drugs and sex: Scene of ambivalence. *Journal of the American College Health Association*, 1973, *21*, 483–488.

This article reports the results of a survey of undergraduate students regarding their sexual experiences and drug use. The most consistent finding was the similarity of attitudes and behavior that men and women share in the major areas surveyed in this study. In their conclusion, the authors assert that their study reaffirmed their "notion that sex and drugs are proper topics for programs of continuing education, reeducation, and sometimes even initial education."

Wieland, W., and Yunger, M. Sexual effects and side-effects of heroin and methadone. Proceedings of the Third National Conference on Methadone Treatment. Washington, D.C.: Public Health Service, U.S. Government Printing Office, No. 2171, 1971, pp. 50–53.

All 70 subjects of this study were former heroin addicts who were on a methadone program at the time of the study. The purpose of the study was to examine sexual effects of both heroin and methadone on the subjects. Results are presented and discussed.

Chapter Nine

Psychiatric and Mental Disorders

Psychiatric Illness / Mental Retardation and Learning Disabilities

Psychiatric Illness

Abernethy, V. D. Sexual knowledge, attitudes, and practice of young female psychiatric patients. *Archives of General Psychiatry,* 1974, *30*, 180–182.

Attitudinal, informational, and behavioral data relating to sexual behavior, fertility, and contraceptive and reproductive patterns were collected. Subjects were 60 women, age 13 to 28, who were either inpatient or day-hospital patients at two public psychiatric hospitals. Results show that women in the study sample had a tendency to engage in contraceptively unprotected sexual intercourse and on the average did not appear to welcome or maintain their pregnancies. Carrying the pregnancy through to a live birth did not contribute to the well-being of the offsprings.

The conclusion was that health-care and social service professionals need to develop family planning counseling programs specifically designed for mentally ill patients.

Abernethy, V. D., and Grunebaum, H. Family planning in two psychiatric hospitals: A preliminary report. *Family Planning Perspectives*, 1973, *5*, 94–99.

Problems involved in family planning and birth control services for sexually active mental patients are discussed and suggestions for improvement are made.

Abernethy, V. D., and Grunebaum, H. Toward a family planning program in psychiatric hospitals. *American Journal of Public Health*, 1972, *62*(12), 1638–1646.

The important role of family planning programs and birth control counseling in psychiatric hospitals is discussed in light of an extensive review of the literature.

Allison, J. B., and Wilson, W. P. Sexual behavior of manic patients: A preliminary report. *Southern Medical Journal*, July 1960, 870–874.

It has commonly been accepted that the manic patient is sexually aggressive. This study of a small sample of patients (n=24) reveals an increased libido and sexual provocativeness in a greater percentage of women than men. Other important factors in determining sexual behavior of patients are the patient's marital status, marital sexual adjustment, and premarital experience.

Apter, A., Tyano, S., Lombroso, D., and Wijsenbeek, H. Sex education in an in-patient adolescent psychiatric ward. Paper read at the Thirteenth World Congress of Rehabilitation International, Tel Aviv, Israel, June 13–18, 1976.

The Adolescent Unit at Geha Hospital is a coeducational ward for severely disturbed adolescents who require therapy in a closed setting. As part of the dynamic approach in the Unit, in-patients were given a series of talks on biological and medical aspects of sex, followed by a lecture-discussion on psychosocial aspects of sex behavior. A follow-up of the 31 patients who took part in the program indicated an increase in factual knowledge, with no significant change in body image and sexual attitudes. In continued individual and group psychotherapy, the subjective impression was that the program had had a beneficial effect, leading to increased frankness and a more open attitude toward sex, thus providing an added avenue of approach in treatment.

Arieti, S. Sexual conflict in psychotic disorders. In C. W. Wahl (Ed.), *Sexual problems: Diagnosis and treatment in medical practice*. New York: Free Press, 1967.

Arieti discusses psychosexual conflicts and their importance in the preschizophrenic and other psychotic patients. The author stresses that "the physician who comes into contact with these psychosexual conflicts must evaluate them in the context of the whole personality and recommend the proper treatment."

Barnett, J. Sex and the obsessive-compulsive person. *Medical Aspects of Human Sexuality*, 1971, *5*(2), 34–45.

Sexual behavior of the obsessive-compulsive person is explored and discussed. This person's sexual life and difficulties "mirror his general personality problems and his problems in relating to people."

Beck, A. T. Sexuality and depression. *Medical Aspects of Human Sexuality*, 1968, *2*(7), 44–51.

A reduction in sexual drive and activity is often a manifestation of depression. The interrelationship between sexuality and depression is discussed and some suggestions for treatment are presented.

Beilin, L. M. Genital self-mutilation by mental patients. *Journal of Urology*, 1953, *70*, 648.

Among the eleven cases of genital self-mutilation reported by the author, six involved amputation of the penis or testicles. In three instances the patients were schizophrenics.

Beilin, L. M. Sexual self-mutilation. *Sexology*, 1959, *25*.

The motives which make psychiatrically disturbed patients sometimes take the rare action of mutilating their sex organs are discussed in light of several case studies.

Beilin, L. M., and Gruneberg, J. Genital self-mutilations by mental patients. *Journal of Urology*, 1948, *59*, 635–641.

This is an attempt to interpret self-mutilations and injuries of the genital organs by mental patients. Five detailed case reports of psychiatric patients are presented and analyzed in light of sexological theory. The act of genital self-mutilation is viewed as a manifestation of either congenital or acquired masochism which may be the end result or a concomitant of various psychic degenerations. The authors conclude that "the practice of sexual self-mutilation constitutes merely one of the symptom-complexes of specific type of psychosis," or it may be one of the characteristics of persistence of infantile sexuality patterns. Some suggestions for the surgical and medical treatment of mutilating wounds of external genital organs are discussed.

Berne, E. The problem of masturbation. *Diseases of the Nervous System*, 1944, *5*, 301–305.

The physician can play a reassuring role in dealing with masturbation and in deciding which patients need detailed psychiatric study. If masturbation is frequently used by a patient as an escape from reality, accompanied by certain "unorthodox fantasies" (i.e., incestuous fantasies), or if certain "unorthodox methods" are used, further psychiatric investigation is needed. This paper presents the results of a survey conducted among 700 psychiatric patients regarding masturbation practices and habits. The percentage of patients reporting they have masturbated was found to be roughly the same as that reported in the general population. No significant differences were found in this survey in the prevalence of masturbation comparing psychotics and neurotics. Other aspects of the survey discussed include the role of guilt and fear in relation to masturbation, methods of masturbation, and the occurrence of nocturnal emissions.

Blacker, K. H., and Wong, N. Four cases of autocastration. *Archives of General Psychiatry*, 1963, *8*, 169–176.

Autocastration is a rare event, and it is most common in the disturbed schizophrenic patient. In this report, the authors present and discuss four case histories of severe genital self-mutilation in borderline or psychotic patients.

Brill, A. A. Sexual manifestations in neurotic and psychotic symptoms. *Psychiatric Quarterly*, 1940, *14*, 9–16.

This is a psychoanalytical account of sexual manifestations in neurotic and psychotic symptoms. The author shows that there is a close relationship between homosexuality and paranoia, insofar as both are narcissistic fixations. Some case histories are presented and discussed.

Brooks, P. A. Masturbation. *American Journal of Nursing*, 1967, *67*(4), 820–823.

The author discusses the nature and the developmental aspects of masturbation. Special attention is given to the needs that masturbation serves in psychiatric patients and the role of the nurse in discussing this issue with patients.

Calnen, T. Gender identity crises in young schizophrenic women. *Perspectives in Psychiatric Care*, 1975, *13*, 83–89.

The author presents and discusses case histories of four schizophrenic women between the ages of 19 and 30 years, illustrating their active desire to change their sex. The author also explores and clarifies the family dynamics that provide the context for and generate the symptoms of transsexual behavior in these patients.

Chapman, A. H., and Reese, D. G. Homosexual signs in Rorschachs of early schizophrenics. *Journal of Clinical Psychology*, 1953, *9*, 30–32.

The Rorschachs of six persons who were developing schizophrenic psychoses were examined at the earliest incipience of their psychoses. The purpose of this study was to examine the psychoanalytic assumption that homosexuality is associated with schizophrenia. As control, the Rorschachs of six persons who were found to be within normal limits on psychiatric diagnostic examination were randomly selected. Results revealed that the Rorschachs of the schizophrenic group showed markedly elevated scores for homosexual responses. The highest number of homosexual signs were found in the following categories: (a) castration and phallic symbols, (b) feminine identification, (c) derealization and mythical distortion, (d) confusion of sexual identification, (e) sexual and anatomical responses, and (f) esoteric and artistic responses. The authors conclude: "It is felt that this evidence tends to support the concept that in the process of a schizophrenic break, the patient passes through a period when homosexual drives are significant and prominent."

Chrzanowski, G. Sex behavior as a clue to mental disease. *Medical Aspects of Human Sexuality*, 1971, *5*(3), 200–209.

According to the author, certain forms of sexual behavior may serve as a clue to the existence of mental illness. He explores and discusses some of these behaviors, and illustrates their association with a mental disorder.

Cleveland, S. E. Three cases of self-castration. *Journal of Nervous and Mental Disease*, 1956, *123*, 386.

The author reports three cases of apparently deliberate and premeditated self-castration in the absence of any overt psychosis, although one of these patients had had a previous psychotic episode. The other two patients had both had previous psychiatric treatment.

Dansak, D. A. Sexual relations of the psychiatrically ill. *Medical Aspects of Human Sexuality*, 1977, *11*(3), 53–54.

The author asserts that we "cannot assume that all psychiatric illness causes sexual dysfunction or that all sexual disorders in the psychiatric patient are the result of the psychiatric condition." Apparently, sexual behaviors of the psychiatrically ill are as diverse as those of the general population. This article presents a guide to sex counseling with psychiatric patients. Some of the steps included in this guide are obtaining a thorough medical history and physical examination; obtaining a history of the emotional disorder; obtaining a baseline of the patient's pre-illness sexual activity; determining the effects of psychotropic medication on sexual behavior; and determining the quality and stability of the patient's relationship with his or her partner.

Dolon, P. T. Sexual symptoms of incipient schizophrenic psychoses. *Medical Aspects of Human Sexuality*, 1976, *10*(11), 69–70.

Sexual disturbances associated with schizophrenic psychoses are multifaceted and common. This brief guide to office counseling identifies and discusses some of the common sexual symptoms accompanying psychotic decompensation, and suggests diagnostic procedures and treatment and counseling guidelines.

Esman, A. H. A case of self-castration. *Journal of Nervous and Mental Disease*, 1954, *120*, 79.

The author describes a case of self-castration in a man, aged 44 years, who was in an acute alcoholic intoxicated state, and who subsequently had no recollection of the act. The author suggests that his patient, who often dressed as a woman when intoxicated, sought a primitive, infantile relationship with a mother figure.

Farley, G. K., and Goddard, L. Sex education for emotionally disturbed children with learning disorders. *Journal of Special Education*, 1970, *4*(4), 445–450.

The authors recognize the importance of children with emotional and learning disabilities having access to accurate sex information and education. In this paper, they report on their experiences in teaching a sex education course to a class of elementary school children with emotional disorders and learning disabilities. The rationale for including the course in the regular curriculum is presented, and some problems encountered in teaching sex education courses to this population are analyzed and discussed.

Freeman, W., and Watts, J. W. *Psychosurgery in the treatment of mental disorders and intractable pain.* Springfield, Illinois: Charles C. Thomas, 1950.

Of special interest is a chapter describing the authors' clinical observations on the relation of prefrontal lobotomy to sexual activity. Both increases and decreases in sexual activity were observed. The authors illustrate their findings with several case studies of postoperative patients who manifested sexual alterations.

Friedlander, J. W., and Panay, R. S. Psychosis following lobotomy in a case of sexual psychopathy. *Archives of Neurology and Psychiatry*, 1948, *59*(1), 302–321.

The authors report and discuss a case study of a sexual psychopath who underwent a lobotomy and became psychotic and then demented. Presented is a comparison of the symptoms and clinical signs exhibited before and after the lobotomy was performed. Before the operation the patient exhibited agitation, tension, apprehension, depression, obsession and compulsion, conscientiousness in work, timidity, anxiety, no hallucinations, and fairly good insight and judgment. In contrast, after the operation the patient exhibited confusion, mild euphoria, shallow affect, irresponsibility, childishness, desire for attention, memory loss, confabulation, suggestibility, circumstantiality, hallucination, no insight, and poor judgment. Also, his sexual behavior changed from overtly masochistic and homosexual to being preoccupied with the same sexual fantasies but exhibiting less overt activity after the lobotomy.

Gantt, W. H. Disturbances in sexual functions during periods of stress. *Proceedings of the Association for Research in Nervous and Mental Diseases*, 1950, *24*, 1030–1051.

This article presents the results of an extensive series of comparative laboratory experiments studying the effects of stress (i.e., neurosis, alcohol, conflicts) on sexual functioning in dogs and cats. The author suggests numerous conclusions based on his findings that can apply to human sexual functioning in periods of psychological stress.

Glueck, B. C., Jr. Early sexual experiences in schizophrenia. In H. G. Beigel (Ed.), *Advances in sex research.* New York: Harper & Row, 1963.

This article examines the question of "how much credence should be given to the evidence that unfolds in the course of treating many schizophrenic patients that suggests the occurrence of overt incestuous sexual activity, involving one or both parents." Observations on several patients are presented and discussed.

Goldfield, M. D., and Glick, I. D. Self-mutilation of the genitalia. *Medical Aspects of Human Sexuality*, 1973, 7(4), 219–236.

The act of genital self-mutilation is always related to severe emotional illness. This is a report and discussion of two case histories of patients who mutilated their genitalia. The first involves genital mutilation in a 22-year-old male, and the second is of a vaginal self-mutilation in a 19-year-old unwed mother.

Grunebaum, H. W., Abernathy, V. D., Rofman, E. S., and Weiss, J. L. The family planning attitudes, practice, and motivations of mental patients. *American Journal of Psychiatry*, 1971, *128*, 740–741.

The purpose of this study was to examine the family planning and sexual practice attitudes and motivations of a sample of female patients (n=21) in a mental institution. There were seven schizophrenics, ten women with neurotic or psychotic depression, and four women diagnosed as borderline. Seven patients reported being "usually" orgasmic in sexual intercourse; five, sometimes; and eight, rarely or never. These findings are comparable to the distribution for the general population of women. Seven patients indicated that sexual relations were very important to them, and another five patients stated that sex was moderately important. Frequency of sexual coitus ranged from once a month to once or twice a day. In general, orgasm was experienced several times a week. Other results relating to attitudes toward family planning, unwanted pregnancies, and motivations and effectiveness of family planning are discussed.

Hemphill, R. E. A case of genital self-mutilation. *British Journal of Medical Psychology,* 1951, *24*, 291.

The author presents a case study of a patient who amputated his penis and one testicle. The patient, aged 66 years, had suffered a number of depressive episodes. It seemed that he was going through a depressive phase at the time of the incident. In a review of relevant literature, the author suggests that most such patients about whom there is adequate psychiatric information appeared to have suffered from an atypical depression.

Hoskins, R. G. Psychosexuality in schizophrenia: Some endocrine considerations. *Psychosomatic Medicine*, 1943, *5*, 3–9.

Various characteristics of schizophrenic psychosis point to an immature level of psychosexual development and functioning. Through a review of the literature on comparative endocrinology and sexuality, this article studies the possibility of deficiency of sex hormones in schizophrenic patients. Numerous theoretical possibilities are raised that attempt to associate the immature psychosexual level in schizophrenia to an immediate abnormality in the amount, balance, or chemical nature of the sex hormones. Based on the literature reviewed, these possibilities cannot prove valid. However, "the possibility remains that abnormal responsivity to these hormones might account for the psychosis and that successful normalization of the responsivity might be an effective therapeutic procedure."

Hoskins, R. G., and Pincus, G. Sex-hormone relationships in schizophrenic men. *Psychosomatic Medicine*, 1949, *11*, 102–109.

Psychosexual development and sex-hormone relationships in schizophrenic patients are discussed in this article. Also reported are the results of a study aimed at the examination of urinary output of androgen, estrogen, and 17-ketosteroids in a group of 29 schizophrenic men.

Kalinowsky, L. B. Effects of somatic treatments on the sexual behavior of schizophrenics. In H. G. Beigel (Ed.), *Advances in sex research*, New York: Harper & Row, 1963.

This chapter examines the sexual behavior of schizophrenic patients following somatic treatment. One group of posttreatment effects consists of changes in potency occurring with convulsive therapy. Many patients are sexually impotent for several weeks following electroshock treatment. Other changes in sexual behavior and functioning are associated with various drugs and lobotomy.

Kiev, A. Depression and libido. *Medical Aspects of Human Sexuality*, 1969, *3*(11), 35–45.

The author suggests that reduced sexual libido and sexual incapacity may be symptoms of depression amenable to chemotherapy. The relationship between depression and sexuality is discussed, along with various treatment modalities, i.e. chemotherapy, psychotherapy.

Klaf, F. S., and Pisetsky, J. E. A son is rendered impotent by his father. *Psychiatric Quarterly*, 1962, *36*, 519–529.

The authors present and discuss a clinical case study of a 25-year-old man who was accidentally rendered paraplegic and sexually impotent by his father. The patient's reactions, and events in his life prior to his injury, are examined carefully in psychodynamic terms which highlight the patient's incestuous wish and his affair with a "mother surrogate," his castration anxiety, and the wish to be punished by his father.

Knoff, W. F. Loss of libido in depressed women. *Medical Aspects of Human Sexuality*, 1975, *9*(11), 119–120.

Loss of libido is one of the most common symptoms of depression. The physician should direct his attention to the underlying depression and treat it. This brief guide to office counseling presents and discusses some specific suggestions for treatment.

Kurland, M. L. Promiscuity in middle-aged men: A reaction to depression. *Medical Aspects of Human Sexuality*, 1977, *11*(11), 79–93.

The author discusses the relationship between depression and sexual promiscuity in middle-aged men. Three case studies are presented along with some suggestions for therapy. It was illustrated that rather than experiencing their problems as depression, the men projected them onto their sex lives and their marriages. The results of therapy with these men were initially poor, since they preferred their sexual acting-out activities to psychiatric treatment.

Lennon, S. Genital self-mutilation in acute mania. *Medical Journal of Australia*, 1963, *50*, 79–81.

The author describes three case histories of psychiatric patients who had mutilated their genitals. Of particular interest is the third case, which is the main subject of this article. Penis amputation in this patient apparently took place during the course of an acute manic episode.

Leviton, D. The significance of sexuality as a deterrent to suicide among the aged. *Omega*, 1973, *4*(2), 163–175.

The author presents his hypothesis regarding the relationship between sexuality and suicide among the aged. In this context, sexuality is not only the ability to enjoy affectionate relationships with others, but also includes seeing oneself as a physically attractive human being. When any aspect of sexuality is lost or diminished significantly, the probability of premature death and/or suicide increases. About one-fourth of recorded suicides per year are in the 65 and older age group. The typical case seems to be that of a male living alone without family ties. The author notes that because few people wish to touch or be touched by the older person, there is a form of deprivation developed that can affect the mental health. The author gives the following recommendations for the improvement of human relationships and sexual expression: (1) the aged need to know they are attractive and able to have affectionate relationships with others; (2) play and recreation are means for improving physical fitness and social interaction; (3) human relationships with all ages should be encouraged; (4) hospital and medical staff need to recognize the therapeutic aspects of a healthy, functioning sexuality; and (5) any medical work-up should include information on the sexual functioning of the patient.

Lukianowica, N. Sexual drive and its gratification in schizophrenia. *International Journal of Social Psychiatry*, 1963, *9*, 250–258.

Sexual drive and activity in 100 schizophrenic patients was studied and compared with a group of normal men and a group of patients suffering from depression. Results show that the schizophrenic subjects retain their sexual drive and its particular direction. They engage in autoerotic sexual activity two to three times as frequently as the males in the normal population. An increase of about 20 percent in the frequency of heterosexual intercourse occurred in the schizophrenic patients, compared to their sexual activity prior to the onset of the psychosis. In depressed patients, there was a very considerable decrease in heterosexual activity. Other findings are presented and discussed.

McNeil, E. B., and Morse, W. C. The institutional management of sex in emotionally disturbed children. *American Journal of Orthopsychiatry*, 1964, *34*, 115–124.

The authors noted that "while the institutional management of sex in emotionally disturbed children constitutes a difficult and delicate psychological problem, it receives surprisingly little systematic delineation in the professional literature." Drawing examples from their clinical experience with emotionally disturbed children, the authors present a series of general principles of adult responses to children's sexual behavior, such as generalized suppression of sexual behavior in the child, a dangerous, self-defeating response, or an objection to sexual acting out in order to "protect the innocent."

Martin, M. J. Impulsive sexual behavior masking insidious depression. *Medical Aspects of Human Sexuality*, 1976, *10*(3), 45–55.

Changes in sexual behavior in a patient should alert the physician to possible depression. The relationship between depression and alteration in sexual behavior is discussed in this article, and suggestions for treatment and counseling are given. Changes in sexual behavior may be impulsive, and may include promiscuity, hypersexuality, compulsive masturbation, homosexuality, and other types of behavior.

Mead, B. T. Depression and sex. In L. Gross (Ed.), *Sexual behavior: Current issues*. New York: Spectrum Publications, 1974.

Psychosocial and sexual manifestations of depression, and various treatment procedures, are described and discussed in this chapter. Impotence in the fifty- or sixty-year-old man is commonly related to his depression. Depression creates a lack of sexual interest and energy, which interferes with sexual functioning and enjoyment in both males and females. The author indicates that "although depression may interfere with sexual feelings, we can always use sexual activity to help prevent or overcome depression." An understanding partner who can express love through affection and sexual relations can help alleviate depression.

Mindek, L. Sex education on a psychiatric unit. *American Journal of Nursing*, 1974, *74*(10), 1865–1868.

Sex education is an important aspect of health care and needs to be an integral part of psychiatric services. The author describes in this report a comprehensive sex education program she developed and implemented for teenage girls in a psychiatric hospital. Short- and long-term goals of the program, as well as the educational process itself, are outlined and discussed. Evaluation of this sex education program revealed that it was a worthwhile experience for the patients.

Morrison, J., Clancy, J., Crowe, R., and Winokur, G. The Iowa 500 I: Diagnostic validity in mania, depression, and schizophrenia. *Archives of General Psychiatry*, 1972, *27*, 457.

This paper presents and discusses the findings of an examination of 100 manic patients who were selected from consecutive admission to a psychiatric hospital. Of these, 30 percent showed increased sexual drive, whereas only 15 percent manifested decreased sexual drive. These data support the general consensus among psychiatrists that manic patients tend to show increased sexual libido and activity.

Nell, R. Sex in a mental institution. *Journal of Sex Research*, 1968, *4*(4), 303–312.

The Country Place is a residential treatment center for patients often referred to as borderline schizophrenics. The majority of the twenty young adults which the center can accommodate are highly intelligent college dropouts who actively participate in policy making and the running of the place. This article discusses sexuality and various instances relating to sex among the residents of this milieu therapy center. The author reports a number of incidents showing that, as is often true outside this environment, the issues involved in male-female encounters are not sexual per se, but relate to human relationships. While the population is limited and somewhat isolated, so that relationships are formed between persons who might otherwise not be attracted to each other, the advantage is that no relationship is free from scrutiny by all others living there. No harmful relationships are continued without confrontation, which so often is not the case outside the therapeutic community. Therefore, even harmful situations can be used therapeutically for significant growth toward health and toward knowing oneself and others.

Norman, J. P. Evidence and clinical significance of homosexuality in 100 unanalyzed cases of dementia praecox. *Journal of Nervous and Mental Disease*, 1948, *107*, 484–489.

The major goal of this study was to examine the prevalence or incidence of homosexuality in schizophrenic patients (n=100) and to test the general validity of the causal psychodynamic connection between paranoid delusions and repressed homosexual drives. Strong conscious and unconscious homosexual tendencies were found in dementia praecox, paranoid patients. There was also evidence that the majority of the patients studied showed a strong Oedipus complex fixation. No proof was found to suggest that the homosexual tendencies in these patients were a primary etiologic factor in the schizophrenic process.

Paykel, E. S., and Weissman, M. M. Marital and sexual dysfunction in depressed women. *Medical Aspects of Human Sexuality*, 1972, *6*(6), 73–101.

In studies conducted by the authors, about 60 percent of depressed patients admitted to some limitation of sexual interest. Other sexual aspects of depression in women are discussed. The authors conclude that some impairment of marital and sexual role-functioning is almost universal in women who are clinically depressed.

Pinderhughes, C. A., Grace, E. B., and Reyna, L. J. Psychiatric disorders and sexual functioning. *American Journal of Psychiatry*, 1972, *128*(10), 1276–1283.

The responses of 18 psychiatrists and 122 psychiatric in-patients to a questionnaire showed that most psychiatrists and 20 to 50 percent of the patients believed that sexual functioning might contribute to psychiatric disorders, that most psychiatric disorders might interfere with sexual functioning, and that sexual activity might retard recovery.

Polatin, P., and Douglas, D. B. Spontaneous orgasm in a case of schizophrenia. *Psychoanalytic Review*, 1953, *40*, 17–26.

The author presents a detailed case study of a 25-year-old white single female diagnosed as schizophrenic who was experiencing recurring spontaneous orgasms. Also presented and discussed are various pertinent reports in the literature identifying spontaneous orgasm. The essential differences in the types of orgasm and their corollaries in psychotic and nonpsychotic states are presented, along with the possible significance of these differences.

Renshaw, D. C. Doxepin treatment of sexual dysfunctions associated with depression. In J. Mendels (Ed.), *Sinequan "Doxe-*

pin HCl": A monograph of recent clinical studies. Amsterdam: Excerpta Medica, 1975, 23–31.

The purpose of this study was to examine the effect of doxepin in the treatment of sexual dysfunctions in depressed patients. A mean dose of 122mg of doxepin was administered at bedtime during a four-week trial to nineteen patients diagnosed as psychoneurotic depressive with concomitant sexual dysfunctions. Results show significant improvement in diverse depressive symptoms, including the sexual dysfunctions. Nine patients experienced some side-effects, all of which disappeared or were tolerated well by the patients. The author concludes that, based on her findings, "it appears that treatment of the underlying depression with doxepin is sufficient to ameliorate concomitant sexual symptoms." A few case histories are also presented to illustrate the successful effect of doxepin therapy.

Renshaw, D. C. Sexuality and depression in adults and the elderly. *Medical Aspects of Human Sexuality*, 1975, *9*(9), 40–62.

Specific sexual dysfunctions related to depression have not been extensively studied, and clinical scrutiny and systematic research regarding sexual dysfunctions are relatively recent. The effective management of sexual dysfunction occurring in depressive disorders continues to pose a significant clinical challenge. While it has been long recognized that incomplete or impaired expression of sexual desire and response is symptomatic of depression, the specific sexual dysfunctions associated with depression have only recently been delineated. This article identifies and discusses various sexual dysfunctions and difficulties believed to be associated with depression. In adults and the elderly the clinical picture may include lowered libido, expressed as loss of desire; secondary impotence; amenorrhea; dyspareunia; situational orgasmic dysfunction; and, in some cases, compulsive masturbation or newly occurring promiscuity. Hypersexuality intermittent with lowered libido should raise suspicion of circular type manic-depressive illness. The depressive illness underlying sexual dysfunction frequently remains undetected.

Renshaw, D. C. Sexuality and depression in infancy, childhood, and adolescence. *Medical Aspects of Human Sexuality*, 1975, *9*(6), 24–25.

Sexual implications of depression in three developmental stages, infancy, childhood, and adolescence, are outlined and discussed. Case histories are presented to illustrate psychosexual difficulties and symptoms associated with depressive states in these stages. In the infant, depression may elicit little or complete lack of self-exploration, including the lack of genital exploration and masturbatory activities, or may elicit constant masturbation or rocking movement. In childhood, sexual problems may be manifested in little or no masturbatory activity, little or no sex exploration activities with peers, or constant masturbation. In adolescence there may be no sex play with same or opposite sex, lowered libido, little or no masturbation or compulsive masturbation, and promiscuous sexual activity. Also presented are suggestions for treatment and management of sexual difficulties associated with depression.

Rosen, M. Conditioning appropriate heterosexual behavior in mentally and socially handicapped populations. *Training School Bulletin*, 1970, *66*(4), 172–177.

Inhibition and control rather than reinforcement of adequate sexual behavior are seen to be typical in sex education programs for the mentally retarded. Since this method has proved ineffective, the author suggests systematic desensitization, programmed heterosexual experience, role playing, reinforcement for sex-related talk, suggestions to masturbate, and aversive conditioning as therapy techniques that may be employed. Each of these techniques is discussed and experimental studies are called for to evaluate specific types of behavioral intervention upon behavioral changes, object choices, and other pertinent indices of psychosexual adjustment.

Rosenzweig, S., and Freeman, H. A. "blind test" of sex-hormone potency in schizophrenic patients. *Psychosomatic Medicine*, 1942, *4*, 159–165.

The authors present and discuss the results of an experiment with 20 schizophrenic patients to examine the effects of sex hormone medication on sexual interest of subjects.

Ruskin, S. H. Analysis of sex offenses among male psychiatric patients. *American Journal of Psychiatry*, January 1941, 955–968.

This study examined the incidence and the interrelationship of sex delinquency and mental illness. Of the 1,932 mental patients who formed the male population of a psychiatric hospital, almost 7 percent were found to be sex offenders, of whom 89 percent gave a history of sexual deviation after the recognized onset of their psychosis. Other statistics and findings are discussed.

Searles, H. F. Sexual processes in schizophrenia. *Psychiatry,* 1961, *24,* 87–95.

Through literature review and his own clinical observation, the author discusses genital and erotic pressures and conflicts in the preschizophrenic person, their etiologic factors and manifestations, and the eventual resolution of these conflicts through transference in psychotherapy.

Seeger, M. K., and Finn, J. Caring for a married couple on the same unit. *Perspectives in Psychiatric Care,* 1965, *3,* 15–21.

The unique and special care to be provided to the hospitalized married couple in order to enhance their relationship, and the role of the nursing staff in such a situation, are the two issues discussed in this paper. To illustrate the problems and concerns involved, the authors present a case study of a couple hospitalized in the same psychiatric treatment unit.

Shulman, B. H. Schizophrenia and sexual behavior. *Medical Aspects of Human Sexuality,* 1971, *5*(1), 144–153.

Schizophrenia can produce significant sexual disturbances. In this article, the author discusses sexual behavior in schizophrenic patients. He concludes that, "in general, the schizophrenic is far less sexually active than the rest of the population and gets less satisfaction out of such activity."

Skopec, H. M., Rosenberg, S. D., and Tucker, G. J. Sexual behavior in schizophrenia. *Medical Aspects of Human Sexuality,* 1976, *10*(4), 32–47.

The authors describe some aspects of sexual behavior found in schizophrenics, and present three case histories for illustration. It is noted that while intellectual preoccupation with sexual matters in schizophrenics may appear excessive, sexual behavior is either normal or reduced. Most sexual activity that exists is either fantasy or masturbation. Also, schizophrenics usually experience their sexual needs on a more primitive psychological level. That is, they prefer caring and comforting rather than overt sexual activity. They are often dependent, and literally cling to people around them. Since a schizophrenic often has distortions of his or her body image and its boundaries, it is difficult to imagine that he or she would enjoy sex with another person. In fact, many schizophrenic males actually avoid sexual intercourse with a female.

Small, I. F., and Small, J. G. Sexual behavior and mental illness. In A. M. Freedman, H. I. Kaplan, and B. J. Sadock (Eds.), *Comprehensive textbook of psychiatry* (Vol. 2). Baltimore: Williams and Wilkins, 1975.

Psychosexual aspects of mental retardation, organic brain syndromes, affective disorders, schizophrenia, neuroses, personality disorders, and other psychiatric disabilities are discussed. An extensive review of relevant literature is presented.

Small, I. F., and Small, J. G. Sexual behavior and mental illness. In B. J. Sadock, H. I. Kaplan, and A. M. Freedman (Eds.), *The sexual experience*, Baltimore: Williams and Wilkins, 1976.

In this chapter, sexual activity and behavior as they occur in association with a wide variety of psychiatric and mental disorders are discussed in light of a thorough literature review. The disorders reviewed include mental retardation, organic brain syndromes, major affective disorders, schizophrenia, neuroses, personality disorders, hysterical personality, antisocial personality, passive-aggressive personality, emotionally unstable personality, psychophysiological disorders, and hypersexuality.

Solms, W. Automutilation with a view to sex transformation. *Wiener medizinische Wochenschrift*, 1952, *102*, 983–986.

The author reports on six patients who wanted to change their sex, two of whom were schizophrenics, and four transvestites. The schizophrenic patients attempted autocastration, whereas the transvestites requested that a surgeon remove their genitals.

Spencer, R. F. Depression and diminished sexual desire. *Medical Aspects of Human Sexuality*, 1977, *11*(8), 51–65.

Loss of libido may be secondary to depression or can be one of its causes. This article discusses the interrelations between depression and sexuality. Five case histories are presented and examined for illustrative purposes. In depression which is secondary to a sexual dysfunction, sex therapy is to be considered and offered. When depression is at the base of the sexual dysfunction, a comprehensive psychotherapeutic approach is indicated.

Tabachnick, N. Sex and suicide. *Medical Aspects of Human Sexuality*, 1970, *4*(5), 48–63.

The relationship between sex and suicide is explored and discussed. The author asserts that "observations of the relationship between these two phenomena lead to the conclusion that generally speaking a happy and gratifying sexual life represents a good protection against suicide."

Tompkins, J. B. Penis envy and incest: A case report. *Psychoanalytic Review*, 1940, *27*, 319–325.

This case report presents a psychiatric patient who had incestuous relations with her father. The author concludes that "it seems evident that the patient's early acquaintance with male anatomy led her to strongly envy the possession of a penis." This penis envy resulted in the fact that "her chosen role became a masculine and rather aggressive one and she developed no interest in feminine anatomy." This patient had suffered also from vaginismus.

Trainer, J. B. Emotional bases of fatigue. *Medical Aspects of Human Sexuality*, 1969, *3*(1), 59–65.

The interrelationship between emotional distress, fatigue, and sexual dysfunction is discussed and some suggestions for treatment and counseling are presented.

Tsung, M. T. Hypersexuality in manic patients. *Medical Aspects of Human Sexuality*, 1975, *9*(11), 83–89.

Hypersexuality is often one of the first signs of manic illness. Sexual thoughts and behavior in manic patients are discussed in this paper along with some suggestions for treatment and counseling. The author concludes that "the manic illness and thus the manifestation of hypersexuality respond to psychiatric treatment."

Wignall, C. M., and Meredith, C. E. Illegitimate pregnancies in state institutions. *Archives of General Psychiatry*, 1968, *18*, 580–583.

A questionnaire on illegitimate pregnancies was developed and sent to 287 state institutions. The actual study sample consisted of responses from 156 state mental institutions (mental hospitals, schools for the retarded). The survey showed that illegitimate pregnancies in institutionalized populations occur at about one-fifth the rate at which they occur in the population at large. This low rate of illegitimate pregnancies in mental institutions "may serve to assure the general public in these cases that the problem is not as threatening as they may imagine it to be."

Willis, S. E. Sexual promiscuity as a symptom of personal and cultural anxiety. *Medical Aspects of Human Sexuality*, 1967, *1*(2), 16–23.

According to the author, sexual promiscuity generally represents diffuse personal anxiety and possibly impending social or cultural disintegration. Psychiatric disturbances associated with promiscuity are discussed in light of several case histories of patients. The author concludes that "sexual promiscuity is one form of pathological self-enhancement by which an individual seeks relief from tension when his sense of security and personal esteem have been disturbed."

Willkower, E. D., and Lester, E. P. Marital stress in psychosomatic disorders. In D. W. Abse, E. M. Nash, and L. M. R. Louden (Eds.), *Marital and sexual counseling in medical practice* (2nd ed). New York: Harper & Row, 1974.

The disturbing effects of psychosomatic illness on marital and sexual relationships are described by the authors, who reflect upon their clinical experience and conclusions they drew from an extensive review of the literature. A circular, self-perpetuating reaction may develop in association with a psychosomatic condition within which marital stress creates somatic illness, and this, in turn, creates marital stress or feeds it. The role of the physician in managing marital problems resulting from psychosomatic disorders is discussed.

Winokur, G., Clayton, P. J., and Reich, T. *Manic depressive illness*. St. Louis: Mosby, 1969.

It is generally accepted among psychiatrists that sexual drive is usually increased in manic patients. The authors analyzed sexual behavior in 100 manic episodes of 61 patients and found that 13 percent of these episodes reveal a decrease in sexual interest; no change was observed in 22 percent of them. The remaining 65 percent of the manic episodes were marked by some sort of hypersexuality. In a minority of these latter cases, the hypersexuality was manifested in promiscuous homosexual and heterosexual behavior. No difference in sexual drive between female and male patients was observed.

Wolfe, S. D., and Menninger, W. W. Fostering open communication about sexual concerns in a mental hospital. *Hospital and Community Psychiatry*, 1973, *24*(3), 147–150.

Homosexual activity of young patients in a mental institution prompted the staff to develop a sex education program that would provide basic knowledge and information on sexuality, and foster more open communication about sexual concerns of patients. The program, consisting of a seminar for staff and one for patients, is described, and its effectiveness is analyzed. It was demonstrated that an open, frank group approach to sex education can be adequately handled by patients and by staff who lack expertise in sex education.

Mental Retardation and Learning Disabilities

Abbott, J. M., and Ladd, G. M. . . . Any reason why this mentally retarded couple should not be joined together. *Mental Retardation*, 1970, *8*(2), 45–48.

The authors describe a residential program aimed at assisting mildly retarded individuals in planning and maintaining married life. The program is based on the premise that many mildly retarded persons are capable of managing a reasonably satisfactory marriage and benefit greatly from this relationship. The program was developed at the Edward R. Johnstone Training and Research Center in New Jersey. Residents who express their desire to get married receive services that help them to define their relationship and determine their goals as a couple. This counseling program consists of both individual and group sessions. Role playing is extensively used to assist the couple in dealing with problems, concerns, and anxieties.

Abelson, R. B., and Johnson, R. C. Heterosexual and aggressive behaviors among institutionalized retardates. *Mental Retardation*, 1969, *5*, 28–30.

Various characteristics of institutionalized mentally retarded persons who were identified as being frequently aggressive were compared to the characteristics of retardates who were described as frequently engaging in heterosexual sex. Results of this study are presented and discussed. The two groups show very little overlap in individuals comprising them and differ markedly on a number of other variables. The heterosexually active group was found to demonstrate superior social competence in various areas.

Alcorn, D. A. Parental views on sexual development and education of the trainable mentally retarded. *Journal of Special Education*, 1974, *8*(2), 119–130.

A questionnaire was constructed to elicit information about parental attitudes toward sex education for their trainable mentally retarded child. Subjects were 206 parents, members of the Nebraska Association for Retarded Children. As in earlier studies, results of this survey showed that parents have much concern or lack of confidence regarding their child's sexual behavior. In most cases, trainable mentally retarded children showed little inclination toward sexual activity and minimal curiosity about sexuality. Some two-thirds of the children did not appear to their parents to be perceptive enough to sex differences or to reveal sexual interests. Although parents believed that they had the responsibility to provide sex education to their retarded children, in reality they did not fulfill this function. They claimed that their retarded children would not understand sex information presented to them. Parents also had little faith in the ability of the trainable retarded to use contraceptives. It was suggested that parents may be less inclined to support voluntary sterilization in their own retarded children than sterilization of the retarded in general. The author concluded that parents need to help their mentally retarded to understand the fundamentals of sexual development and sexuality. Sex education for mentally retarded persons is an essential aspect in normalization and humanization of this population.

Andron, L., and Sturm, M. L. Is "I DO" in the repertoire of the retarded? A study of the functioning of married retarded couples. *Mental Retardation*, 1973, *11*(1), 31–34.

The marriages of twelve couples in which at least one partner was mentally retarded were studied to determine their levels of daily functioning, interpersonal relationships, social adjustment, and self-reliance. Most of the couples seemed able to function adequately, although they relied on parents, other relatives, neighbors, or social workers for help with major personal or financial difficulties. The companionship of marriage was overwhelmingly preferred to single life, in spite of difficulties experienced by some. Most of the couples had been sterilized, and some doubt is expressed as to whether they had understood this operation when it was performed.

Attwell, A. A., and Clabby, D. A. *The retarded child: Answers to questions parents ask*. Burbank, California: Eire Press, 1969.

The book answers a wide variety of questions relating to mental retardation, its terminology, diagnosis, prognosis, and other psychological, social, and familial aspects. Of particular interest is a chapter discussing sexual development and sex education.

Bass, M. S. Attitudes of parents of retarded children toward voluntary sterilization. *Eugenics Quarterly*, 1967, *14*(1), 41–53.

The attitudes of parents of retarded children toward voluntary sterilization were examined (n=132). Results show that some 60 percent of the subjects approved of sterilization; approval was positively related to information on sterilization. Over a third of the subjects erroneously believed that sterilization and castration were synonymous and as a result showed lower approval. The author argues for the need for appropriate counseling for parents of retarded children.

Bass, M. S. Developing community acceptance of sex education for the mentally retarded. *SIECUS Report*, 1972.

The author asserts that education and habilitation services for mentally retarded persons should help them to attain their maximum potential for living a normative community life, and yet protect them from responsibilities that are beyond their capacity to handle. Within this context, sex education for the mentally retarded is of great importance. Literature expressing the importance of sex education for the retarded is reviewed. There seems to be an urgent need to develop sex education programs for retarded children, since most parents do not provide such needed sex information. This article outlines a program for several meetings with parents to introduce them to the importance of and the need for sex education for retarded children. It is vital to enlist the parents' cooperation in planning and developing such a program.

Bass, M. S. Marriage, parenthood, and prevention of pregnancy. *American Journal of Mental Deficiency*, 1968, *68*(3), 318–331.

This is a comprehensive review of the literature discussing marriage for the retarded, parenthood and limitation of offspring, medical, psychological, and eugenic indications for sterilization, deterrents to sterilization, and the legal aspects of sterilization for the retarded. In her conclusion, the author asserts that "marriage can be recommended for retarded individuals in an appreciable per cent of cases, but that it is often advisable to prevent parenthood for the individual and his potential child." The lack of information in this area is pointed out.

Bass, M. S. Marriage for the mentally deficient. *Mental Retardation*, 1964, *2*(4), 198–202.

Many authorities have recognized the importance of marriage for mentally retarded persons. This paper discusses various aspects of marriage for the retarded in light of the increasing acceptance of birth control. Although marriage may prove very beneficial to many retarded persons, it is agreed upon by many that they should not have children, since their capacity to care for them adequately is diminished. Studies are cited to suggest that retarded persons have marriages that are more satisfying when they do not have children. It is suggested that every case be studied individually before making a recommendation for marriage. The ability of the person to maintain an independent and sound existence in the community should be carefully studied before making recommendations.

Bennett, B., Vockell, E., and Vockell, K. Sex education for EMR adolescent girls: An evaluation and some suggestions. *Journal for Special Education of the Mentally Retarded*, 1972, *9*, 3–7.

The purpose of this study was to implement and evaluate a sex education program for educable mentally retarded girls in a day center. Subjects were seven girls between 17 and 23 years of age, with IQs ranging from 58 to 81 and with a mean IQ of 69.1. The study subjects were interested in acquiring information about sex and were willing to participate in a group situation. The study class met for one hour three times a week for a period of four weeks to discuss topics that included menstrual hygiene, body hair and acne, human reproduction, sexual feelings, masturbation, premarital sex, sexual deviance, contraception, and venereal diseases. Results showed a considerable increase in the subjects' abilities to discriminate between sexes, in their understanding of biological sexual facts, in their knowledge about venereal diseases, in specific aspects of sexual intercourse, and in birth control.

A bibliography of resources in sex education for the mentally retarded. New York: Sex Information and Education Council of the U.S., 1973.

This bibliography is intended as a supplementary resource for persons concerned with educating, helping, and understanding the needs of the retarded for sexual expression and sex education. The bibliography includes items concerned with sexuality and the retarded, resources for parents, sexual reproduction, attitudes and values, marriage and parenthood, sex education, and other related topics.

Biller, H. B., and Borstelmann, L. J. Intellectual level and sex role development in mentally retarded children. *American Journal of Mental Deficiency*, 1965, *70*(3), 443–447.

The relation between sex role development and intelligence among 73 retarded children ranging in age from 7 to 15 and in IQ from 37 to 70 was examined in this study. The results are discussed, along with some conclusions.

Bowden, J., Spitz, H. H., and Winters, J. J. Follow-up of one retarded couple's marriage. *Mental Retardation*, 1971, *9*(6), 42–43.

As a result of this follow-up, the authors concluded that "the dreary reality that was revealed by the follow-up of this marriage contrasts rather sharply with the hopes presented in the original paper" (which presented a more positive and encouraging picture). They stress that great caution should be observed before institutionalized retardates are encouraged to marry.

Burt, R. A. Legal restrictions on sexual familial relations of mental retardation: Old laws, new guesses. In F. F. de la Cruz and G. D. LaVeck (Eds.), *Human sexuality and the mentally retarded.* New York: Brunner/Mazel, 1973.

Several kinds of state laws currently limit the freedom of the retarded person to engage in sexual relations, to marry, and to rear children. These laws are identified and discussed in this presentation, which was made at a conference held by the National Institute of Child Health and Human Development to study sexuality and the retarded person.

Carruth, D. G., Human sexuality in a halfway house. In F. F. de la Cruz and G. D. LaVeck (Eds.), *Human sexuality and the mentally retarded.* New York: Brunner/Mazel, 1973.

The author reports the results of a survey examining sexual attitudes of the staff and sexual activity of the residents of a halfway house for mentally retarded persons. This presentation was made at a conference held by the National Institute of Child Health and Human Development to study sexuality and mental retardation.

Clark, E. T. Sex role preference in mentally retarded children. *American Journal of Mental Deficiency*, 1973, *67*, 606–610.

This study examined the hypothesis that older retarded boys and those with higher IQs would express greater masculine sex role preferences than younger boys and those with lower IQs. Younger female retardates and those with lower IQs were expected to show greater feminine sex role preference. Subjects were 66 male and 50 female retardates with a chronological age mean of almost 12 years for males and over 12 years for females. Relatively dichotomous patterns of sex role preferences were found to exist between these male and female retardates. No exclusively feminine patterns of sex role preference were found in either male or female retarded subjects. However, exclusively male preferences were found in both groups. Sex role preferences in the retarded do not differ from normal, since boys generally express a greater preference for the masculine sex role than girls do for the feminine sex role. Other results are discussed.

Culley, W. J. Age and body size of mentally retarded girls at menarche. *Developmental Medicine and Child Neurology,* 1974, *16*, 209–213.

Mentally retarded girls, particularly the profoundly retarded, were found to reach menarche at an older age than nonretarded girls, regardless of the cause of retardation. Based on his findings, the author concludes that "some determinant must become operative after a certain age which allows menarche to occur, even though the critical body weight has not been attained."

Deisher, R. W. Sexual behavior of retarded in institutions. In F. F. de la Cruz and G. D. LaVeck (Eds.), *Human sexuality and the mentally retarded.* New York: Brunner/Mazel, 1973.

This chapter reports the results of a survey of sexual attitudes of personnel and actual sexual behavior of the residents in two large institutions for mentally retarded persons. Basic information was obtained through the use of a questionnaire that was answered by twenty-five persons from each institution. The results of this survey are presented and discussed. The author stresses the need for more realistic sex education programs for the retarded person, both in institutions and in the community. This presentation was made at a conference held by the National Institute of Child Health and Human Development to study sexuality and the mentally retarded person.

de la Cruz, F. F., and LaVeck, G. D. (Eds.). *Human sexuality and the mentally retarded.* New York: Brunner/Mazel, 1973.

To meet the need for authoritative information and guidance in the area of human sexuality and the mentally retarded, the National Institute of Child Health and Human Development held a conference on this topic. This book consists of the proceedings of that conference. Chapters by participants include the examination of the biological, psychosocial, and institutional aspects of sexual behavior and attitudes as they apply to the special needs of the retarded. Issues discussed are the effects of institutionalization, sex education, marriage, contraception, moral and ethical implications of sex and the retarded, and new directions in research. The concept of normalization was an underlying premise of the entire discussion.

Doherty, E. Sex education for the handicapped. *Special Education*, 1971, *60*, 27–28.

The need for sex education for mentally handicapped children and adults is expressed by the author, who also presents suggestions for the implementation of sex education programs for this population.

Edgerton, R. B. Some socio-cultural research considerations. In F. F. de la Cruz and G. D. LaVeck (Eds.), *Human sexuality and the mentally retarded*. New York: Brunner/Mazel, 1973.

The author identifies various areas of needed research in sexuality and the mentally retarded person. The first research priority is to determine the relationship of various kinds of sexual behavior to different intelligence and adaptive behavior levels. Other areas of research focus are sexual behavior and self-esteem, self-control of sexual behavior, population control, marriage and parenthood, public attitudes about the sexuality of the retarded person, and sex education.

Edgerton, R. B., and Dingman, H. F. Good reason for ban supervision: "Dating" in a hospital for the mentally retarded. *Psychiatric Quarterly Supplement*, 1974, *38*, 221–233.

In most facilities for the mentally retarded there is close supervision of the patients. This article examines the consequences of permitting male-female interaction to take place without close supervision. The experiment took place at Pacific State Hospital, a large California state institution, which houses approximately 3,000 patients in forty-seven wards scattered over a 500-acre campus. Only 400 patients, whose IQs ranged from 40 to 70 and who were not greatly physically handicapped, were involved in this program. These individuals were provided a system of passes which permitted them free access to large areas of the hospital grounds during certain hours of the day. For a period of one year intensive and systematic observations of the range of interaction between male and female patients were carried out. No significant changes were made in the pattern of male and female interaction during the course of the year's research. The results were essentially favorable.

Edmonson, B., and Wish, J. Sex knowledge and attitudes of moderately retarded males. *American Journal of Mental Deficiency*, 1975, *80*(2), 172–179.

Eighteen moderately retarded men were examined to determine their understanding of pictures of homosexual embrace, masturbation, dating, marriage, intercourse, pregnancy, childbirth, and their knowledge of anatomical terminology. Results of this study and some conclusions are presented.

Fischer, H. L., Krajicek, M. J. Sexual development of the moderately retarded child: How can the pediatrician be helpful? *Clinical Pediatrics*, 1974, *13*, 79–83.

In this paper, material is provided to equip the pediatrician with information needed by a moderately retarded child concerning sexual development. "Sexual development" refers to more than sexual anatomy, sexual functions, or physical maturation. It includes the child's understanding of and reactions to body changes and his appreciation of culturally accepted sex roles. The concepts of dating, marriage, expressing affection, and parenthood should also be considered. Responsibility for one's own behavior must be stressed. The pediatrician should assume the initiative in discussing these questions with the parents and the child, and it should be done before the onset of puberty.

Fischer, H. L., and Krajicek, M. J. Sexual development of the moderately retarded child: Level of information and parental attitudes. *Mental Retardation*, 1974, *12*, 28–30.

The main purpose of this study was to examine the level of sexual knowledge in moderately retarded children (n=16). The subjects' parents were also studied in relation to their knowledge and attitudes regarding sexuality and their children. Both children and parents responded in direct interviewing to questions and pictures concerning sexual identification, body parts and functions, emotional functions, pregnancy, and birth. Results of the study and their implications for sex education are discussed.

Fischer, H. L., Krajicek, M. J., and Borthick, W. A. *Sex education for the developmentally disabled: A guide for parents, teachers, and professionals.* Baltimore: University Park Press, 1973.

This guide provides visual and verbal representations of sexual concepts, functions, and structures for the purpose of eliciting information from the developmentally disabled or mentally retarded person.

The interview hints which accompany the simple line drawings are designed to assist the interviewer in determining the level of the handicapped person's information about sexuality and the accuracy of his concepts, in order to correct any misinformation and to elaborate on any questions that the retarded person may ask.

Terms that present a more concrete way of understanding concepts common to many developmentally disabled are suggested. However, this guide is not considered appropriate for use with the severely or profoundly retarded or with totally nonverbal persons. Covered are sexual identification, body parts, emotional functions, bodily functions, pregnancy, and birth.

Fischer, H. L., Krajicek, M. J., and Borthick, W. A. *Teaching concepts of sexual development to the developmentally disabled: A guide for parents, teachers, and professionals.* Denver, Colorado: The Universty of Colorado Medical Center, 1973.

It is the view of the authors that what has been missing in the field of sex education for the handicapped are materials that help the parent, teacher, or other professional more directly and concretely in their efforts to communicate necessary information about sexuality to the developmentally handicapped person. The present guide attempts to provide such material. Sets of questions are developed that cover a broad range of topics related to a broad definition of sexuality. These topics are: sexual identification, body parts, emotional functions, bodily functions, pregnancy, and birth. Closing sections emphasize the parents' role in sex education, organizational hints for conducting sex education workshops, and bibliographic material.

Fisher, G. M. Sexual identification in mentally retarded male children and adults. *American Journal of Mental Deficiency*, 1960, *65*, 42–45.

On the assumptions that sexual identification is learned, that learning is dependent upon intellectual level, and that sex of the first-drawn figure in the Draw-a-Person test is related to sexual identification, the author hypothesized that: (1) mentally retarded males would draw the male figure first less frequently than would non-retarded males; (2) retarded persons would be less reliable in the sex of the first-drawn figure; and (3) the more severe the retardation, the less frequently would the male figure be drawn first. The procedure and results of this study are discussed, and conclusions are presented.

Fisher, G. M. Sexual identification in mentally subnormal females. *American Journal of Mental Deficiency*, 1961, *66*, 266–269.

This study examined the effects of age and intelligence on the frequency with which females draw the female figure first in the Draw-a-Person test. This test provides some information about the sexual identification of subjects tested. Specific hypotheses examined in this study were: (1) mentally retarded females would draw the female figure first less frequently than would non-retarded female subjects; and (2) the more severe the retardation, the less frequently would the female figure be drawn first. Procedures and results of this study are presented and discussed.

Floor, L., Rosen, M., Baxter, D., Horowitz, J., and Weber, C. Sociosexual problems in mentally handicapped females. *Training School Bulletin*, 1971, *68*, 106–112.

The results reported in this article were part of a follow-up study of previously institutionalized mentally handicapped women. The purpose of the study was to obtain information regarding the social, vocational, and economic adjustment of the subjects (n=49). These subjects, living independently in the community, were studied to determine occurrence of sex-related problems leading to social and economic repercussions. A relationship between sex-related incidents at the institution and sociosexual problems occurring shortly after discharge was found. The authors conclude that "sexual acting out within the institution appears to signal a need for guidance in appropriate heterosexual behaviors, an area so far not sufficiently stressed in rehabilitation programs."

Friedman, E. Missing in the life of the retarded individual—sex: Reflections on Sol Gordon's paper. *Journal of Special Education*, 1971, *5*(2), 365–368.

In a preceding article, Sol Gordon points out that mentally retarded children are in greater need of sex education than are normal children because, under conditions of sexual repression and denial, the retarded become increasingly bewildered and anxious in our society, which is filled with sexual stimuli. This article presents the author's response to Sol Gordon's discussion. It is pointed out that before we can set realistic goals for sex education for the retarded, we must first educate ourselves. What is needed is society's complete and unconditional acceptance of the handicapped person as a sexual human being.

Fujita, B., Wagner, N. N., and Pion, R. J. Sexuality, contraception, and the mentally retarded. *Postgraduate Medical Journal*, 1970, *47*(2), 193–197.

In the past, science and the public in general have been in opposition to the retarded having children. In contrast to past thought, however, scientists now realize that conclusive proof of the hereditability of mental ability is still lacking. In addition to the genetic factors, science has come to recognize the importance of sociopsychologic factors in the development of a person. This and other areas of sexuality and contraception as they relate to the mentally retarded are further discussed.

Gebhard, P. H. Sexual behavior of the mentally retarded. In F. F. de la Cruz and G. D. LaVeck (Eds.), *Human sexuality and the mentally retarded*. New York: Brunner/Mazel, 1973.

This presentation was part of a conference held by the National Institute of Child Health and Human Development to study sexuality in the retarded person. In this chapter the author examines and discusses sexual behavior and activities of mentally retarded persons interviewed by the staff of the Institute for Sex Research in Bloomington, Indiana. The sample consisted of 84 white males who had IQs ranging from 31 to 70, and who were primarily from penal institutions. Results analyzed and discussed deal with prepubertal sexual activity, masturbation, orgasm in sleep, premarital petting and coitus, coitus with prostitutes, marital coitus, homosexuality, animal sexual contact, and sexual knowledge. Results obtained from the study sample were compared with results from a control group of 477 white males of grammar or high school education who had never been convicted of a crime, imprisoned, or sent to a mental institution.

Gendel, E. S. Sex education of the mentally retarded child in the home. Arlington, Texas: National Association for Retarded Citizens, 1969.

Aimed at parents of mentally retarded children, this booklet presents numerous suggestions for adequate sex education at home. Parents are advised that sex education starts very early in the child's life, and that the principles of sex education are not different for parents of retarded children. The parents' lack of adjustment to the impact of retardation may present some difficulties in implementing an effective sex education program at home.

Ginsberg, L. H. The institutionalized mentally retarded. In H. L. Gochros and J. S. Gochros (Eds.), *The sexually oppressed.* New York: Association Press, 1977.

The sexual concerns and rights of the institutionalized mentally disabled are discussed in this chapter.

Goodman, L. The sexual rights of the retarded: A dilemma for parents. *The Family Coordinator*, 1973, *22*, 472–474.

Personal factors that reflect parents' unresolved sexual conflicts, lack of knowledge about sexual matters, and discomfort in discussing sexual subjects are some of the difficulties involved in affirming the sexual rights of the retarded person. These and other conflicts frequently found in parents of mentally retarded children and adults are discussed and suggestions for improvement are made.

Goodman, L., Bunder, S., and Lesh, B. The parents' role in sex education for the retarded. *Mental Retardation*, 1971, *9*(1), 43–45.

The authors report the views of 15 parents of retarded adolescents interviewed in depth. The parents had made only minimal efforts—or none at all—to give sexual instruction, showed marked anxiety over the dangers facing their retarded children in this area, had themselves only a limited knowledge of sexual function, and felt inadequate in giving their children sexual information. Greater concern and more readiness to participate in a sex education program were exhibited with their retarded child than with their normal children. Parents were strongly in favor of a sex education program not only for the retarded, but for themselves as well. While the interviews were conducted to obtain information, they proved to be cathartic and therapeutic for nearly all parents. Previously unvoiced fears and feelings were expressed. Parents of girls talked about contraception and about the possibility of sterilization to enable their child to have the interpersonal gratification of marriage and a satisfying sex life without conception.

Goodman, R. Family planning programs for the mentally retarded in institutions and community. In F. F. de la Cruz and G. D. LaVeck (Eds.), *Human sexuality and the mentally retarded.* New York: Brunner/Mazel, 1973.

The author describes his experiences in developing and implementing family planning programs for mentally retarded individuals. Programs developed in a sheltered workshop, a public school, a state hospital, and an urban day activity center are discussed. In his conclusion, the author stresses the importance of trained professional personnel, the involvement of parents of the mentally retarded, the cooperation of physicians, and administrative clarity on what constitutes delivery of a family planning service. This presentation was part of a conference held by the National Institute of Child Health and Human Development to study sexuality and the mentally retarded person.

Gordon, S. Telling it like it is. Paper presented at a Conference on Sexuality and the Mentally Retarded, State University of New York College at Potsdam, September 21–22, 1972.

The author discusses sexual development and behavior, homosexuality, masturbation, marriage, and other aspects of sexuality as they relate to the mentally disabled person. The overall message of this presentation is that the retarded person, like all other human beings, has sexual feelings and needs that should be expressed and met.

Gordon, S., and Green, J. Sexuality in courtship, marriage, and parenthood among the retarded. Paper presented at the Nineteenth Annual Convention of the Association for Mental Deficiency, Minneapolis, May 18, 1972.

Various aspects of sexuality as they relate to the mentally retarded are presented in light of the view that the mentally retarded person is a sexual human being.

Green, R. Mental retardation and sexuality: Some research strategies. In F. F. de la Cruz and D. G. LaVeck (Eds.), *Human sexuality and the mentally retarded.* New York: Brunner/Mazel, 1973.

Four areas of potential study regarding sexuality in mental retardation are identified and discussed in this chapter. These are: psychosexual differentiation; prenatal gonadal hormones and intellectual development; sex-hormone-dependent social behavior; and sex chromosomes, intellectual development, and social behavior. This presentation was made at a conference held by the National Institute of Child Health and Human Development to study sexuality and the retarded person.

Hall, J. E. Bibliography: Sexual behavior of the mentally retarded. Birmingham, Alabama: Center for Developmental Learning Disorders (no date).

This bibliography consists of over 250 references in the field of sexuality in mental retardation. Marriage, sterilization, homosexual and heterosexual behavior, special sex education programs, sex role development, sexual development, sexual identification, sexual knowledge, masturbation, sexual problems, and other related areas are covered.

Hall, J. E. Sexual behavior. In J. Wortis (Ed.), *Mental retardation and developmental disabilities.* New York: Brunner/Mazel, 1974.

In recent years there has been a growing interest in the sexuality of the mentally retarded. In this extensive chapter, the author discusses various aspects of human sexuality as they relate to the mentally retarded person. Sterilization, sexual development, reproductive capacity, masturbation, sexual misbehavior, marriage, care of children, contraception, and sex knowledge and attitudes in both retardates and their parents are some of the topics thoroughly discussed. Finally, the need for adequate sex education programs is stressed. These programs "should be administered with attitudes of support and understanding; they should be regarded as a requirement in every educational facility and not as a luxury."

Hall, J. E. Sexuality and the mentally retarded. In R. Green (Ed.), *Human sexuality: A health practitioner's text.* Baltimore: Williams and Wilkins, 1975.

Sociosexual aspects of mental retardation are discussed in view of parents' and professionals' typical reactions to sexual expression in the retarded individual. Various responses are identified, including the denial of sexuality, the moralistic attitude, and the overprotective attitude. Problems associated with sexual development, masturbation, sexual exploitation, homosexuality, and venereal disease are raised and alternative solutions to these problems are presented. Also discussed are topics relating to sterilization, contraception, and marriage and their legal aspects.

Hall, J. E., and Morris, H. L. Sexual knowledge and attitudes of institutionalized and noninstitutionalized retarded adolescents. *American Journal of Mental Deficiency*, 1976, *80*(4), 382–387.

This article presents and discusses the results of a study aimed at the evaluation of sexual attitudes and knowledge among institutionalized (n=61) and noninstitutionalized (n=61) mentally retarded adolescents. Also studied were the subjects' self-concepts.

Hall, J. E., Morris, H. L., and Barker, H. R. Sexual knowledge and attitudes of mentally retarded adolescents. *American Journal of Mental Deficiency*, 1973, *77*(6), 706–709.

Parents' perceptions of their mildly and moderately retarded adolescents' knowledge and attitudes about sex were compared with the adolescents' actual responses to a psychometric questionnaire covering these topics. Subjects were 61 noninstitutionalized retardates with a chronological age range of 10 to 24 years, a mental age range of 5 to 13 years, and an IQ range of 41 to 95. The retarded respondents were significantly more liberal in sexual ethics than their parents predicted, but parents accurately predicted their children's scores on knowledge and self-concept questionnaires. A need is seen for education of both parents and retarded adolescents in certain areas, particularly the areas of conception, contraception, and venereal disease.

Hamilton, J. The retarded adolescent: A parent's view. *Family Planning Perspectives*, 1976, *8*(6), 257.

This brief article presents a parent's concerns with recent trends which call for the increase of sex education for the retarded adolescent.

Hamilton, J., Allen, P., Stephens, L., Davall, E. Training mentally retarded females to use sanitary napkins. *Mental Retardation*, 1969, 40–43.

This article discusses a method of training mentally retarded women to use sanitary napkins. Also presented and discussed are the results of an evaluation of this method which was based on behavioral components.

Hammar, S. L., and Barnard, K. E. The mentally retarded adolescent: A review of the characteristics and problems of 44 noninstitutionalized adolescent retardates. *Pediatrics*, 1966, *38*(5), 845–857.

The purpose of this study was to further examine the characteristics of the adolescent retarded person and his specific human needs. Subjects were 44 adolescent patients who had been referred to the University of Washington Adolescent Clinic between 1963 and 1965. A thorough medical, psychological, mental, and family evaluation was conducted. In those cases in which sexual misbehavior was noted, much sexual stimulation was found in the home situation. This promoted exaggerated interest in sex and in sexual acting out. Parents' complaints about the sexual acting out of their retarded adolescents involved exhibitionism and masturbation in the males and sexual promiscuity, masturbation, and pregnancy for the females.

Hammar, S. L., Wright, L. S., and Jensen, D. L. Sex education for the retarded adolescent: A survey of parental attitudes and methods of management in fifty adolescent retardates. *Clinical Pediatrics*, 1967, *6*(11), 621–627.

In order to study parental attitudes and practice regarding sex education for mentally retarded adolescents, parents of 50 retarded home-reared adolescents were interviewed in three areas: (1) management of the adolescent's sex education by the family; (2) sexual behavior, heterosexual interest, and incidence of sexual misbehavior; (3) the parents' attitudes towards marriage, reproduction, and contraception for their retarded child. It was found that 88 percent of the retarded girls had received some preparation for their sexual changes and menarche, while only 32 percent had received any type of sex education. Parental anxiety concerning the possibility of sexual misbehavior by their retarded child was high, although the actual incidence of sexual problem behavior was low. Seventy percent of the parents considered some type of prevention of reproduction to be imperative for their child's adjustment and satisfaction. Most parents were found to be uninformed about the various methods available for contraception or sterilization.

Helbig, D. W. Physical and biological aspects. In F. F. de la Cruz and G. D. LaVeck (Eds.), *Human sexuality and the mentally retarded*. New York: Brunner/Mazel, 1973.

The author answers the question "how does reproductive capacity—meaning both fecundity (the physical capacity to reproduce) and the social capacity to bear and raise children—differ between normal persons and mentally retarded persons of varying degrees of severity and various diagnoses?" In studying the fertility of the mentally retarded person, the following factors should be considered: the etiology of the retardation, the degree of its severity, the person's age, the couple's marital status, time elapsed since sexual activity began, frequency of sexual activity, and socioeconomic status. This presentation was made at a conference held by the National Institute of Child Health and Human Development to study sexuality and mental retardation.

Hildek, R. Sex education for the mentally retarded. Rehabilitation Counselor Internship Training Program, Nebraska Psychiatric Institute, Omaha, Nebraska, 1970.

This paper deals with personal and sociosexual aspects in the rehabilitation process of mentally retarded persons. A basic philosophy supporting sex education with this population is presented and discussed along with some basic findings relating to the retardates' sexual behavior and the extent to which they can benefit from sex education programs. Two examples of functioning, effective sex education programs are also summarized. The author concludes that, "assuming that sex education can be effective, and all indications and studies point in this direction, it should always be considered an important, essential aspect of vocational preparation as a means of insuring vocational success with the mentally retarded."

Howley, P. L. Attitudes of parents, career personnel, and volunteers toward sex education and sex participation for the mentally retarded. Unpublished Doctoral Dissertation, The Florida State University, 1974 (*Dissertation Abstracts*, 1974, 1808–A).

The purpose of this study was to investigate the attitudes held by parents of retarded children, by career personnel, and by volunteers toward sex education and participation for the mentally retarded person. The Sex Education and Sex Participation Attitude Scale, a Likert-type questionnaire, was developed specifically for this study. Results show that different attitudes can be expected based on age and religion. Younger non-Christian subjects had significantly more positive attitudes toward sex education and participation for the mentally retarded than did older, Christian subjects. Other results are discussed.

Jennings, A. N., Balandin, R., and Mills, M. Sex and the mentally retarded. *Rehabilitation in Australia*, 1970, *7*(4), 15–18.

The authors discuss the sexual problems of the mentally handicapped, and community attitudes toward these problems. They see the family as the most important influence in teaching from infancy what should be learned about modesty, sex differences, family relationships, heredity, love, restraint, dress, chastity, promiscuity, morals, romance, and marriage.

Johnson, W. R. Mental retardation and masturbation. *Sexology,* 1967, *33*(9), 596–599.

The author discusses some myths and misconceptions relating to masturbation and the mentally retarded. He calls for better sex education and counseling programs for the mentally retarded, who should be allowed normative sexual expression. The author asserts that masturbation is a normal and harmless function.

Johnson, W. R. Mental retardation and masturbation. In I. Rubin and L. A. Kirkendall (Eds.), *Sex in the childhood years*. New York: Association Press, 1970.

Some realistic suggestions regarding the handling of masturbation in mentally retarded children are presented. The author suggests that those responsible for the behavior of the mentally retarded person should come to terms with their own sexuality so that they are more effective in dealing with the retarded person's sexuality.

Johnson, W. R. Sex education and the mentally retarded. *Journal of Sex Research*, 1969, *5*, 179–185.

In this article, the author discusses various topics of his sex education program with parents of mentally retarded children. He also comments on some controversial issues concerning dating, marriage, and parenthood of mentally retarded persons and makes suggestions as to possible ways of utilizing sexual interests to facilitate and enhance educational and developmental processes in this population.

Johnson, W. R. Sex education of the mentally retarded. In F. F. de la Cruz and G. D. LaVeck (Eds.), *Human sexuality and the mentally retarded*. New York: Brunner/Mazel, 1973.

This chapter represents a presentation made at a conference held by thc National Institute of Child Health and Human Development to study sexuality and mental retardation. In this chapter the author discusses sex education of the mentally retarded person by examining the characteristics of the learner, of the subject matter, and of the sex educators. He stresses that "the need for appropriate sex education is clearly urgent" in order to add quality to the life of the mentally retarded person.

Kaplan, O. J. Marriage of mental defectives. *American Journal of Mental Deficiency*, 1944, *48*, 379–384.

This article presents the results of a follow-up analysis of marriages involving patients who had left Sonoma State Home, a California institution for the mentally defective. It was done to show some relationship between intelligence and marital success. The study involved fifty-six of the sixty-one patients who married during the period 1941–1942. Those marriages considered "satisfactory" were couples living together in a manner judged satisfactory by the social worker's observation. The "unsatisfactory" marriages were those which the social worker judged unsatisfactory, and those who were divorced, separated, or living together in a relationship considered destructive. In 14.3 percent of the cases the nature of the couple's adjustment was unknown. Results and conclusions are presented.

Kempton, W. Marriage, parenthood and birth control for the mentally retarded. Paper presented at a Conference on Sexuality and the Mentally Retarded, State University of New York College at Potsdam, September 21–22, 1972.

Sexuality, marriage, parenthood, and birth control are discussed in relation to the mentally retarded person and in light of principles of normalization. Also presented are some important questions and answers about birth control for the mentally retarded.

Kempton, W. The mentally retarded. In H. L. Gochros and J. S. Gochros (Eds.), *The sexually oppressed.* New York: Association Press, 1977.

Factors in the sexual oppression of the mentally retarded by professionals and by society in general are discussed, and new approaches to securing sexual rights of the retarded person are presented.

Kempton, W. *A teacher's guide to sex education for persons with learning disabilities.* North Scituate, Massachusetts: Duxbury Press, 1975.

This is a detailed, step-by-step guide for sex education for persons with learning disabilities. The material presented in this book was gathered from various previously developed resources and from the author's own experiences. The book includes questions, examples, and techniques which are based on the author's experiences as a sex educator and counselor. Each chapter in the book consists of a discussion of certain topics, followed by questions and answers and specific practice exercises. Topics discussed include sex education, attitudes toward sexuality, characteristics of the sex educator, the sex education program, techniques of teaching, and other related areas. Also included is an extensive resource guide for audio-visual aids, written materials, and other teaching aids for sex education with special groups.

Kempton, W., and Forman, R. *Guidelines for training in sexuality and the mentally handicapped.* Philadelphia: Planned Parenthood Association of Southeastern Pennsylvania, 1976.

This book presents a training program for sex education with mentally handicapped persons. The main purpose of the program is to assist the mentally retarded person to better understand his or her sexuality and develop responsible attitudes toward it. The book is designed primarily for those who are interested in preparing training programs in sexuality for staff, aides, parents, and others who are involved with the mentally handicapped person. The material presented in this book is, for the most part, what the authors have found to be effective in training courses and sex education programs. The authors also suggest audio-visual materials to be used with the guidelines listed and discussed. The book includes guidelines for nine training sessions, including specific topics to be discussed in each, practice exercise tests, and bibliography.

Kempton, W., Bass, M. S., and Gordon, S. *Love, sex and birth control for the mentally retarded: A guide for parents.* Philadelphia: Planned Parenthood Association of Southeastern Pennsylvania, 1975.

The authors are convinced that "parents of handicapped children must assume the responsibilities of being informed and keeping their children informed in this crucial area of human interaction," i.e., love, sex, and birth control. The retarded individual has the same love and sexual feelings, emotions, thoughts, and needs as other persons. To assist parents of handicapped children to adequately satisfy the sexual curiosity of their children, the authors prepared this booklet, which discusses a wide range of topics, including masturbation, preparing a child for puberty, dating and its merits, sexual intercourse, venereal diseases, birth control, contraceptive methods, abortion, marriage, and having children.

LaVeck, G. D., and de la Cruz, F. F. Contraception for the mentally retarded: Current methods and future prospects. In F. F. de la Cruz and G. D. LaVeck (Eds.), *Human sexuality and the mentally retarded.* New York: Brunner/Mazel, 1973.

Current fertility-regulating methods available to the mentally retarded person, and some future prospective developments, are discussed in this chapter. The authors conclude that "increased fundamental and directed research during the past five years has resulted in a number of leads that eventually could result in new drugs, devices, and methods of contraception." This presentation was made at a conference held by the National Institute of Child Health and Human Development to study sexuality in the mentally retarded person.

Livingston, V., and Knapp, M. E. Human sexuality: A portfolio for the mentally retarded. Planned Parenthood of Seattle-King County, 1974.

This is a training aid to assist instructors in sex education programs with mentally retarded populations. It includes illustration plates that are large enough to be seen by a group of six people, and topics of discussion associated with each plate. Also included are specific suggestions for further discussion. Plates illustrating the similarities and differences between male and female anatomy are suitable in discussing bodily functions, development, and growth. Also included are plates pointing up male and female sexual parts, male and female masturbation, and sexual intercourse.

Mattinson, J. *Marriage and mental handicap.* Pittsburgh: University of Pittsburgh Press, 1970.

This book is a comprehensive report of a research study aimed at examining the marriages of a small number of mentally handicapped couples. The structure of the interpersonal relationships within these marriages, the existence and use of familial and friendship networks, and success and failure in marriage are some of the specific aspects studied.

Mattinson, J. Marriage and mental handicap. In F. F. de la Cruz and G. D. LaVeck (Eds.), *Human sexuality and the mentally retarded.* New York: Brunner/Mazel, 1973.

The author discusses the results of an intensive follow-up study examining 32 married couples in which both partners had at one time in their lives been designated mentally retarded. This presentation was made at a conference held by the National Institute of Child Health and Human Development to study sexuality in mental retardation. In her conclusion, the author stressed that in most of the couples she studied, the partners "were able to reinforce each other's strengths and established marriages which, in the light of what had happened to them previously, were no more, no less, foolish than many others in the community."

Menolascino, F. J. Sexual problems of the mentally retarded. *Sexual Behavior*, 1972, *2*(11), 39–41.

This article discusses the sexual problems faced by the mentally retarded individual. The author asserts that mentally retarded people are looked on by much of society as being subhuman and are not recognized as having the basic human needs for love, friendship, and affection. Two case histories are presented to support the statement that mentally retarded persons have the same needs as "normal" people have. Sex education is recommended for the retarded living in the community as well as for those retarded who are institutionalized.

Menolascino, F. J. Sexual problems of the mentally retarded. In L. Gross (Ed.), *Sexual behavior: Current issues.* New York: Spectrum Publications, 1974.

This is a reprint of the same article that appeared in the November 1972 issue of the journal *Sexual Behavior* (1972, *2*(11), 39–41).

Meyen, E. L. Sex education for the mentally retarded: Implications for programming and teacher training. *Focus on Exceptional Children*, 1970, *1*(8), 1–5.

The author asserts that public response to sex education for the mentally retarded tends to be restricted to parents. In this article, the author presents sex education as the responsibility of teachers. He describes two approaches to the training of teachers in the area of sexuality and the retarded. The first approach was developed and incorporated into a statewide in-service training program for teachers of educable mentally retarded in Iowa. The second approach was a two-week workshop aimed at changing teachers' behavior. The purposes, processes, experiences, and results of both approaches are discussed.

Meyen, E. L., and Retish, P. M. Sex education for the mentally retarded: Influencing teachers' attitudes. *Mental Retardation*, 1971, *9*(1), 46–49.

The authors describe the utilization of a workshop approach to instruct and influence attitudes of teachers toward sex education for the mentally retarded. Participants included 42 teachers, of whom 16 were special class teachers. Although a slight trend toward conservatism was noted at the conclusion of the two-week period, the participants found the program valuable.

Meyerowitz, J. H. Bridge over troubled waters. Paper read at a Conference on Sexuality and the Mentally Retarded, State University of New York College at Potsdam, September 21–22, 1972.

The author discusses sexuality in three different levels of mental retardation.

Meyerowitz, J. H. Sex and the mentally retarded. *Medical Aspects of Human Sexuality*, 1971, *5*(11), 95–118.

In this article, the author discusses sexuality and sexual behavior in mentally retarded persons. The author strongly reacts to some observers who report "abnormal sexual behavior" on the part of the mentally retarded person. Sexual development as it relates to the retarded person is described and discussed in light of research and clinical findings. The need for adequate sex education for retarded individuals is argued.

Money, J. W. Some thoughts on sexual taboos and the rights of the retarded. In F. F. de la Cruz and G. D. LaVeck (Eds.), *Human sexuality and the mentally retarded.* New York: Brunner/Mazel, 1973.

The author stresses that "there should be greater understanding of the importance of allowing the mentally retarded an opportunity for expressing tenderness, affection, and love even to the point of sexual activity." This presentation was made at a conference held by the National Institute of Child Health and Human Development to study biological and psychosocial aspects of sexuality in the retarded person. The author discusses social attitudes toward teaching sex education, and explicit sexual pictures and pornography and their relations to the sexuality of the mentally retarded person. The author argues for nonjudgmentalism in developing sex education programs for the retarded.

Money, J. Special sex education and cultural anthropology, with reference to mental deficiency, physical deformity, and urban ghettos. *Journal of Special Education*, 1971, *5*(4), 369–372.

In this article, the author discusses the difficulties faced by handicapped persons in their attempts for sexual expression. He asserts that in our culture sex is dealt with by exclusion and duplicity. Some sexual subjects are not to be discussed and some sexual behaviors are not to be tolerated. Those with the most warped ideas about sex are the very ones who insist there should be no sex education. The author complains that alternative and innovative programs for the severely mentally retarded are rejected without any apparent consideration of the joy possible for retarded persons from forming and/or sustaining an intimate relationship. Also, physically handicapped persons are not helped to get to know each other, but are often isolated and are not aware of others of the opposite sex similarly handicapped. In addition, they are given little or no help in the mechanics of how to achieve a full and joyful sex life within the limits of their handicap. The author discusses some ideas to bring about improvement in this area.

Morgenstern, M. Community attitudes toward sexuality of the retarded. In F. F. de la Cruz and G. D. LaVeck (Eds.), *Human sexuality and the mentally retarded.* New York: Brunner/Mazel, 1973.

The author obtained information about attitudes toward the sexuality of the retarded from various sources, e.g., literature reviews and interviews. He found three main categories of attitudes: (1) the subhuman attitude, reflected by those who believe the retarded have to be segregated in closed institutions; (2) the child-innocent attitude, which reflects a view of the retarded as eternal child; and (3) the developing person attitude, a progressive view that sees the retarded person as having full rights for development and growth. Other observations are discussed by the author.

Morgenstern, M. The psychosexual development of the retarded. In F. F. de la Cruz and G. D. LaVeck (Eds.), *Human sexuality and the mentally retarded.* New York: Brunner/Mazel, 1973.

This presentation was made at a conference held by the National Institute of Child Health and Human Development to study the biological and psychosocial aspects of sexuality and the mentally retarded individual. This chapter examines the psychosexual developmental process in the mentally retarded person from birth to adulthood. The author suggests that the psychosexual development of the retarded person is similar to that of the nonretarded.

Morgenstern, M. Sexuality, marriage, and parenthood among the retarded. *Journal of Clinical Child Psychology*, 1973, *2*(1), 27–28.

In this article, the author discusses sex, marriage, and the possibility of parenthood for mentally retarded persons. He points out that society has a dual image of mentally retarded individuals. One concept is that they are sexless and inert, and the other is that, because of their retardation, they are oversexed and the community must be protected from them. Parents are skeptical of their retarded child's ability to develop warm, friendly relationships, and they fear promiscuity will be the result. In an attempt to deny their child's sexuality, the very behavior they fear is produced. The need for sex education is stressed.

Morgenstern, M. Sexuality and the mentally retarded. Paper presented at a Conference on Sexuality and the Mentally Retarded, State University of New York College at Potsdam, September 21–22, 1972.

Various aspects of sexuality and marriage in the mentally retarded are discussed in light of information obtained from the literature. The author concludes that from the limited information we have, "the sexual needs of most retarded persons are essentially the same as their normal peers."

Mosier, H. D., Grossman, H. J., and Dingman, H. F. Secondary sex development in mentally deficient individuals. *Child Development*, 1962, *33*, 273–286.

This report presents the results of a survey conducted to define the relation between mental deficiency and secondary sex development. Examination of an institutionalized male and female population showed that there is a tendency for a delay in the appearance of secondary sex features in the mentally retarded, when compared with a cross section of the population at large. Differences within four diagnostic groups and three IQ groups of the patients were compared. Results showed no significant differences, with the exception of axillary hair for the mongoloid girls between 14 and 17 years of age.

Mulhern, T. J. Survey of reported sexual behavior and policies characterizing residential facilities for retarded citizens. *American Journal of Mental Deficiency*, 1975, *79*(6), 670–673.

This report presents and discusses the results of a survey conducted in 82 residential facilities for mentally retarded persons. The survey concerned sexual behavior among residents, and the attitudes of the professional personnel toward various sexual activities of residents. The author asserts that the results of this survey suggest "that a commitment to principles of normalization encounters severe strains in the area of sexual behavior." He adds that there is a need for conceptual clarification directed both at defining normative behavior in this area and at applying the principles of normalization to those behaviors.

Narot, J. R. The moral and ethical implications of human sexuality as they relate to the retarded. In F. F. de la Cruz and G. D. LaVeck (Eds.), *Human sexuality and the mentally retarded.* New York: Brunner/Mazel, 1973.

Jewish religious attitudes, ethics, and morality regarding sexuality and the retarded are presented and discussed in this chapter by Rabbi Narot of the reformed Temple Israel in Miami. This presentation was made at a conference held by the National Institute of Child Health and Human Development to study sexuality in the retarded person.

Ortinau, M. C. Some considerations in planning a sex education program for the trainable mentally handicapped. Paper presented at a Conference on Sexuality and the Mentally Retarded, State University of New York College at Potsdam, September 21–22, 1972.

This presentation is concerned with the interrelationships of the home, school, church, and community in planning a sex education program for the trainable mentally retarded.

Pallister, P. D., and Perry, R. M. Reflections on marriage for the retarded: The case for voluntary sterilization. *Hospital and Community Psychiatry*, 1973, *24*(3), 172–174.

Issues relating to marriage and sterilization for the retarded person are discussed in light of research findings and concepts of normalization in human services.

Pattullo, A. W. Puberty in the girl who is retarded. Arlington, Texas: National Association for Retarded Children, 1969.

This booklet is an attempt to deal with some of the questions and concerns that parents may have when their retarded daughter reaches puberty. Presented in the form of questions often asked, the booklet provides answers on a wide range of topics, such as physical changes in puberty, menstruation, sexual behavior, masturbation, contraceptives, marriage, protection against sexual aggression, menstrual hygiene, and others. Also included are specific suggestions for the use of sex education material for teaching about various sexual organs and functions.

Pattullo, A. W., and Barnard, K. E. Teaching menstrual hygiene to the mentally retarded. *American Journal of Nursing*, 1968, *68*, 2572–2575.

This paper presents a report of the learning experiences of 14-year-old mentally retarded girls, and data gathered from 25 mothers of retarded girls regarding menstrual hygiene. Both the learning experiences and the data collected from these mothers show how highly structured the teaching plans must be for mentally retarded teen-aged girls and what kind of help their mothers need from nurses and sex educators. The authors conclude that the "explanation to the retarded girl that menstruation is a sign of growing up and her mastery of the task of menstrual grooming" help her to meet her need for independence and adulthood.

Perske, R. About sexual development: An attempt to be human with the mentally retarded. *Mental Retardation,* 1973, *11*(1), 6–8.

It is noted that past attitudes toward the sexual development of the mentally retarded have tended toward brutal insensitivity and callous repression of their sexuality. In order to forestall a possible trend toward the equal extreme of forcing concentrated sex education upon retardates who are unprepared to cope with such "crash courses," a humane and understanding approach is advocated. This approach would recognize the right of each retarded individual to achieve his highest reasonable potential on the continuum of human sexual development, at his own pace, throughout his lifetime.

Perske, R. Sexual development. In R. Perske (Ed.), *New directions for parents of persons who are retarded.* New York: Abingdon Press, 1973.

This chapter discusses sexual development and psychosexual aspects in mentally retarded persons. It is written primarily for parents of retarded children who want to deal with their child's sexuality in an effective way.

Reed, S. C., and Anderson, V. E. Effects of changing sexuality on the gene pool. In F. F. de la Cruz and G. D. LaVeck (Eds.), *Human sexuality and the mentally retarded.* New York: Brunner/Mazel, 1973.

Understanding the factors maintaining the frequency of mental retardation in the general population is important to any consideration of policies regarding the sexual behavior of the mentally retarded person. A review of relevant literature and analyses of studies in this area are presented in this chapter. The authors conclude that "at present, retarded parents produce 17 percent of all retarded children, and it is improbable that there will be any large deviation in this proportion in the immediate future." This presentation was made at a conference held by the National Institute of Child Health and Human Development to study sexuality in the mentally retarded person.

A resource guide in sex education for the mentally retarded. Washington D.C.: American Association for Health, Physical Education and Recreation, 1971.

This working guide, designed to help educators, counselors, parents, and others concerned with the growth of the mentally retarded, provides materials applicable to educable retarded of all ages and levels of development. Resource materials and curriculum concepts are presented in the areas of awareness of self, physical changes and understanding of self, peer relationships, and responsibility to society as men and women. A detailed coded listing of resources is provided, including printed materials, films, filmstrips, transparencies, slides, records, teaching aids, tapes, and other materials appropriate to sex education programs for the mentally retarded. Concepts are presented sequentially from the basic and easy to the difficult and more sophisticated.

A resource guide in sex education for the mentally retarded. New York: American Association for Health, Physical Education and Recreation, and Sex Information and Education Council of the U.S., 1973.

This publication includes guidelines for the development of sex education programs for retarded individuals, and resources that can facilitate the planning and implementation of these programs.

Salerno, L. J., Park, J. K., and Giannini, M. J. Reproductive capacity of the mentally retarded. *Journal of Reproductive Medicine*, 1975, *14*(3), 123–129.

Ninety-seven mentally retarded females were examined in order to evaluate aspects of physical growth and sexual development. The areas studied were anthropometric, bone age, and sexual maturation, i.e., breast development, pubic hair, axillary hair, menarche, menstrual pattern, and patterns of ovulation. Results showed that, in general, mental retardation is associated with marked retardation in physical growth, in the development of secondary sex characteristics, and in the achievement of menstrual regularity and ovulation.

Scally, B. G. Marriage and mental handicap: Some observations in Northern Ireland. In F. F. de la Cruz and G. D. LaVeck (Eds.), *Human sexuality and the mentally retarded*. New York: Brunner/Mazel, 1973.

The author discusses the results of an intensive study examining marriage among mentally retarded persons in Northern Ireland. Also discussed is the suitability of retarded persons as parents. This presentation was made at a conference held by the National Institute of Child Health and Human Development to study sexuality and mental retardation.

Secker, L. Sex education and mental handicap. *Special Education,* 1973, *62*, 27–28.

The author asserts that placing mentally handicapped persons in the community "without preparing them as much for the sexual aspects of life as for other situations seems to fail to provide a full education." This paper discusses the school's aims to adopt a natural approach both to sex education and to dealing with sexual behavior and problems in mentally handicapped children and adults.

Selznick, H. M. Sex education and the mentally retarded. *Exceptional Children*, 1966, *32*, 640–644.

Sex education is an important part of the responsibilities confronting the educator charged with providing appropriate learning experiences for the mentally retarded. Various methods and aspects of sex education programs for the mentally retarded are presented and discussed, along with some objectives to be included in such programs.

Sengstock, W. L., and Vergason, G. A. Issues in sex education for the retarded. *Education and Training of the Mentally Retarded*, 1970, *5*, 99–103.

The authors assert that "the school has many advantages for teaching sex education to the retarded." This paper discusses the urgent need for sex education in the special class curriculum. This should include the psychosocial aspects of sex as well as the biological processes. The authors present ways of selecting and preparing teaching staff to handle sex education effectively, and offer suggestions for involving parents.

Sexuality and the mentally retarded. Watertown, New York: Planned Parenthood of Northern New York, 1975.

This book consists of the proceedings of a Conference on Sexuality and the Mentally Retarded held at the State University of New York College at Potsdam, on September 21 and 22, 1972. Various aspects of sexuality, marriage, sterilization, parenthood, and sex education programs were discussed by conference leaders.

Shaw, C. H., and Wright, C. H. The married mental defective: A follow-up study. *Lancet*, January 1960, 273–274.

The authors report and discuss the results of a follow-up study aimed at the assessment of the marriages of 242 mentally retarded persons. Most of the marriages were found to be "reasonably happy and stable." Divorce was reported in 20 percent of the subjects.

Shindell, P. E. Sex education programs and the mentally retarded. *Journal of School Health*, 1975, *45*(2), 88–90.

Various aspects of sex education for the mentally retarded, and factors in the development of programs in this area, are discussed in light of a review of the literature.

Thaller, K. E. Attitudes toward sexuality of the mentally retarded. Paper read at a Conference on Sexuality and the Mentally Retarded, State University of New York College at Potsdam, September 21–22, 1972.

This paper presents the results of a study aimed at the examination of basic knowledge about and attitudes toward the sexuality of the mentally retarded person. Subjects were the participants at a conference on sexuality and the retarded who were evaluated before and after the conference.

Thorne, G. D. Sex education of mentally retarded girls. *American Journal of Mental Deficiency*, 1957, *62*, 460–463.

This is a follow-up report of an earlier article which described a new sex education program at Caswell Training School in North Carolina. The program included only those who were considered "high grade" females ranging in age from twelve years to over fifty years. Each class was composed of girls with similar ages, IQs, and reading levels. A very "natural" approach was taken, and subjects related to sex were integrated into other home economics subjects without launching immediately into full-blown discussions of sex. The objective was to provide essential information without focusing undue attention on normally determined physiological or psychological characteristics. The author points out that staff involved in this program find it "most necessary" to provide students with information basic to their ability to cope with life.

Thurman, R. L., Bassin, J., and Ackermann, T. Sexuality, sex education and the mentally retarded: One educational approach. *Mental Retardation*, 1976, *14*(1), 19.

Convinced that parents and teachers must be comfortable with and knowledgeable in sexuality, the authors developed a model for sex education that is described in this article. The authors suggest that this program can be generalized to include other populations.

Turchin, G. Sexual attitudes of mothers of retarded children. *Journal of School Health*, 1974, *44*, 490–492.

Mothers (n=44) of trainable mentally retarded children were interviewed to examine their attitudes toward various sexual issues relating to their children, i.e., sexual behavior, sex education, birth control, marriage, and dating. It was found that religion has a great impact on mothers' attitudes toward masturbation. Although many of the mothers expected that their children would develop the ability to date, most of them felt that their children would never be able to marry. Mothers indicated that they wanted sex education taught in the schools. They also desired some help in understanding their child's sexuality.

Turner, E. T. Attitudes of parents of deficient children toward their child's sexual behavior. *Journal of School Health*, 1970, *40*, 548–550.

The purpose of this study was to examine the attitudes of parents (n=53) of mentally deficient children toward various aspects of sexuality as they relate to their child. It was found that only one-third of the parents discussed sex with their child, and the majority of these parents only discussed the birth process. Those who had not discussed sex stated that their child was not ready for discussing sex. The parents were asked if their child was having difficulty adjusting to sex, and 20 percent felt that their child was having difficulty. Those having difficulty were the emotionally disturbed and brain-damaged children, and the most difficulty was found to be with "excessive masturbation." Half of the parents had discussed their child's excessive behavior with their spouse, and 25 percent had discussed it with their physicians. Eight percent of the parents had sterilization proposed to them for their brain-damaged or mongoloid child.

Valente, M. Sexual advice for the mentally retarded and their families: Brief guide to office counseling. *Medical Aspects of Human Sexuality*, 1975, *9*(10), 91–92.

The role of the physician in counseling the mentally retarded and their families is discussed, and office counseling procedures are outlined in this article. The author asserts that sexual counseling with teen-aged and adult retarded and their families "is best done in a group situation supervised by those experienced in the field." Supervisors may be physicians, social workers, psychologists, nurses, educators, or occupational therapists. These persons must "come to grips" with their own sexual attitudes and feelings before attempting to counsel the retarded person regarding sexuality.

Vockell, E., and Mattick, P. Sex education for the mentally retarded: An analysis of problems, programs, and research. *Education and Training of the Mentally Retarded*, 1972, *7*, 129–134.

In this article, the authors analyze and discuss the many problems associated with the development and implementation of sex education programs for mentally retarded persons. Specific difficulties faced by retarded children, their parents and their teachers, as well as specific programs of sex education, are critically evaluated. The authors conclude that their analysis of the literature reveals that most of it presents theoretical aspects rather than scientific data and is concerned with adolescents rather than younger children. Recommendations for further research and development in this area are made.

Walker, G. H. Some psychosexual considerations of institutionalized mental defectives. *American Journal of Mental Deficiency*, 1948, *53*, 312–317.

All too often we neglect the sexual development of patients in institutions for the mentally retarded. In an effort to sensitize those professionals working with the retarded, normal sexual development is compared with that noted by the author to occur with the retarded. The model used for comparison is psychodynamic in nature. It seems certain that sexual development in the retarded is not given the full significance and consideration it warrants. Further attention should be directed at the sexual adjustment problems of these individuals.

Weingold, J. T. Some considerations on sexuality and the mentally retarded. Paper read at a Conference on Sexuality and the Mentally Retarded, State University of New York College at Potsdam, September 21–22, 1972.

Various aspects of sexuality, birth control, and marriage as they relate to the mentally retarded person are discussed.

Whalen, R. E., and Whalen, C. K. Sexual behavior: Research perspectives. In F. F. de la Cruz and G. D. LaVeck (Eds.), *Human sexuality and the mentally retarded.* New York: Brunner/Mazel, 1973.

The authors present selected excerpts from interviews conducted with two mentally retarded adults regarding various sexual issues. The excerpts demonstrate that the retarded adults had knowledge about sexual functioning and had concerns over appropriate sexual behavior.

At the same time, the interviews revealed that they had minimal sex education and general confusion regarding many sexual matters. These interviews are followed by an extensive review and analysis of various studies examining the biological basis of sexuality and sexual differentiation. Finally, the authors discuss some research perspectives. Two areas of needed research are identified: the neurohormonal control of reproduction, and the neurohormonal control of sexual behavior.

Wish, J. Socio-sexual beliefs and attitudes of moderately retarded male adults. Unpublished Master's thesis, Ohio State University, 1974.

Attitudes and beliefs held by moderately retarded men regarding various sociosexual variables were studied. Results and conclusions are presented and discussed.

Zelman, D. B., and Tyser, K. Elementary adult sex education for the mentally retarded: EASE Curriculum. Madison, Wisconsin: The Madison Opportunity Center, Inc., 1976.

The EASE Curriculum was designed to be a comprehensive teaching guide for sex education with mentally retarded adults. The curriculum consists of instructional objectives which were grouped into four major units: (1) biological, (2) sexual behavior, (3) health, and (4) relationships. Each unit includes a series of instructional objectives and an objective test based on the instructional content of the unit.

Chapter Ten

Sex and the Aged

Amulree, L. Sex and the elderly. *Practitioner*, 1954, *172*, 431–435.

Sexual behavior and functioning in the elderly is discussed in this article in light of the clinical and research findings of the author and other researchers.

Armstrong, E. B. The possibility of sexual happiness in old age. In H. G. Beigel (Ed.), *Advances in sex research.* New York: Harper & Row, 1963.

Sexual functioning in the aged is discussed in light of common myths and research-based facts. While the former hold that the aged are sexless, the latter reveal that older persons have sexual needs, interests, and ability.

Bastani, J. B. Sexuality in later life. *Nebraska State Medical Journal*, 1977, *62*(3), 62–64.

The importance of sexual expression and changes that occur in sexual responsivity and functioning in later life are the topics discussed by the author. Aimed primarily at physicians, this article identifies the role of the health-care practitioner in sex counseling with the elderly.

Benjamin, H. Impotence and aging. *Sexology*, 1959, *26*(3), 238–243.

This paper discusses the problem of impotence in the aging male in light of research and clinical findings. Some treatment modalities and counseling suggestions are presented.

Benjamin, H. The role of the physician in the sex problems of the aged. In H. G. Beigel (Ed.), *Advances in sex research.* New York: Harper & Row, 1963.

Sexual problems of the aged and the role of the physician in assisting patients to achieve sexual adjustment are discussed, along with some treatment modalities. Several clinical case studies are presented for illustration.

Blazer, D. Adding life to years: Late life sexuality and patient care. *Nursing Care*, 1977, *10*(7), 28–29.

The main thrust of this article is that sexuality is ageless and is to be enjoyed in later life as it is enjoyed by the young. The author describes changes and problems that might be experienced by some older patients and outlines the role of the nurse in alleviating their difficulties.

Bowers, L. M., Cross, R. R., and Lloyd, F. A. Sexual function and urologic disease in the elderly male. *Journal of the American Geriatrics Society*, 1963, *11*, 647–652.

According to the authors, previous studies of sexual function in the elderly male, conducted primarily with patients, have been biased. The survey reported in this article concerns the sexual function and behavior and the medical status of a sample of elderly men who were not patients (n=157). Subjects' ages ranged from 60 to 74 years. The sexual and urologic histories and the results of physical examinations and urinalyses were recorded, and are presented in this paper. The incidence of impotence was found to rise progressively from 30 percent in the youngest patients to 60 percent in patients who were 70 to 74 years of age. However, the potent males at these ages continue to experience coitus approximately 20 times per year.

Bowman, K. M. The sex life of the aging individual. *Geriatrics*, 1954, *9*, 83–84.

Sexuality in old age, and the need for extensive studies of sexual functioning and behavior in older people, are discussed.

Bowman, K. M. The sex life of the aging individual. In M. F. DeMartino (Ed.), *Sexual behavior and personality characteristics*. New York: Citadel Press, 1963.

This chapter was reprinted from *Geriatrics*, 1954, *9*, 83–84. It discusses changes in sexual activity and behavior in old age, and the need for extensive studies in this area.

Burnside, I. M. Sexuality and aging. *Medical Arts and Sciences*, 1973, *27*(3), 13–27.

This paper presents a comprehensive literature review on the topic of sexuality in the aging person. Cultural and social attitudes toward the aging and sexuality, the attitudes of the aged toward sexuality, and the institutionalized aged are some of the areas covered in this review. Suggestions for intervention and improvement are discussed. These include the increase of sexual knowledge and self-awareness in order to improve attitudes, and improvement in the aged person's environment for better sociosexual expression. The author makes the plea "that each of us increase our own knowledge about sexuality and strive for a more open, sensible, and sensitive approach in matters of sexuality in the elderly."

Butler, R. N. Sexual advice to the aging male. *Medical Aspects of Human Sexuality*, 1975, *9*(9), 155–156.

Sexual problems in the elderly are discussed in this article and some specific suggestions for office counseling are given. Common causes of loss of sex drive in later years may include depression, anxiety, boredom, fear of heart attack, alcohol abuse, antidepressants, tranquilizers, poor physical fitness, obesity, and diabetes.

Butler, R. N., and Lewis, M. E. *Sex after sixty: A guide for men and women for their later years.* New York: Harper and Row, 1976.

This is a practical book aimed at guiding older persons in "enjoying—to whatever degree and in whatever way they wish—the satisfactions of physical sex and pleasurable sensuality." The authors answer questions such as: What happens to the body sexually as it ages? Will the changes affect sexual functioning? Also discussed are the impact of heart conditions on sexual functioning, other common medical problems and sex, common emotional problems and sexual functioning, where to go for sexual counseling, and other related topics.

Calderone, M. S. The sexuality of aging. *SIECUS Newsletter*, 1971, *7*(1).

Society's view of the aging person and its impact on sexuality in later years are the topics discussed in this brief communication.

Cauldwell, D. O. When does sex life end? *Sexology*, 1958, *25*, 250–253.

More and more, it is being realized that age is not the decisive factor in ending sex interest and activity. This is the main message of this article, which discusses sexual activity, function, and dysfunction in old age.

Cavan, R. Speculations on innovations to conventional marriage in old age. *Gerontologist*, 1973, *13*, 409–411.

Research findings show that the elderly have needs for sexual expression, dependency relationships, inclusion in a peer group, and participation in a family life. The author believes that the personal needs of the elderly are very similar to the personal needs of the young, and that the innovations being tried out by the young may also be very applicable to the elderly. Some of these innovations include nonmarital cohabitation, homosexual or lesbian companionships, group marriage, communes, and comarital contracts. This article is a review of some of these concepts as applied to the personal and emotional needs of the elderly. The author concludes that at present only the young approve of the innovations, and only a small number of middle-age persons accept these methods. If the innovations are to be effective in satisfying the needs of the aged, a more tolerant public opinion will first be required.

Chapman, R. H. Comment and controversy no longer at risk: Sex among the elderly. *Family Planning Perspectives*, 1976, *8*(5), 253.

Aging persons are too often deprived of opportunities for sexual expression. This article addresses this problem and discusses the need for a more optimistic view of sexuality in the elderly.

Christensen, C. V., and Johnson, A. B. Sexual patterns in a group of older never-married women. *Journal of Geriatric Psychiatry*, 1973, *7*, 80–98.

This article presents the results of a study aimed at the examination of sexual behavior in a group of older women who were never married (n=70).

Claman, A. D. Sexual difficulties after 50: Panel discussion. *Canadian Medical Association Journal*, 1966, *94*, 207.

This article presents a panel discussion on sexual dysfunction and difficulties in older persons.

Clark, L. M. Sex life in the middle-aged. *Marriage and Family Living*, 1949, *11*, 58–60.

Changes in sexuality of middle-aged men and women are discussed.

Clark, L. M. Sex life of the middle-aged. In M. F. DeMartino (Ed.), *Sexual behavior and personality characteristics*. New York: Citadel Press, 1963.

Changes that occur in the psychological, emotional, and physiological aspects of sexuality in middle life are discussed. This chapter was reprinted from *Marriage and Family Living*, 1949, *11*, 58–60.

Clover, B. H. Family practice and problems of aging: Sex in the aging. *Postgraduate Medicine,* 1975, *57*(6), 165–169.

This article discusses psychosocial and sexual aspects in the aged in light of clinical and research findings. The psychological effects of age seem to be more important than the physical aspects in most instances. Opportunities for sexual expression should not be limited for the elderly in nursing homes and other institutions.

Cole, T. M. The physician's role in working with the sexuality of the elderly. In J. T. Kelly and J. H. Weir (Eds.), *Perspectives on human sexuality*. Minneapolis: Craftsman Press, 1976.

The content and style used by the author in approaching the topic of sexuality and in counseling aged patients regarding their sexual concerns are outlined and discussed.

Comfort, A. Sex and aging. *Resource Guide*, 1976, *1*(1), 4–7 (Published by Multi Media Resource Center).

In this article, Comfort discusses the changes that occur in both male and female sex responses as a result of aging. The aging male needs more direct physical stimulation to achieve an erection, but can maintain it for a prolonged time. Sexual potency is normally lifelong, and the most common cause of impotency among older men is their thinking that it should occur. Sexual desire and performance seem to persist in women to a greater degree than they do in men.

Comfort, A. Sexuality and aging. *SIECUS Report*, 1976, *4*(6), 1, 9.

Comfort expands in this article on a statement issued by the Sex Information and Education Council of the U.S. which indicates that "aging people are too often deprived of opportunities for sexual companionship and expression, which they need despite unscientific beliefs to the contrary. Society has an obligation to create conditions conducive to the fulfillment of these needs." The general message of this article is that sexuality and sexual functioning are lifelong. The author presents results of research studies to confirm this message, and concludes: "We can at least stop mocking, governessing, and segregating the old and the aging; it is to their sexuality, after all, that we owe our own existence, and that sexuality is honorable."

Comfort, A. Sexuality in old age. *Journal of the American Geriatrics Society*, 1974, *22*(10), 440–442.

The everpresent myths of society are compared with the results of studies showing that among married couples in their 70s, between 70 and 80 percent were still sexually functioning and active. The author asserts that older people should experience sexuality as a continued source of self-value in institutional settings, such as nursing homes and hospitals.

Cooley, E. E. Psychosocial aspects of sex and aging. In J. T. Kelly and J. H. Weir (Eds.), *Perspectives on human sexuality*. Minneapolis: Craftsman Press, 1976.

Among the problems faced by the aged, one area of concern that has been inadequately treated and researched is that of sexuality. The author discusses the psychosocial and sexual aspects of aging in light of societal attitudes surrounded by myths, and in light of research-based information. The author concludes that contrary to common misconception, healthy elderly persons are physiologically capable of and interested in sexual activity.

Costello, M. K. Sex, intimacy and aging. *American Journal of Nursing*, 1975, *75*(8), 1330–1332.

The importance of the gratification of sexual needs and the desire for intimacy is discussed in light of the author's clinical observations of a 70-year-old male patient who had Parkinson's disease. The author indicates that the nurse must be comfortable with her own sexuality so that she can help patients express their sexual problems and concerns. She concludes that "the elderly like any age group have sexual needs. One is the opportunity to express themselves without condemnation or ridicule."

Daly, M. J. Sexual attitudes in menopausal and postmenopausal women. *Medical Aspects of Human Sexuality,* 1968, *2*(5), 48–53.

Sexual attitudes, function, and responsiveness in menopausal and postmenopausal women are discussed and suggestions for treatment and counseling are presented.

Dean, S. Geriatric sexuality: Normal, needed, neglected. *Geriatrics,* 1974, *29*, 134–137.

The author discusses the need of the elderly for sexual and interpersonal relationships. Older men often request erotic activity with prostitutes when their wives will not participate. Medical doctors have been remiss in not treating aging and its sexual consequences. Decline in sexual activity is psychosocial rather than physiologic. The author also discusses the trend for senior citizens to live together, instead of marrying, in order to maintain their Social Security benefits, and reviews legislation which discriminates against quality of life for the elderly.

De Nigola, P., and Peruzza, M. Sex in the aged. *Journal of the American Geriatrics Society*, 1974, *22*(8), 380–382.

Sexual activity and habits in the aged are analyzed and discussed in light of observations made on 85 subjects and a review of the literature. Subjects' ages ranged from 62 to 81 years. The impact of diseases and the importance of environmental, social, and psychological factors in connection with sexual activity in older years are discussed. Sexual activity in the aged is not exceptional and may give serenity to aging. The authors conclude that "medical, social, and psychologic prophylatic counseling should be applied as early as possible by geriatricians in collaboration with sexologists."

Dresen, S. E. The middle years: The sexually active middle adult. *American Journal of Nursing*, 1975, *75*, 1001–1005.

This article examines some facts and fallacies regarding sexuality in middle years. In light of recent research findings, the author discusses sexual patterns in middle age, sexual dysfunctions, and sexual difficulties associated with chronic health problems. Aimed primarily at practicing nurses, the article includes some suggestions and recommendations for counseling and advising patients regarding sexual difficulties. The author asserts that "the nurse's own attitudes about sexuality will largely determine her ability to counsel people with sexual problems."

Dunn, A. P. Liberating the aged. III. *Nursing Times,* 1975, *71,* 1086–1087.

Some myths and misconceptions regarding the aging person, and the mistreatment the aged receive in nursing homes, are discussed in this report. One area of mistreatment is sexuality. Institutionalized aging persons, most of whom are separated from their spouses, are expected to live a life of celibacy. The author calls for better treatment of the aged and for the realization that older persons have sexual needs to be acknowledged and satisfied.

Ellis, W. J., and Grayhack, J. T. Sexual function in aging males after orchiectomy and estrogen therapy. *Journal of Urology,* 1963, *89*(6), 895–899.

The sexual function of patients with carcinoma of the prostate who have been subjected to orchiectomy, estrogen therapy, or both, was studied (n=82). Only 46 percent of the patients were sexually potent prior to therapy, and only 26 percent of these were active sexually. Following treatment, 42 percent of the patients who were potent before therapy retained their sexual potency. Those treated by estrogen alone showed a greater tendency to remain potent than those subjected to orchiectomy or to a combination of both therapeutic modalities.

Fellman, S. L., Hasting, D. W., and Miller, W. W. Viewpoints: Should androgens be used to treat impotence in men over 50? *Medical Aspects of Human Sexuality*, 1975, *9*(7), 32–43.

This article presents the clinical opinion of the authors regarding treatment with androgens of impotence in males over fifty years of age. An appropriate diagnostic and endocrine evaluation has to be made before this treatment can be prescribed. According to Fellman, the successful effect of this treatment does not result from direct enhancement of erectile ability by the androgen. Rather, it relates to the sense of well-being associated with anabolic androgenic substances, the physician's confidence that the impotence is treatable, and the reduction of anxiety during the course of treatment. Some reservations concerning this treatment are presented and discussed. With these reservations, "androgens are considered beneficial in the treatment of impotence in the male over 50 years of age."

Felstein, I. *Sex in later life*. Baltimore: Penguin Books, 1973.

First published in 1970 as *Sex and the Long Life*, this book is devoted to the discussion of physical, mental, and sexual changes in the aged. The author, in nonmedical language, answers such questions as: To what age is sexual activity likely to continue? Can and should sexual activity be prolonged indefinitely? How far do ideas and conceptions about youth and aging inhibit the expression of married love in the elderly? The book gives advice and reassurance to the elderly in the area of love and sexual expression.

Finkle, A. L. Emotional quality and physical quantity of sexual activity in aging males. *Journal of Geriatric Psychiatry,* 1973, *6*, 70–79.

Sexual responsivity, functioning, and concerns of the aging male are discussed in this paper in light of a review of the literature and several case histories of geriatric patients. In conclusion, the author asserts that "aging men who have been sexually active for much of their lives may be expected to maintain sexual interest and activity even to an advanced age." The role of the physician in alleviating sexual concerns in the aging patient is also discussed.

Finkle, A. L., and Moyers, T. C. Sexual potency in aging males. IV. Status of private patients before and after prostatectomy. *Journal of Urology*, 1960, *84*(1), 152–157.

This study examined sexual functioning in patients diagnosed and treated surgically for prostatic symptoms. Subjects were 101 male patients ranging in age from 30 to 92 years, whose post-prostatectomy status was reviewed. Only 50 percent of the patients were sexually active preoperatively. Of those, approximately 70 percent retained their sexual function after surgery. The authors conclude that the physician's attitude toward preservation of the patient's potency greatly influences the patient.

Freeman, J. T. Sexual aspects of aging. In E. V. Cowdry and F. U. Steinberg (Eds.), *The care of the geriatric patient*. St. Louis: C. V. Mosby, 1971.

Sexual functioning and disturbances in aging are discussed in light of some case histories and a review of relevant literature. Effects on sexuality of various drugs, i.e., amphetamines, sedatives, androgens and estrogens, are presented. In conclusion, the author stresses that "each individual has a personal array of sexual capacities, but the general trend with aging is one of reduced incentive, lessened ability, fewer opportunities, and reasonable acceptance of the senescent situation."

Gaitz, C. M. Sexual activity during menopause. *Medical Aspects of Human Sexuality*, 1974, *8*(12), 67–68.

Psychological and sexual aspects in menopausal women are discussed in this brief guide to office counseling. Also presented are some specific suggestions for counseling and advice by the physician.

Glover, B. H. Disorders of sexuality and communication in the elderly. *Comprehensive Therapy*, 1977, *3*(6), 21–25.

Sexual difficulties most frequently encountered by the elderly are presented. Treatment of communication problems and counseling methods for sexual problems are also discussed. This article is aimed at physicians, and emphasizes the importance of sex counseling with the elderly.

Glover, B. H. Sex counseling of the elderly. *Hospital Practice,* 1977, *12*(6), 101–113.

Aging people are too often deprived of opportunities for satisfying their sexual needs. This article describes changes in sexual functioning induced by aging, identifies some of the problems encountered by the elderly, and discusses counseling efforts to alleviate these difficulties.

Goldfarb, A. F., Daly, M. J., Lieberman, D., and Reed, D. M. Sex and the menopause. *Medical Aspects of Human Sexuality,* 1970, *4*(11), 64–89.

With the increase in the number of people between the ages of 40 and 60, medicine is increasingly faced with the problems of sexuality within the total health care of patients. Participants in this roundtable, which is narrated by the main author, discuss sexuality in older women and some treatment modalities to enhance it.

Herrick, E. H. Sex changes in aging. *Sexology,* 1957, *24,* 248–253.

Physiological and hormonal changes in the sexual systems of aging men and women are described.

Jones, D. M. Sex: Not for youngsters only. *Journal of Practical Nursing,* 1976, *26*(3), 30–31.

Elderly people have sexual drives and needs. However, "nurses and other staff members in long-term care facilities often find themselves unprepared to deal with the sexual behavior presented by the residents." In this article, the author presents some sexual aspects of aging, and discusses the role of the nurse and the administration in long-term care facilities in dealing with the sexual behavior and concerns of patients. The author concludes that "every human being wants to be needed and loved. Our nursing home residents are no exception."

Kahn, E. The REM sleep and other characteristics of the aged. Unpublished Doctoral Dissertation, Yeshiva University, 1968.

This investigation was aimed at studying the sleep EEG, the amount of REM erection, the amount of dream recall, and the reported sexual behavior in 21 healthy males aged 71 to 96 years. Results showed that 45 percent of the recorded REM periods were accompanied by full or moderate erection, compared to some 80 percent reported for young adults. Not all the elderly showed reduced erection; 5 of the 12 subjects aged 71 to 80 had amounts of erection similar to that reported for the young adult. Of the 3 oldest subjects, aged 87, 95, and 96, 2 still had some REM erections. There was no relationship between the amount of REM sleep and the reported frequency of sexual outlet. However, the amount of REM sleep did correlate significantly with the amount of full erection. The author concludes that "the function of REM sleep remains ambiguous, and all that can be said is that in the healthy aged, amount of REM sleep appears to be related to the general physiological vigor of the individual."

Kahn, E., and Fisher, C. Amount of REM sleep erection in the healthy aged. *Journal of Geriatric Psychiatry*, 1969, *2*(2), 181–199.

Eighteen male subjects aged 71 to 96 years were each studied for three or two nights using the strain gauge method to measure penile erection. Full or moderate erections were observed in 45 percent of REM periods, while in the remaining 55 percent erections were either slight or nonexistent. Correlations between amount of full erection and reported current sexual behavior or the ability to enjoy sex just missed statistical significance.

Kahn, E., and Fisher, C. Dream recall and erections in the healthy aged. *Psychophysiology*, 1968, *4*(3), 393–394.

This study examined dream recall and sleep erections in 13 healthy males aged 70 to 96 years. During the study period, dream recall was recorded in 41 percent of the instances. Of the three oldest subjects, aged 87, 95, and 96, two still showed REM-period erections, while the 95-year-old showed no erection.

Kahn, E., and Fisher, C. REM sleep and sexuality in the aged. *Journal of Geriatric Psychiatry*, 1969, *2*(2), 181–199.

The purpose of this study was to examine penile erection during periods of rapid eye movements (REM) in the aged. Subjects were eighteen healthy males aged 71 to 96 years who were observed and examined during several nights. Results showed that in 45 percent of REM periods subjects had full or moderate erections, while in the remaining 55 percent erections were slight or absent. Five of the twelve subjects aged 71 to 80 years had amounts of erections similar to that of young adults. The authors concluded that "although amount of REM erection is lowered in the 70's, in individual cases it may be maintained as late as 80 to a degree approximating that of the young man."

Kahn, E., and Fisher, C. Some correlates of rapid eye movement sleep in the normal aged male. *Journal of Nervous and Mental Disease*, 1969, *148*(5), 495–505.

The purpose of this study was to examine the effects of cognitive and drive functioning on the amount of REM sleep in the aged. The level of drive was operationally defined by the subject's proportion of REM periods accompanied by full erection and by his reported frequency of sexual outlet. Sleep data were available from 16 healthy male subjects, aged 71 to 95 years. Results showed that the amount of REM sleep correlated significantly with the proportion of REM periods accompanied by full erection. Due to difficulties in interpreting these correlations in terms of a drive theory, these significant results were not considered confirmation of the drive hypothesis. The authors conclude that their findings "reflect a general physiological decline with age, affecting amount of REM sleep, erection, cognition and other aspects of functioning, and probably due to the deterioration of the central nervous system."

Kassel, V. Sex in nursing homes. *Medical Aspects of Human Sexuality,* 1976, *10*(3), 126–131.

The author discusses sex and the elderly, and asserts that "many elderly people residing in nursing homes have erotic feelings which continue to seek expression." He presents several case studies to illustrate the inadequate approach to sexuality and the aged in nursing homes. The author concludes that "aged people with active sexual interests are restricted from expressing a normal life when living in a nursing home."

Kirkendall, L. A., and Rubin, I. Sexuality and the life cycle: A broad concept of sexuality. New York: Sex Information and Education Council of the U.S., 1969.

Of particular interest in this booklet is a chapter discussing sexuality in later life.

LaToor, R. A., and Kear, K. Attitudes toward sex in the aged. *Archives of Sexual Behavior*, 1977, *6*(3), 203–213.

The purpose of this study was to evaluate the attitudes toward sex for the aged in university students (n=80) and in staff members of a nursing home for the aged (n=40). Results show an absence of negative attitudes, although sex in the aged was perceived as less credible than sex in young people.

Le Mon, C. Sex life of the middle aged. *Marriage and Family Living*, 1949, *11*, 58–60.

Physiological, psychological, and sexual changes in middle-aged men and women are discussed in this article.

Lief, H. I., Israel, S. L., Garcia, C. R., and Charny, C. W. Roundtable: Sex after 50. *Medical Aspects of Human Sexuality*, 1968, *2*(1), 41–47.

This roundtable, narrated by the major author, discusses sexual function and behavior in aging men and women. Also discussed are some sexual dysfunctions and concerns commonly experienced by aging patients.

Lindsay, H. B. The male and female climacteric. *Diseases of the Nervous System*, 1962, *23*, 149–151.

This study included 46 male and 30 female patients who were treated with heterosexual hormones for climacteric symptoms. Results of treatment were favorable. There was some improvement noticed in sexual functioning following treatment.

Martin, C. E. Marital and sexual factors in relation to age, disease, and longevity. In R. D. Wirt, G. Winokur, and M. Roff (Eds.), *Life history research in psychopathology (Volume 4)*. Minneapolis: University of Minnesota Press, 1975.

As part of the Baltimore Longitudinal Study of Aging, the author developed an interview schedule to secure systematic information about the marital and sexual experiences of the subjects participating in this program. This chapter presents and discusses the results of this effort. The main objectives of this study were to describe the effects of aging on sexual reactivity and functioning, to determine whether individual differences in sexual functioning may be related to some aspects of health, and to discover whether any attribute of sexual experience and functioning may be associated with the occurrence of disease. Data from 603 interviews with men ranging in age from 20 to 79 years are presented and discussed. The results were tabulated statistically in seven tables. A wide range of aspects were considered. With increasing age there were more reports of marital dissolution, a reduction in the quantity and kind of sexual activity, a decrease in certain sexual stimuli, and recurrent erectile impotence. The author felt the study revealed a definite decline in sexual expression with increasing age, as well as an increase in disturbances of sexual functioning.

Masters, W. H., and Ballew, J. W. The third sex. *Geriatrics*, 1955, *10*(1), 177–180.

The authors assert that "there is a third sex or 'neutral gender' existent and rapidly multiplying in our society today," referring to persons reaching old age. The various aspects of long-range sex steroid replacement therapy in this population are discussed in this article. The purpose of this treatment is to develop happier, better adjusted, more useful members of this "neutral gender."

Miller, M. Sexuality in the aged. *Forum*, Wisconsin Psychiatric Institute, University of Wisconsin-Madison, 1972, No. 2.

The author notes that "sex encompasses all the physical and psychological ways in which couples enhance each other's total well-being and contentment. Old age brings changes in physiology, in attitudes, and in environment, but the potential for sexuality remains." He further discusses sexuality in old age and outlines some specific suggestions for sexual counseling of the aged. It is noted that when older couples are institutionalized or not in a home of their own, it is important that some arrangement be made for their privacy.

Millet, J. A. P. Sexuality after 60: Unmasking the myths. *Medical Insight*, 1972, *4*, 24–27.

The author studies some common myths and misconceptions regarding the sexuality of the aged in relation to actual medical and psychological facts. One common myth is that sexuality among elderly people is negligible or unimportant. Contrary to this misunderstanding, continuing sexual activity is regarded as one of the most important signs of healthy aging.

Mozley, P. D. Woman's capacity for orgasm after menopause. *Medical Aspects of Human Sexuality*, 1975, *9*(8), 104–110.

Psychosexual concerns and sexuality in postmenopausal women are discussed in this article. The mature woman will accept the loss of her procreative ability and may enjoy sex increasingly, while the immature woman with previous sexual difficulties may find her problems intensified. Hormonal therapy and other therapeutic and counseling modalities are presented.

Newman, G., and Nichols, C. R. Sexual activities and attitudes in older persons. *Journal of the American Medical Association*, 1960, *173*, 33–35.

This paper reports the results of a comprehensive, interdisciplinary study of geriatric subjects (n=250), regarding their sexual activity and attitudes. Subjects ranged from 60 to 93 years of age, with an average age of 70 years. Seven percent of the single subjects were sexually active, compared to 54 percent of married subjects who reported being sexually active. This confirms the value that marital status has on sexual activity and responsivity. There was an abrupt lessening of sexual activity in the group of subjects aged 75 years and older. The authors attribute this to the fact that many subjects in this group had chronic illnesses such as heart disease, arthritis, and diabetes. The authors conclude that "given the conditions of reasonably good health and partners who are also physically healthy, elderly persons continue to be sexually active into their seventh, eighth, and ninth decades."

Newman, G., and Nichols, C. R. Sexual activities and attitudes in older persons. In M. F. DeMartino (Ed.), *Sexual behavior and personality characteristics*. New York: Citadel Press, 1963.

This chapter was reprinted from the *Journal of the American Medical Association*, 1960, *173*, 33–35, and presents the results of a study examining sexual activity and attitudes in a geriatric population (n=250).

Person, M. M. Middle-aged male crises. *Medical Aspects of Human Sexuality*, 1968, *2*(8), 6–13.

Psychological and sexual reactions to middle age in men are discussed and some suggestions for counseling are presented.

Pfeiffer, E. Geriatric sex behavior. *Medical Aspects of Human Sexuality*, 1969, *3*(7), 19–28.

Sexual function and activity in the aged are discussed in light of research findings. Some implications for clinical practice are presented.

Pfeiffer, E. Sex and aging. In L. Gross (Ed.), *Sexual issues in marriage: A contemporary perspective*. New York: Spectrum Publications, 1975.

Healthy older people continue to have sexual and affectional needs. This chapter discusses the importance of sexual expression in the aged, and the social and cultural taboos inhibiting them. Results of the Masters and Johnson study of sexuality in the aged are presented and discussed. Also presented are the findings of a study conducted at Duke University to examine sexual activity among older persons. It was found that sexual interests and activities in the study group were common. Four out of five men who retain good health were sexually interested past age 65. While two out of three men in their sixties were still sexually active, only one in five was still active in his eighties. There were fewer women than men who were sexually active and interested in their sixties. The author concludes that "it is certainly clear that the activity is physically possible, and there is no reason why sexual expression should not be an important source of emotional reward." He adds that "the aged must be granted their own sexuality with accompanying dignity."

Pfeiffer, E. Sexuality in the aging individual. *Journal of the American Geriatrics Society*, 1974, *22*(11), 481–484.

The author presents results of studies examining sexual activity and functioning in the aged, and discusses their implications for health-care practice. Statistics show that at age 68 about 70 percent of men still regularly partake in sexual relations, while at age 78 about 25 percent are still sexually active. While for men the married state is not a necessary factor for continuing sexual activity, very few unmarried older women report regular sexual activity. The practitioner should take sexual needs into consideration when counseling the aging patient. It is important to improve the quality of life and not merely to prolong life.

Pfeiffer, E., Verwoerdt, A., and Davis, G. C. Sexual behavior in middle life. *American Journal of Psychiatry*, 1972, *128*(10), 1262–1267.

This investigation was part of a larger, multidisciplinary, longitudinal study examining some of the determinants of adaptation to middle age. The subjects for this study were 261 white males and 241 white females aged 45 to 69 years at the time of selection for the study. The data on sexual behavior and functioning were gathered as part of a self-administered medical history questionnaire. Results reported in this paper do not indicate how individuals change over time, but rather how groups of persons in a given age function in comparison with groups of persons of a different age. Results showed dramatic differences between men and women of the same age in regard to almost all indicators of sexual behavior studied, with the men generally reporting greater interest and activity than the women. While there was a general pattern of decline in sexual interest and activity with advancing age, sex still continued to play an important role in the lives of most subjects. Other results are discussed.

Pfeiffer, E., Verwoerdt, A., and Davis, G. C. Sexual behavior in middle life. In A. M. Juhasz (Ed.), *Sexual development and behavior*. Homewood, Illinois: Dorsey Press, 1973.

This chapter was reprinted from the *American Journal of Psychiatry*, 1972, *128*(10), 1262–1267.

Pfeiffer, E., Verwoerdt, A., and Wang, H. Sexual behavior in aged men and women. I. Observations on 254 community volunteers. *Archives of General Psychiatry*, 1968, *19*, 753–758.

This paper is one in a series of reports on sexual behavior of aged men and women who were studied repeatedly over an extended period of time. Subjects were 254 community volunteers who were 60 years old or older at the inception of the study. Data on sexual behavior and activity were elicited during a structured interview. Results relating to sexual activity, frequency of sexual intercourse, continued sexual interest, and other variables are presented and discussed.

Raskind, M. A., and Preston, C. A. Sexual counseling of the elderly. *Medical Aspects of Human Sexuality*, 1975, *9*(5), 153–154.

In this brief communication, the authors discuss sexual problems in the elderly male, and sexual and gynecologic problems in the elderly woman. Also presented are some suggestions for counseling by the physician.

Renshaw, D. C. Sex after sixty. *Alive and Well*, December 1974, 19–20.

The article discusses various sexual responses and changes associated with aging. The overall message of this paper is that sexuality can be enjoyed in old age. Furthermore, for many, sex may become a more pleasurable activity in later years than it was when they were younger. Some of the changes that may be expected in the aging male are: slowed erection of the penis, somewhat weaker erections, decrease in the quality and force of ejaculation, and longer periods between erections. These changes are normal and should be accepted comfortably. Finally, the author suggests that nursing homes should improve their attitudes toward the sexuality of the elderly and provide respectful consideration of their sexual desires and needs.

Rubin, I. Sex and aging men and women. In C. E. Vincent (Ed.), *Human sexuality in medical education and practice*. Springfield, Illinois: Charles C. Thomas, 1975.

This article focuses on the responsibility of the physician to help destroy the myth of "the sexless older years" and to help establish the right of older persons to express their sexuality freely and without guilt. The author presents research data that attest to the fact that older persons can still be sexually active well into their seventh, eighth, and even ninth decades. Factors responsible for diminished or lack of sexual response in the older person include boredom with the partner, mental and physical fatigue, overindulgence in food and alcohol, fear of failure, and various diseases. On the part of the aging woman, physiological and psychological changes due to cessation of menses are stressed. These changes include decrease in length and width of vagina and diminishing vaginal lubrication. The author asserts that regular sexual activity is important in maintaining sexual functioning. Another important factor is combating the many myths and misconceptions associated with sexuality and the aging person. The importance of counseling in this area is also stressed.

Rubin, I. The search for rejuvenation. *Sexology,* 1959, *25,* 558–561.

Sexuality in old age is the topic discussed in this paper.

Rubin, I. Sex over 65. In H. G. Beigel (Ed.), *Advances in sex research.* New York: Harper & Row, 1963.

Various studies examining sexual functioning and behavior in persons over 65 years of age are reviewed and conclusions are drawn. This review illustrates the need for health-care practitioners who work with aging persons to give serious consideration to the sexual needs of their aging patients.

Rubin, I. The "sexless older years": A socially harmful stereotype. *Annals of the American Academy of Political and Social Science*, March 1968, 87–95.

The author discusses the origin, nature, and the harmful influence of the stereotype about the "sexless older years." A comprehensive review of the literature was conducted to provide research data on sexual activity and functioning in aging. The general finding of most studies reviewed was that given physical and mental health and a positive attitude toward the aging process and sexuality, a person is capable of being sexually responsive and active until a very advanced age. Special attention is given in this article to the sexuality of the unmarried elderly, who also have sexual needs. The author urges improvement of society's attitudes toward the elderly and concludes that "unless our entire culture recognizes the normality of sex expression in the older years, it will be impossible for older persons to express their sexuality freely and without guilt."

Rubin, I. *Sexual life after sixty.* New York: Basic Books, 1965.

The author indicates that the purpose of this book "is to try to help establish the atmosphere required to allow sex play its proper role in the older years without being distorted or thwarted by a prejudiced and hostile environment." Presented and discussed are research data about sexual activity after sixty, myths and misconceptions regarding sex and the elderly, the sexual aging process, and special sexual and psychological problems of the later years. Of particular interest are sections discussing the effects of sex-organ surgery, heart disorders, hypertension, and diabetes on sexual functioning and activity.

Rubin, I. Sexual life in the later years. New York: Sex Information and Education Council of the U.S., 1970.

According to the author, the purpose of this publication is to "stimulate educators and counselors to help our society recognize the normality of sexuality and sexual expression in the later years." Specific topics discussed include myths about the sexuality of the older person, the importance of regular sexual expression, research findings, impotence, and other related subjects.

Sexuality and the aging: A selective bibliography. *SIECUS Report,* 1976, *4*(6), 5–8.

This extensive annotated bibliography includes the description of a wide variety of books, articles, and chapters in books discussing sexual behavior in older persons.

Spence, A. W. Sexual adjustment at the climacteric. *Practitioner,* 1954, *172*, 427–430.

Sexual functioning and changes in sexual activity in climacteric women and in middle-aged men are discussed in light of clinical and research findings. Some treatment modalities for sexual dysfunction are also presented.

Stokes, W. R. Sexual function in the aging male. *Geriatrics,* 1951, *6*, 304–308.

The author comments on Kinsey's findings regarding sexual functioning and behavior in the aging male. His commentary is based on psychoanalytic views of sexual behavior in western societies. The author concludes that "basic improvement of male potency and the extension of it in the life cycle must depend upon deeper understanding of how our cultural pattern affects the physiology of sex."

Stokes, W. R. Sexual function in the aging male. In M. F. DeMartino (Ed.), *Sexual behavior and personality characteristics.* New York: Citadel Press, 1963.

This chapter was reprinted from *Geriatrics*, 1951, *6*, 304–308, and deals with the physiological and psychosocial aspects of sexuality in the aging male.

Sviland, M. P. Helping elderly couples attain sexual liberation and growth. *SIECUS Report*, 1967, *4*(6), 3–4.

This article presents a sex therapy program designed for elderly couples who want to improve their sex life and enhance their sex pleasure. The program focuses on attitude restructuring concepts and is aimed at the removal of sexually negative self-labels and at improving interpersonal relationships. The author describes the various steps of the program.

Swartz, D. Sexual difficulties after 50: A urologist's view. *Canadian Medical Association Journal*, 1966, *94*, 208–210.

The purpose of this article is to discuss sexual functioning and difficulties in males after age 50. The author points out that in assessing sexuality, one needs to realize the difference between growing old and aging. Growing old, he states, is a process of maturing and results in a natural slowdown. To age, however, is pathological, and thus regressive. The author asserts that "given the right heredity, hormonal patterns and nutrition, sexual power is no more weakened in man by advancing years than are other bodily processes." He cites a study that shows that two-thirds of men ages 55 to 70 are still potent, and one-third of those over 70 are still active sexually. The author gives a detailed explanation of the processes of erection and ejaculation and also the effect of prostatectomy on sexual functioning. With the increase in life span, he feels that sexual functioning can also be prolonged.

Uerback, A. Sexual patterns in later years of life. *Arizona Medicine*, 1970, *27*, 13–16.

This article presents an attempt to abolish some common myths and misconceptions regarding sexuality, or the lack of it, in older people. Many believe sex in the older person to be negligible and unimportant, and the old person to be sexless. The author presents the findings of several studies that contradict these mistaken beliefs. Studies conducted by Masters and Johnson demonstrated very clearly that those men in good physical and mental health who had positive, healthy attitudes regarding the aging process were capable of a satisfying sexual life even beyond the age of 80. Other studies showed that people who were regularly active sexually in their earlier years continued to have strong sexual interests and active sex lives until very advanced age. In women, those who had achieved orgasmic ability in earlier years were more interested in continuing their sexual activity than women who could not reach orgasm. Similarly, men who were sexually active through adolescence, either through masturbation or intercourse, continued at a higher frequency rate than men who started their sexual experiences at a later age. The author presents findings that, contrary to popular belief, individuals who masturbate actively in adolescence or those who masturbate in adult life when intercourse activity is not available continue to have a high degree of sexual interest and activities until advanced age. Health-care professionals should not ignore the sexual needs expressed by older people, but need rather to reassure these persons.

Walker, K. The critical age in men. *Sexology*, 1964, *30*(1), 705–707.

Does a man pass through a climacteric or critical age, resembling that which occurs in women who have reached the second half of their lives? This question is answered in this article written by a British sexologist.

Wallin, P., and Clark, A. L. A study of orgasm as a condition of women's enjoyment of coitus in the middle years of marriage. *Human Biology*, 1963, *35*, 131–139.

This study investigated the extent to which women in middle or late years of marriage enjoy sexual relations in the absence of orgasm. Data were collected through a questionnaire from 417 women who had been married for between 17 and 20 years. Results of the study revealed a positive correlation between frequency of orgasm and the extent of enjoyment of coitus. However, the data also showed that orgasm is not necessary for the enjoyment of sexual intercourse; 17 percent of the subjects showed very high enjoyment even though they had "none or few" orgasms. Other data are discussed.

Weinberg, J. Sexual expression in late life. *American Journal of Psychiatry*, 1969, *126*, 159–162.

Sexual drive, function, and activity in old age are discussed in light of research and clinical findings and two case histories. The author concludes that "chronological age is no barrier to the continued sexual life of the old when opportunity and sanction are present."

Weinberg, J. Sexuality in later life. *Medical Aspects of Human Sexuality*, 1971, *5*(4), 216–227.

Sexual function and activity in old age is discussed in this article in light of research and clinical findings and society's attitudes toward the elderly.

Weinberg, M. S. The aging homosexual. *Medical Aspects of Human Sexuality*, 1969, *3*(12), 66–76.

Psychosocial and social difficulties faced by the aging homosexual are discussed.

Whiskin, F. E. The geriatric sex offender. *Medical Aspects of Human Sexuality*, 1970, *4*(4), 125–129.

Society's prejudicial attitudes toward older people are explored in relation to the geriatric sex offender. The incidence, etiology, and nature of the sexual offenses committed by older people are discussed in view of research findings and several case studies.

Yeaworth, R. C., and Friedman, J. S. Sexuality in later life. *Nursing Clinics of North America*, 1975, *10*(3), 565–574.

The authors discuss biophysical changes with aging and their impact on sexual functioning in light of society's attitudes and influence. They note that "while sexual interest and sexual thoughts decline, they do not disappear." Regularity of sexual activity is a very important factor in maintaining sexual capacity and functioning for both males and females. Aging patients who are concerned about their sexuality should be provided adequate sex counseling and advice. The role of the practicing nurse in this context is identified and discussed.

Chapter Eleven

Sex Education with the Disabled

Bass, M. S. Sex education for the handicapped. *Family Coordinator*, 1974, *23*, 27–33.

Sex education for the handicapped person is timely and important since current trends in rehabilitation and social services call for greater normalization and humanization of the disabled. The retarded individual has the right to live a normative community life, but at the same time there are obligations and responsibilities. There is need for a comprehensive educational program on sexuality and family planning to resolve problems and questions relating to possible conflicts between the retarded person's rights and responsibilities. The author cites several studies showing that handicapped persons have better adjustment following courses and programs in sex education and family planning. The author also outlines the basic principles that apply to a sound sex education for handicapped persons, and lists special considerations for blind, deaf, and neurologically disabled students.

Blom, G. E. Some considerations about the neglect of sex education in special education. *Journal of Special Education*, 1975, *5*(4), 359–361.

Based on the premise that rational beliefs and actions should be fostered to promote sex education in special education settings, the author identifies several irrational beliefs, myths, misconceptions, and negative attitudes causing neglect of this subject: (1) people assume that the exceptional child is more likely to act out his sex impulses; (2) teachers feel uncomfortable teaching exceptional children about sex; (3) many myths about the sexual behavior of handicapped children exist among parents and teachers; (4) people believe that providing sex information leads to and fosters sexual acting-out behavior;

(5) it is felt that not talking about sex suppresses sexual expression; and (6) people think that sex education is a very private matter and should be left to parents and the church. The author concludes that through realistic sex information and comfortable discussion one can foster more adequate expressions of sexuality among exceptional children.

Bloom, J. L. Sex education for handicapped adolescents. *Journal of School Health*, 1969, *39*, 363–367.

The major purpose of this study was to examine the effect of a sex education course on a group of physically disabled (n=31) and a group of emotionally disturbed (n=33) adolescents. More specifically, there were four hypotheses in the study: (1) disabled adolescents who had been removed from the regular school situation would show deficits in sex knowledge when compared to a control group; (2) the study groups would show a significant difference in sex knowledge after the presentation of a sex education course; (3) the groups would show a significant difference in their level of manifest anxiety after having had this course; and (4) there would be no significant difference in sex knowledge or anxiety between the two study groups. Results of the study are presented and conclusions are drawn.

Bloom, J. L. Sex education for the physically handicapped. *Sexology*, January 1970, 62–65.

The author asserts that "it is most difficult for parents of handicapped children to accept the fact that their children are sexual beings with needs and desires of normal children." This attitude presents some difficulties in the child's psychosexual development. Some of these difficulties are discussed along with the need for sex education for the physically handicapped child. The author concludes that parents of handicapped children should realize that their task in sex education is not essentially different from that of parents of nonhandicapped children, although their problems will be greater.

Cook, R. Sex education program service model for the multihandicapped adult. *Rehabilitation Literature*, 1974, *9*, 264–271.

A comprehensive sex education program for male and female cerebral palsied patients and their parents is described. The program has seven components: recognition of specific needs expressed by patients; personal awareness; board or agency support; staff training; parental involvement; development of program services, including parents' meetings and individual counseling sessions; and, program evaluation. These components are discussed in detail. The program described was developed at United Cerebral Palsy of Denver, Denver, Colorado.

Delp, H. A. Sex education for the handicapped. *Journal of Special Education*, 1971, *5*(4), 363–364.

Responding to a preceding article by Sol Gordon, the author of this paper asserts that sex education for the handicapped is missing in schools. Home sex education is as equally repressed, because parents tend to wish for dependency from the handicapped. He adds that discussion about sex must be in understandable terms and without use of euphemisms. Parents must be given proper information and education to deal with the problems.

Dickman, I. Sex education for the disabled person. New York: Public Affairs Committee Inc., 1975.

Dickman emphasizes that physically or mentally handicapped persons are much more like than unlike "normal" people. He includes in the category of similarities the rights to sex education and to appropriate expressions of affection. In this pamphlet he examines societal, institutional, and parental attitudes that have served to deny or inhibit the sexuality of the disabled. Arguments supporting the desirability of sex education for all persons are considered and Dickman also suggests attitudes necessary for those who would teach sex education.

Special concerns of persons with disabilities, including marriage, genetic counseling, family planning, and voluntary sterilization, are examined. Dickman concludes with a statement on the universal right to personal fulfillment. A bibliography and a list of organizations concerned with this topic are included.

Dupras, A., and Tremblay, R. Sexual handicappism and sex education of the handicapped children: Path analysis of the attitudes of parents, educators and professionals. Paper read at the Thirteenth World Congress of Rehabilitation International, Tel Aviv, Israel, June 13–18, 1976.

The purpose of this study was to identify and analyze certain factors that may explain attitudes toward sex education of the handicapped child. The authors identified five sets of causes that could account for approval or resistance toward sex education in schools: general sexual attitudes; attitudes toward premarital sex of the handicapped; attitudes toward dating, marriage, and reproduction for the handicapped; and, finally, prejudices toward the sexuality of the handicapped. The attitudes of parents of handicapped children, special educators, social workers, and psychologists were examined. Results and conclusions are discussed.

Eisenberg, M. G. Sex education and the handicapped: An examination of a sex re-education program in the VA: A preliminary report. *Newsletter for Research in Psychology*, 1972, *14*(4), 15–16.

A sex re-education program for spinal-cord-injured patients was developed by the author. This paper presents the basic assumptions underlying the program and a preliminary report on its function.

Fox, J. Sex education—but for what? *Special Education*, 1971, *60*, 15–17.

The author discusses the realities in the life of the handicapped child that guide the relevance and content of sex education. Differences among handicapped children concerning sexual behavior and sex education are identified, along with some questions concerning a sex education approach that can prepare severely handicapped children for adulthood. The author asserts that "discussions about sex education are useless, meaningless, and beside the point unless we face up squarely to the question: education for what?"

Garett, J. Sex education: A second opinion. *Special Education*, 1971, *60*(4), 16–17.

In this article the author strongly argues for the inclusion of sex education for handicapped children. In his school, Garett encourages his teachers to be accurate and frank and yet sensitive when answering any questions asked by the children. In addition, the handicapped in the school are given as much freedom in their emotional life as are the nonhandicapped, while the teachers try to help them conform to the accepted standards of society. The author further discusses the problems of older handicapped persons, who need to come together so that they can make contact with the opposite sex on an equal basis. For those unable to live independently, the author suggests that many more boarding accommodations are needed. They should cater to both men and women and give them as much opportunity as possible to be independent and to live a full emotional life.

Gordon, S. Missing in special education: sex. *Journal of Special Education*, 1971, *5*(4), 351–354.

Gordon defines sex education as an integral and necessary part of the special education curriculum, noting that handicapped and otherwise disadvantaged children have an even greater need than do their normal peers for information to help them understand and cope with their adolescent sexuality.

Several commentaries on this article are also published in this issue of the *Journal of Special Education.*

Handy, J. S. Sex education: The psychological approach—who and where. Paper presented at a meeting of the American Association on Mental Deficiency, Denver, 1967.

Psychological aspects in sex education of mentally retarded individuals is the topic discussed in this presentation.

Johnson, W. R. *Sex education and counseling of special groups: The mentally and physically handicapped, ill and elderly*. Springfield, Illinois: Charles C. Thomas, 1975.

Part I of this book is directed specifically to the mentally and physically handicapped, the chronically ill, and the elderly as they are affected by recent sociocultural developments and changes in sociosexual attitudes. The author discusses the effects of the "sexual revolution" on these special groups, the concept of sexual normality, and some philosophies and precautions concerning sex education and counseling of these groups.

In Part II Johnson considers a range of sex-related topics, discussing each first in general terms, then in relation to special population members as appropriate, and finally, using a question-and-answer format, he pinpoints typical concerns. Some of the topics discussed are: physical contact, circumcision, masturbation, menstruation, child molestation, venereal diseases, sexual intercourse and sex without intercourse, abortion, and marriage and parenthood by special group members.

Kempton, W. Sex education: A cooperative effort of parent and teacher. *Exceptional Children,* May 1975, 531–535.

The author outlines some suggestions for conducting an effective sex education program for mentally retarded persons. She stresses the need for cooperative relations between parents and teachers of retarded children for the purpose of improving sex education. She concludes that "parents and teachers have separate but complementary roles in helping to make the child's sexuality a positive part of his total sense of self."

Maddock, J. Sex education for the exceptional person: A rationale. *Exceptional Children*, 1974, *40*(4), 273–278.

Unlike many who believe that the retarded person should be protected from knowledge about sex, the author argues in this article in its favor, and presents a comprehensive rationale to support sex education for exceptional persons. The central thesis is that the sexuality of any exceptional person should be confronted positively. Most adults working with children who have special emotional and physical needs do not respond positively to the child's sexual expression for three reasons: concern over possible reproductive capacities of the handicapped; fear of sex as an undisciplined drive; and the "custodial" mentality, which has prevailed especially in institutions. These negative attitudes are disputed and the concepts of self-fulfillment and individuality of persons are espoused. Guidelines are presented in a positive frame of reference that is intended to replace the more traditionally repressive orientation, which is seen as having dominated the general point of view.

Morlock, D. A., and Tovar, C. S. Sex education for the multiple handicapped as it applies to the classroom teachers. *Training School Bulletin*, 1971, *68*(2), 87–96.

The authors contend that sex education should be offered in accordance with the age and the intellectual capacity of the individual. In the case of educating the retarded and multiply handicapped, this places a special responsibility on the instructor to set his approach at the ability level of his students and to be sensitive to the special environment in which they live. Three pages of references and a pamphlet bibliography are included.

Nordqvist, I. Education of disabled people and their families. Paper presented at the Thirteenth World Congress of Rehabilitation International, Tel Aviv, Israel, June 13–18, 1976.

The author describes a sex education program for disabled persons developed by the Swedish Committee on Sex and the Disabled in Stockholm. Some recommendations and suggestions for an effective sex education program are presented.

Reich, M. L., and Harshman, H. W. Sex education for handicapped children: Reality or repression. *Journal of Special Education*, 1971, *5*, 373–377.

This paper is in response to a preceding article by Sol Gordon dealing with the need for sex education programs for handicapped children. The authors assert that the goal of sex education for handicapped children must be the same as for all individuals, i.e., to develop people who are not only sexually fulfilled persons but who also understand themselves, their behavior, and their value systems. The authors offer the following guidelines for an effective sex education program: (1) sex education must be communicated to children in each grade; (2) the material should be "team-taught"; (3) parents should be included in and participate in the sex education experiences; (4) ample opportunity for feedback should be allowed so that distortions of reality are either minimized or prevented; (5) sex education should be given on an individual as well as a group basis. It is especially true that for emotionally disturbed children, individual counseling will be more effective than group discussion.

Chapter Twelve

Media Review

compiled and edited by
Susanne M. Bruyer

*Devices are never media in and of themselves. They become media only when associated with those peculiar processes of human behavior which we have termed the transmission of information.**

The opening quotation succinctly summarizes a critical key in the successful use of media to convey information. Media of any form can be useful learning tools, but are only effective in transmitting information when used in a context which provides the receiver with an opportunity to personalize the material being offered. Literature in the area of adult education suggests that the adult learner be approached in an *andragogical* fashion; that is, we, as conveyors of information, should try to respond to the unique learning needs of each person, drawing upon the experiences and perceptions of adult learners in a manner that will allow each to better personalize the material we present.

In the area of sexuality and disability, it is particularly critical that sex educators and counselors be sensitive to the learning needs, unique experiences, and values of each person with whom they work. We must, therefore, carefully choose both the learning tools and the learning situations, mindful of our target population. It is my hope that the media reviews offered in this section provide you with information to make more appropriate choices of media to use in your work.

The films chosen for review were selected from the Multi Media Resource Center in San Francisco, and the Medical Rehabilitation Research and Training Center of the Department of Physical Medicine and Rehabilitation, University of Minnesota.

**The New Media and Education: Their Impact on Society*. P. H. Rossi and B. J. Biddle, eds. Chicago: Aldine, 1966, pp. 3–4.

Multi Media Resource Center, Inc., has been providing media material on human sexuality to educators, counselors, researchers, and therapists since 1970. Its library includes over 100 films, slides, tapes, and educational guides on sexuality. The sole distributor of materials developed by the National Sex Forum in San Francisco, the Center also distributes the work of the University of Minnesota and of independent filmmakers. Multi Media Resource Center publishes a Resource Guide three times yearly, which contains a complete catalog of their film, videotape, and other audiovisual resources, as well as articles on current affairs and new techniques for education and therapy in the sex field. Information on purchase or rental of films, or a copy of the Resource Guide may be obtained from:

Multi Media Resource Center
1525 Franklin St.
San Francisco, California 94109
Telephone: (415) 673-5100

Send in orders at least four weeks before the planned show date, to ensure their reservations, or a late charge applies.

The Medical Rehabilitation Research and Training Center of the Department of Physical Medicine and Rehabilitation, University of Minnesota, produces and distributes films on physical rehabilitation, some of which deal with sexuality. Films are available for purchase or rental (five working days). A three-week interval between the date of request and the showing date is required. Available media and rental and purchase information may be obtained from:

Medical Rehabilitation Research and Training Center
Physical Medicine and Rehabilitation Department
Box 297 Mayo Building
University of Minnesota
Minneapolis, Minnesota 55455
Telephone: (612) 373-8990 or 373-9198

Give It a Try

Produced in 1975 by Mary Briggs, this film, a project of the Region V Office of Rehabilitation Services, Center for Continuing Education, was directed by Theodore and Sandra Cole, and filmed in cooperation with the Program in Human Sexuality and the Department of Physical Medicine and Rehabilitation of the University of Minnesota Medical School.

Give It a Try concerns the troubled relationship between a recently injured quadriplegic male and his able-bodied wife as they attempt to reestablish the physical aspect of their marriage. The film begins as they acknowledge concern and frustration over sexual issues and decide to see a counselor. A sexual counseling program is established and an advocate counseling couple is integrated into the counseling format.

The film illustrates the professional's approach to gathering background information on a disabled individual's sexual behavior, and the use of an advocate counseling couple, who discuss their own struggle to reestablish their marriage following the spinal-cord injury of one partner. The advocate couple discuss the importance not only of open communication between partners regarding sexuality, but also of exploring new ways to experience each other sexually. Home assignments are emphasized to ensure that the couple incorporate the material from the counseling sessions into their behavior. The film ends as they are applying some of their newly acquired communication techniques to their relationship—beginning to "give it a try."

Although sexually nonexplicit, this is a very informative, supportive, and personal film which portrays early reactions to disability as it relates to sexuality in an ongoing relationship. It is recommended for use in the training of rehabilitation counselors, social workers, and disabled individuals. *Give It a Try* would interest disabled individuals and their partners, and could be used by counselors to illustrate the benefits of and approaches to sex counseling.

Program information:

33 minutes
color film with sound
16mm (reel)

Can be obtained from:

Multi Media Resource Center
1525 Franklin St.
San Francisco, California 94109
Telephone: (415) 673-5100
Purchase: $395 Rental: $55

or

Physical Medicine & Rehabilitation Department
Box 297 Mayo Building
University of Minnesota
Minneapolis, Minnesota 55455
Telephone: (612) 373-8990 or 373-9198
Purchase: $385 Rental: $25

Bringing It Up

Bringing It Up was produced in 1974 by the Program in Human Sexuality and the Department of Physical Medicine and Rehabilitation of the University of Minnesota in Minneapolis. This film demonstrates a doctor's approach to introducing sex counseling to a spinal-cord-injury patient. The patient, still in the acute phase of hospital care, is being seen for the first time by the consultant physician in rehabilitation. James Boen, Ph.D., shares emotions and concerns that he had when he was injured several years ago with Theodore Cole, M.D., who suggests some questions and issues that should be raised with spinal-cord-injured patients. The interview moves in gradual stages from a discussion of the patient's injury to his current status and future potential. The patient is encouraged to think about present and future capabilities, sexual and otherwise, while the doctor emphasizes that such thoughts are normal and that questions will be welcomed and answered as fully as possible.

This teaching film on spinal-cord injury focuses on the right time, place, and manner in which a counselor can begin to discuss with the patient his or her future as a sexual being. It would be useful not only for the training of rehabilitation and hospital personnel—physicians, psychologists, physical and occupational therapists, nurses, social workers, rehabilitation counselors—who work with recently disabled persons, but also for disabled persons themselves.

Program information:
17 minutes
color film with sound
16mm (reel)

Can be obtained from:
Multi Media Resource Center
1525 Franklin St.
San Francisco, California 94109
Telephone: (415) 673-5100
Purchase: $240 Rental: $40

or

Physical Medicine & Rehabilitation Department
Box 297 Mayo Building
University of Minnesota
Minneapolis, Minnesota 55455
Telephone: (612) 373-8990 or 373-9198
Purchase: $120 Rental: $15

Touching

This film was produced by the National Sex Forum in 1972, under the coordination of Dr. Theodore Cole of the University of Minnesota Medical School in Minneapolis. *Touching* shows the physical expression of sexuality between a man with a C-6 spinal-cord injury and his able-bodied female partner. The setting is a bedroom with a waterbed; background music is the only sound. The man has sensation in only two areas below his shoulders: under the coronal ridge of his penis, and the area immediately around his anus. There is a high emphasis on oral sexuality in the film, which graphically conveys several of the forms of sexual expression possible for individuals with limited sensation and mobility due to spinal-cord injury. The couple are obviously comfortable with a range of sexual expression, and display evident affection and enjoyment of each other.

This film is quite explicit, but sensitively done. It would be useful in couples' groups where one or both of the partners have physical disabilities and are interested in exploring alternative approaches to sexual activity. Professionals who provide sexual counseling to physically disabled individuals and their partners would find this an instructive training film.

Program information:
16 minutes
color film with sound (music only)
16mm (reel) and video

Can be obtained from:
Multi Media Resource Center
1525 Franklin St.
San Francisco, California 94109
Telephone: (415) 673-5100
Purchase: $240 Rental: $40

If Ever Two Were One

Dr. Theodore Cole, University of Minnesota Medical School Minneapolis, coordinated this film, produced in 1974 by the National Sex Forum. *If Ever Two Were One* was planned as a companion film to *Touching*. A couple in their early thirties, a paraplegic man and his able-bodied partner, are shown engaging in slow, pleasurable sex. The man has a muscular torso and good mobility, and is able to have partial erections. The female partner uses the "stuffing" technique, and there is mutual sharing of oral-genital sexual activity. The pace is relaxed, and the couple show much warmth and caring for each other.

This film is recommended for use with couples where one or both of the partners have physical disabilities. This film is sensitively done and valuable in its explicit representation of alternative ways for individuals with physical disabilities to approach sexual activity.

Program information:
14 minutes
color film with sound (music only)
16mm (reel)

Can be obtained from:
Multi Media Resource Center
1525 Franklin St.
San Francisco, California 94109
Telephone: (415) 673-5100
Purchase: $224 Rental: $35

Just What Can You Do

Just What Can You Do, produced in 1972 by the National Sex Forum, shows a group discussion of sexuality and what it means to spinal-cord-injured individuals, led by Dr. Theodore Cole. The group includes two paraplegics, a quadriplegic, their wives, and a female quadriplegic, who center their discussion around the "forced identity crisis" that the spinal-cord-injured persons have had. They share frankly their concerns and experiences on topics such as marriage, physical attractiveness, sexual fulfillment, and incontinence during sexual activity, illustrating the discussion with personal and often humorous anecdotes. The couples discuss problems and possibilities inherent in a marriage where one person is disabled, emphasizing the importance of open communication to get to know each other better as individuals and to enhance sexual intimacy. The general consensus is that cord-injured people can be sexually active and fulfilled, if they are willing to accept new ways of sexual expression.

Technically, the sound track can occasionally be difficult to understand, but the film is well done and aptly demonstrates the sense of trust and support which group sharing can give to individuals. It would be a good film to use in counseling with couples where one or both of the partners are physically disabled. It also could be used as a training film for professionals to illustrate the therapeutic use of a peer group in sex counseling.

Program information:
23 minutes
color film with sound
16mm (reel) and video

Can be obtained from:
Multi Media Resource Center
1525 Franklin St.
San Francisco, California 94109
Telephone: (415) 673-5100
Purchase: $300 Rental: $50

Artist's Fantasy

Artist's Fantasy was produced in 1975 by Sandra Cole and Ted Cole, M.D., of the Program in Human Sexuality and the Department of Physical Medicine and Rehabilitation at the University of Minnesota Medical School in Minneapolis. Through the narration of the sole character, a man with cerebral palsy confined to a wheelchair, this film depicts the thoughts and feelings of a person with a severe physical disability about sex and body image. He describes his interest in sexuality and depicts his sexual fantasies in his drawings. A masturbation experience is shared, showing techniques which a severely disabled individual might use to obtain sexual satisfaction, including the use of a vibrator and varied stroking techniques to comfortably bring pleasure, despite some physical limitations of this man's hands.

This film is explicit, but sensitively done. It would be useful in a training session for human service professionals working in sexuality education or counseling with physically disabled individuals. It could also be used with disabled individuals themselves, to initiate group discussion on such topics as perception of self as a sexual being and body image.

Program information:
15 minutes
color film with sound
16mm

Can be obtained from:
Physical Medicine & Rehabilitation Department
Box 297 Mayo Building
University of Minnesota
Minneapolis, Minnesota 55455
Telephone: (612) 373-8990 or 373-9198
Purchase: $225 Rental: $35

A Bridge to Disability

This film was produced by the Program in Human Sexuality and the Department of Physical Medicine and Rehabilitation, University of Minnesota at Minneapolis. *A Bridge to Disability* shows the trauma of a car accident and subsequent hospitalization through the eyes of the accident victim. Using background voices and visual scene changes, it traces an individual's impressions of what has happened to him through the feedback provided, often insensitively, by hospital staff and family members. The crisis of learning that he will never walk again is discussed. The film closes on a more positive note showing a variety of situations in which men in wheelchairs are engaging enthusiastically in athletic activities.

This is an excellent film to spur discussion of the need for responsibility and sensitivity by professionals who are initially involved with individuals who have had a traumatic and disabling accident. It could be recommended for use by human service professionals in the medical and rehabilitation area, as well as with other groups of individuals, as a tool to generate discussion of what it might be like to have a seriously disabling accident.

Program information:
10 minutes
color film with sound
16mm

Can be obtained from:
Physical Medicine & Rehabilitation Department
Box 297 Mayo Building
University of Minnesota
Minneapolis, Minnesota 55455
Telephone: (612) 373-8990 or 373-9198
Purchase: $175   Rental: $30

Don't Tell the Cripples About Sex

Don't Tell the Cripples About Sex is a two-part film program produced in 1974 at the Human Sexuality Program, University of Minnesota Medical School at Minneapolis. These films show an interview conducted with four individuals with cerebral palsy by Theodore Cole, M.D., of the Human Sexuality Program. These films, showing two men and two women with varying degrees of both physical impairment and communication difficulties, illustrate the ways in which cerebral palsy may affect a person's physical functioning and communication ability, as well as the range of personal experiences and backgrounds of disabled people.

Prompted by questions from Dr. Cole, the four participants share frankly their most private feelings, creating a feeling of intimacy and a sense of respect in the viewer. In Part I they discuss their developmental years and how sexuality was dealt with by their families, hospital staff, and other professionals, and how each may have turned to activities such as high achievement in school to compensate for little or no socialization and opportunity for sexual expression. In Part II the discussion revolves around their adult experiences with sexuality. They share how they learned about sex, became aware of their own sexual needs, and found ways to become more self-confident socially, sexually, and vocationally. The discussion also brings out the problems incurred in fighting anti-sexual social attitudes, and the tendency by some disabled people to consider asexuality an expected role that must be assumed by individuals with a disability.

Although the discussion can at times be difficult to understand, due to the varying communication abilities of the four participants, in general both films move well over many topics of importance to individuals with disabilities and to professionals who work with them. These films would be useful both to facilitate open discussion among disabled people in a group experience and as a training resource for human service professionals to heighten sensitivity to the sexuality-related problems of disabled people.

Program information:
Part I: 16 minutes
Part II: 23 minutes
color film with sound
16mm and video

Can be obtained from:
Physical Medicine & Rehabilitation Department
Box 297 Mayo Building
University of Minnesota
Minneapolis, Minnesota 55455
Telephone: (612) 373-8990 or 373-9198

Purchase:		Rental:	
	Part I: $240		Part I: $40
	Part II: $275		Part II: $45
	Parts I & II: $485		Parts I & II: $75

Possibilities

Possibilities was produced in 1973 by the National Sex Forum in San Francisco. This film provides a visual illustration and background description of the sexual relationship of a male quadriplegic with a C5-6 spinal injury and his female partner. In the soundtrack he talks about the impact which his injury has had on his sex life and how he went about rediscovering his sexuality in the past year, after going through a period of no sexual activity. He describes where his body has sensation, what he likes sexually, and his new confidence in himself, evolving from his present opportunity for sexual expression.

The film is explicit, showing the sexual techniques developed between this quadriplegic man and his female partner. Breast stimulation, caressing, and oral sex in several positions are demonstrated. The sensitivity and caring of the couple for each other come through clearly.

This film would be very useful in groups of individuals with quadriplegia or paraplegia. The candid self-disclosure of the film could very well facilitate more open discussion and personal sharing by group members. It would be most helpful as a tool to stimulate discussion on how individuals can, subsequent to a severely disabling injury, initiate socialization, create opportunities for sexual relationships to develop, and explore alternate forms of sexual expression.

Program information:
12 minutes
color film with sound
16mm and video

Sexuality and Physical Disability

This is a series of seven color video tapes produced in 1975 by Sandra S. Cole and Theodore M. Cole, M.D., of the Program in Human Sexuality, Department of Physical Medicine and Rehabilitation, University of Minnesota Medical School. The series is designed to stimulate discussion and facilitate a deeper consideration of sexuality and why it may be important to the physically disabled and the professionals who work with them, such as the nurse, counselor, social worker, psychologist, physician, therapist, or student of these professions. The presentations explore several important aspects of human sexuality and how it influences and is influenced by disability. They are conducted by various staff members of the Program in Human Sexuality, the Department of Physical Medicine and Rehabilitation of the University of Minnesota Medical School, and physically disabled men and women.

For maximum utilization of the information presented, it is recommended that the tapes be presented in a context where an opportunity for discussion is afforded, and that a leader or trainer with expertise in the area of human sexuality, particularly as it relates to those with disabilities, be on hand to address specific questions raised by viewers. Each of the tapes are 30–45 minutes in length and can be used independently.

This series of video tapes can be obtained from two sources:

Multi Media Resource Center
1525 Franklin Street
San Francisco, California 94109
Phone: (415) 928-1133

Available in ¾″ color video cassette only.
Rental: $30.00 each; Purchase: $200.00 each.

and

Audio Visual Library Service
Continuing Education and Extension
University of Minnesota
3300 University Avenue, S.E.
Minneapolis, Minnesota 55414
Phone: (612) 373-3810
Available in both ¾″ cassette or ½″ reel.
Rental/preview: $25.00 each; Purchase $200.00 each.

Program #1. *Orientation to Sexuality of the Physically Disabled* (38 min.).

This introductory program is based on the experiences of Sandra Cole and Dr. Theodore Cole at the University of Minnesota Hospitals and the Program in Human Sexuality, as well as their work nationwide in the area of sexuality. Several fundamental assumptions and objectives of sexuality and disability sex education/treatment programs are discussed. Basic to the discussion are two questions: Should sex be discussed with the client who has a disability? and, Who is the best person to discuss sexuality with a disabled person? This tape emphasizes the importance of counselors' first examining their own sexuality values as a basis for being able to deal comfortably with sexuality in a counseling situation. The presentation ends with representative questions which may facilitate discussion of sexuality and rehabilitation.

This tape would be particularly useful as a discussion stimulus for a training program for counselors who will be working in a rehabilitation setting.

Program #2. *Anatomy and Physiology of Sexual Response Cycles* (44 min.).

This presentation focuses on the premise that to be comfortable in discussing sex with others and in exploring one's own sexuality, a person must first be aware of his or her own physiology and anatomy. Mary Briggs and Theodore Cole, M.D., utilizing schematic artwork and photographs of models, describe the anatomy of adult sex organs and their function during sexual arousal. The four stages of the sexual response cycle—excitement, plateau, orgasm, and resolution—are explained.

The language and explanations in this program are at times technical, and for this reason it would be recommended for use with professionals and selected client/patient populations.

Program #3. *Medical and Institutional Aspects* (39 min.).

Dr. Theodore Cole presents the issue of sexuality of the physically disabled person through the perspectives of past and current institutional practices and the medical information now available. He explores the various rationalizations which institutions and professionals often use to avoid dealing with sexuality in the rehabilitation process, and encourages greater recognition by professionals of the fact that dealing with sexuality as a natural part of the rehabilitation process can increase the overall level of confidence and functioning of the individual, thereby facilitating gains in other rehabilitation areas. A classification is offered, dividing disability groups by age and rapidity of onset, which aids in understanding the impact of specific physical disabilities on sexual functioning. Slides and photographs are used to highlight the presentation. Dr. Cole also briefly presents a sampling of devices used to deal with altered sexual performance.

This presentation would be a particularly useful one with professionals in various rehabilitation settings to illustrate that sexuality is often affected by disability, and therefore must be seen as an important concern to be dealt with in the rehabilitation process.

Program #4. *Body Image* (37 min.).

A panel of five physically disabled men and women, whose disabilities range from minimal to severe, discuss their feelings about self and sexuality in relation to their handicaps. The panelists explore the pressures people with physical disabilities experience in trying to meet other people's expectations in areas such as dating, social development, social acceptance by peers, and the ways in which they deal with problems incurred in these areas. The discussion is supplemented with slides which show some of the physical characteristics of individuals with disabilities, and an exploration of the possible ramifications of these characteristics on an individual's body-image and comfort in physical expression. The tape also addresses the differences in body-image development that may be associated with time of onset of disability (e.g., congenital vs. later in life).

This presentation would be a good way to sensitize rehabilitation personnel to the feelings of disabled individuals about their body-images and perceptions of self as sexual beings. It could also be useful to promote discussion with a group of disabled individuals.

Program #5. *Sexual Counseling of Physically Disabled Adults* (40 min.).

Four rehabilitation professionals (a medical practitioner, two counseling psychologists, and a community resource coordinator) discuss why they believe that it is important in their work to include sex counseling or discussion with patients/clients. They exchange ideas on how to initiate and carry on a discussion focusing on sexuality, including the importance of permission-giving in the initiation of discussion surrounding sexuality and extending either limited information, specific suggestions, or intensive therapy to the patients, depending upon the nature of the presenting sexual concern and the skills of the professional. The group compares how they deal with people from different life styles and situations, and also explore the ways in which their own personalities, attitudes, and professional roles influence their work.

Emphasizing the importance of professionals being comfortable with their own sexuality and able to discuss sex with others, this presentation would be valuable for use with health-care practitioners working in rehabilitation settings as a tool to facilitate discussion.

Program #6. *Sexuality and Disability Adjustment* (30 min.).

A physician, a psychologist, and a disabled man and woman explore the relationship of an individual's sexuality to his or her attitude toward disability, emphasizing how satisfactory sexual adjustment to disability is related to the overall success of the individual in the rehabilitation process, how variations in perception of sexuality may influence social interactions, and how discrepancies in attitudes toward sexuality may introduce conflicts between the health-care team and the disabled individual. The importance of understanding one's dependency and need for protection, as contrasted with one's strength or assertiveness, is underscored as central to both sexual health and overall adjustment to physical disability.

This program might be particularly useful as a stimulus for discussion on the area of sexual adjustment in groups of physically disabled individuals.

Program # 7. *Sexual Variations* (39 min.).

This program deals with the varieties of human sexual behavior in our society, which has customarily focused on "normal sex," that is, sexual intercourse between husband and wife for procreation. Any other sexual expression has been labeled abnormal by psychology, unlawful by statutes, and immoral by religions. Tom Maurer, lecturer in the Program in Human Sexuality at the University of Minnesota, addresses questions from a group of disabled and nondisabled individuals. He traces the evolution of information about sexuality, and discusses current legislation prohibiting certain kinds of sexual activity and other ways that society seeks to impose conformity on sexual activity, thus instilling guilt and impinging upon an individual's sexual fulfillment. Theories of how innate makeup and early learning experiences shape our sexual preferences are discussed. The professional is seen as having an obligation to be aware of the full range of sexual behavior, such as transvestism, exhibitionism, transsexuality, homosexuality, bisexuality, etc.

This presentation is not necessarily focused on disability and sexuality; rather, with an emphasis on homosexuality, it explores the impact of society on sexual behavior and seeks to dispel some myths about sexual variety and to increase overall acceptance and understanding.

Appendix

A Selected List of Primary Sources

The following primary sources may also be found in the annotated bibliography, but are listed here for the convenience of those persons who wish to obtain a quick list of references that will give a broad overview of the subject of human sexuality and disability. A number of conferences and their published proceedings are also listed here, while the individual presentations and papers from these conferences are listed in their appropriate sections in the annotated bibliography. A few journals primarily concerned with sexuality and disability are listed for the reader's convenience.

Primary Sources

Abse, D. W., Nash, E. M., and Louden, L. M. R. (Eds.). Marital and sexual counseling in medical practice (2nd ed.). New York: Harper and Row, 1974.

Al-Anon Family Group. The dilemma of the alcoholic marriage. New York: Al-Anon Family Group Headquarters, Inc., 1971.

Attwell, A. A., and Clabby, D. A. The retarded child: Answers to questions parents ask. Burbank, Cal.: Eire Press, 1969.

Ayrault, E. W. Helping the handicapped teenager mature. New York: Association Press, 1971.

Beigel, H. G. (Ed.). Advances in sex research. New York: Harper and Row, 1963.

Brenton, M. Sex and your heart. New York: Coward-McCann, 1968.

Butler, R. N., and Lewis, M. E. Sex after sixty: A guide for men and women for their later years. New York: Harper and Row, 1976.

Cowdry, E. V., and Steinberg, F. U. (Eds.). The care of the geriatric patient. St. Louis: C. V. Mosby, 1971.

de la Cruz, F. F., and LaVeck, G. D. (Eds.). Human sexuality and the mentally retarded. New York: Brunner/Mazel, 1973.

DeMartino, M. F. (Ed.). Sexual behavior and personality characteristics. New York: Citadel Press, 1963.

Egg, M. The different child grows up. New York: The John Day Company, 1969.

Enby, G. Let there be love: Sex and the handicapped. New York: Taplinger, 1975.

Felstein, I. Sex in later life. Baltimore: Penguin Books, 1970. (Original title, Sex and the long life.)

Fischer, H. L., Krajicek, M. J., and Borthick, W. A. Sex education for the developmentally disabled: A guide for parents, teachers, and professionals. Baltimore: University Park Press, 1973.

Fischer, H. L., Krajicek, M. J., and Borthick, W. A. Teaching concepts of sexual development to the developmentally disabled: A guide for parents, teachers, and professionals. Denver: University of Colorado Medical Center, 1973.

Freedman, A. M., Kaplan, H. I., and Sadock, B. J. (Eds.). Comprehensive textbook of psychiatry (Vol. 2). Baltimore: Williams and Wilkins, 1975.

Friedman, A. I. Fat can be beautiful. New York: Berkeley Publishing Corporation, 1974.

Friedman, A. I. How sex can keep you slim. Englewood Cliffs, N.J.: Prentice-Hall, 1972.

Gochros, H. L., and Gochros, J. S. (Eds.). The sexually oppressed. New York: Association Press, 1977.

Green, R. (Ed.). Human sexuality: A health practitioner's text. Baltimore: Williams and Wilkins, 1975.

Green, R., and Money, J. (Eds.). Transsexualism and sex reassignment. Baltimore: The Johns Hopkins University Press, 1969.

Gross, L. (Ed.). Sexual behavior: Current issues. New York: Spectrum Publications, 1974.

Gross, L. (Ed.). Sexual issues in marriage: A contemporary perspective. New York: Spectrum Publications, 1975.

Heslinga, K., Scheller, A. M., and Berkuyl, A. Not made of stone: The sexual problems of handicapped people. Springfield, Ill.: Charles C. Thomas, 1974.

Johnson, J. Disorders of sexual potency in the male. Oxford: Pergamon Press, 1968.

Johnson, W. R. Sex-education and counseling of special groups: The mentally and physically handicapped, ill and elderly. Springfield, Ill.: Charles C. Thomas, 1975.

Juhasz, A. M. (Ed.). Sexual development and behavior. Homewood, Ill.: Dorsey Press, 1973.

Kelly, J. T., and Weir, J. H. (Eds.). Perspectives on human sexuality. Minneapolis: Craftsman Press, 1976.

Kempton, W. A teacher's guide to sex education for persons with learning disabilities. North Scituate, Mass.: Duxbury Press, 1975.

Kempton, W., and Forman, R. Guidelines for training in sexuality and the mentally handicapped. Philadelphia: Planned Parenthood Association of Southeastern Pennsylvania, 1976.

Kempton, W., Bass, M. S., and Gordon, S. Love, sex and birth control for the mentally retarded: A guide for parents. Philadelphia: Planned Parenthood Association of Southeastern Pennsylvania, 1975.

Lancaster-Gaye, D. (Ed.). Personal relationships, the handicapped and the community: Some European thoughts and solutions. London: Routledge and Kegan Paul, 1972.

Leibel, B. S., and Wrenchall, G. A. (Eds.). On the nature and treatment of diabetes. Amsterdam: Excerpta Medica Foundation, 1965.

Little, N., Stewart, L., Simmins, G., and Nobles, B. (Eds.). Rehabilitation of the spinal cord injured. Fayetteville: Arkansas Rehabilitation Research and Training Center, University of Arkansas, 1974.

Mattinson, J. Marriage and mental handicap. Pittsburgh: University of Pittsburgh Press, 1970.

Meyer, J. K. (Ed.). Clinical management of sexual disorders. Baltimore: Williams and Wilkins, 1976.

Mooney, T. O., Cole, T. M., and Chilgren, R. A. Sexual options for paraplegics and quadriplegics. Boston: Little Brown, 1975.

Nordqvist, I. Life together: The situation of the handicapped. Stockholm: The Swedish Central Committee for Rehabilitation, 1975. (English translation)

Nursing management of spinal cord injuries. National Paraplegia Foundation, 1974.

Perske, R. (Ed.). New directions for parents of persons who are retarded. New York: Abingdon Press, 1973.

Rehabilitating the person with spinal cord injury. Washington, D.C.: Veterans' Administration, Department of Medicine and Surgery, 1972.

Rubin, I. Sexual life after sixty. New York: Basic Books, 1965.

Rubin, I., and Kirkandall, L. A. (Eds.). Sex in the childhood years. New York: Association Press, 1970.

Sadock, B. J., Kaplan, H. I., and Freedman, A. M. (Eds.). The sexual experience. Baltimore: Williams and Wilkins, 1976.

Scheingold, L. D., and Wagner, N. N. Sound sex and the aging heart. New York: Human Science Press, 1974.

Schoenber, B., Carr, A. C., Peretz, D., and Hutscher, A. H. (Eds.). Loss and grief: Psychological management in medical practice. New York: Columbia University Press, 1970.

Sex and the handicapped: A selected bibliography (1927–1975). Cleveland, Ohio: Veterans' Administration Hospital, 1975.

Sex education for the visually handicapped in schools and agencies. New York: American Federation for the Blind, 1975.

Sexuality and the mentally retarded. Watertown, N.Y.: Planned Parenthood of Northern New York, 1975. (Proceedings of a Conference on Sexuality and the Mentally Retarded, State University of New York College at Potsdam, September 21–22, 1972.)

Spock, B., and Lerrigo, M. O. Caring for your disabled child. New York: Macmillan, 1965.

Vincent, C. E. (Ed.). Human sexuality in medical education and practice. Springfield, Ill.: Charles C. Thomas, 1975.

Wahl, C. W. (Ed.). Sexual problems: Diagnosis and treatment in medical practice. New York: Free Press, 1967.

Walsh, J. J. Understanding paraplegia. Philadelphia: J. B. Lippincott, 1964.

Woods, N. F. Human sexuality in health and illness. St. Louis: C. V. Mosby, 1975.

Wortis, J. (Ed.). Mental retardation and developmental disabilities. New York: Brunner/Mazel, 1974.

Conferences and Proceedings

American Association on Mental Deficiency, Denver, 1967.

Annual Meeting of the American Psychosomatic Society, Boston, Massachusetts, March 24–25, 1956.

Association for Research in Nervous and Mental Diseases, 1950. Proceedings.

Clinical Spinal Cord Injury Conference, U.S. Veterans' Administration, October 1962. Proceedings.

Conference on Continuing Education in the Treatment of Spinal Cord Injuries, Milwaukee, Wisconsin, June 28–29, 1972. Proceedings.

Conference on Sexual Interviewing with the Spinal Cord Injured and Their Sexual Partners. Special Seminar, Indiana University Medical School, Indianapolis, May 8–9, 1976.

Conference on Sexuality and the Mentally Retarded, State University of New York College at Potsdam, September 21–22, 1972. Proceedings. (Sexuality and the Mentally Retarded. Watertown, N.Y.: Planned Parenthood of Northern New York, 1975.)

European Dialysis and Transplant Association Annual Conference, 1970. Proceedings.

Fifth International Congress of Nephrology, Mexico, 1972. Proceedings.

International Cerebral Palsy Society, April 1971.

International Conference on Psychology and Human Development, Jerusalem, Israel, December 30, 1976.

National Conference on Methadone Treatment, 1973. Proceedings.

Nineteenth Annual Convention of the Association for Mental Deficiency, Minneapolis, May 18, 1972.

Rehabilitation Counselor Internship Training Program, Nebraska Psychiatric Institute, Omaha, Nebraska, 1970.

Seventh Congress of the International Diabetes Federation, Buenos Aires, August 23–28, 1970.

Seventieth Annual Meeting of the American Sociological Association, August 25–29, 1977.

Symposium of the Royal College of Surgeons, at Edinburgh, June 1963. Proceedings.

Third Annual Indiana Epilepsy Conference, Indianapolis, November 4–6, 1976.

Third National Conference on Methadone Treatment, Washington, D.C.: U.S. Government Printing Office, 1970. Proceedings.

Thirteenth World Congress of Rehabilitation International, Tel Aviv, Israel, June 13–18, 1976.

Thirty-fifth Annual Assembly of the American Academy of Physical Medicine and Rehabilitation, Washington, D.C., October 24, 1973.

Twelfth World Congress of Rehabilitation International, Sydney, Australia, 1972.

Workshop on Sex: Rehabilitation's Stepchild, Indianapolis, June 23, 1973. Proceedings.

Journals

Fertility and Sterility
Journal of Sex & Marital Therapy
Journal of Sex Education and Therapy
Journal of Sex Research

Medical Aspects of Human Sexuality
Sexology
Sexuality and Disability (first published in April 1978; quarterly)
SIECUS Newsletter
SIECUS Report